LINCOLN CHRISTIAN UNIVERSITY

EARLY CHILDHOOD EDUC

Sharon Ryan, Edi

ADVISORY BOARD: Celia Genishi, Doris Fromberg, C. ....er, Dominic Gullo, Amita Gupta, Beatrice Fennimore, Sue Grieshaber, Jackie Marsh, Mindy Blaise, Gail Yuen, Alice Honig, Betty Jones, Stephanie Feeney, Stacie Goffin, Beth Graue

(continued)

What If All the Kids Are White?

Anti-Bias Multicultural Education with Young Children and Families

SECOND EDITION

LOUISE DERMAN-SPARKS
PATRICIA G. RAMSEY

with Julie Olsen Edwards

Foreword by Carol Brunson Day

Teachers College
Columbia University
New York and London

Published by Teachers College Press, 1234 Amsterdam Avenue, New York, NY
10027

Copyright © 2011 by Teachers College, Columbia University

All rights reserved. No part of this publication may be reproduced or transmitted
in any form or by any means, electronic or mechanical, including photocopy,
or any information storage and retrieval system, without permission from the
publisher.

Library of Congress Cataloging-in-Publication Data

Derman-Sparks, Louise.
    What if all the kids are white? : anti-bias multicultural education with young
children and families / Louise Derman-Sparks, Patricia G. Ramsey ; foreword
by Carol Brunson Day. — 2nd ed.
        p. cm. — (Early childhood education series)
    Includes bibliographical references and index.
    ISBN 978-0-8077-5212-8 (pbk. : alk. paper)
    1. Multicultural education—United States. 2. Racism—Study and teaching
(Early childhood)—United States. 3. Whites—Race identity—United States. I.
Ramsey, Patricia G. II. Title.
    LC1099.3.D47   2011
    370.117—dc22   2010049621

ISBN 978-0-8077-5212-8 (paper)

Printed on acid-free paper
Manufactured in the United States of America

18   17   16   15   14   13   12   11   8   7   6   5   4   3   2   1

From Louise:

To *Dorothy Healey*,
who taught me that analysis and practice
must always be partners

From Patty:

In memory of *Leslie Williams*,
beloved friend, wise mentor,
and fun-loving adventurer

2277

127042

CHOTHI

Contents

Foreword

What do you do when you want to attract a broad audience of readers interested in anti-bias and multicultural education and at the same time pique the interest of Whites to examine themselves? Louise Derman-Sparks and Patricia Ramsey's bold and provocative title is no doubt one good way if it creates for you, as it did for me, a cognitive imbalance that gets curiosity and emotion churning. For, to the extent that our approach to the study of racism only admonishes Whites to change their behavior toward its victims, it also directs curiosity and emotion away from Whites examining their own Whiteness.

But this examination is a necessary one, growing out of what we have discovered about the complexities of how racism perpetuates itself. These writers' conviction that we *can* be comfortable with Whites retreating into their Whiteness and focusing on a deeper understanding of it is a step that can bring us closer to our ultimate goal. For Derman-Sparks and Ramsey offer an alternative vision for White identity that breaks the mold and refuses to accept the unspoken assumptions for Whites being White. Their challenge is for Whites to become critical thinkers about the history that they learned in school and that they continue to relearn. They examine the most difficult of topics—and explore the long-overdue treatment of Whites *not* as homogeneous, but as a group with intricate variety, unraveling privilege and social class differences in depth, acknowledging that the material advantages of being White are not equally distributed.

In the process, they provide plenty of concrete suggestions and ideas with which to engage and struggle. Yet, their expert message comes with plenty of assurance that this is no recipe book. Rather the participants in the process will construct the solutions for change.

Derman-Sparks and Ramsey's personal histories and professional trajectories demanded that they write this book. And the current status of our anti-bias work demands we read it and use it well.

Are Whites ready to learn how to have the conversation about racism among themselves? Though I am not White, I feel strongly that it is time. And I believe that the presence of this book in your hands represents a marker for a maturity point in the anti-bias multicultural movement in early childhood education. I feel thankful to have an approach with such integrity—integrity made possible by the work that has been accomplished in early childhood education so far, work that has as its highest goal solidarity among activists of all backgrounds who want to build a just and sustainable society with equitable distribution of resources.

—Carol Brunson Day, Ph.D.

Acknowledgments

Over the decades, many friends, colleagues, and sister/fellow anti-racism activists inspired, informed, and supported our work. We pay homage to them. They include Joe Barndt, Babette Brown, Brad Chambers, Ron Chisom, Carol Brunson Day, Robette Dias, Catherine Goins, Jane Lane, Sandra Lawrence, Glenda Mac Naughton, Mary Pat Martin, Deborah Menkart, Sonia Nieto, Helen Robb, Anne Stewart, Beverly Daniel Tatum, Nahdiyah Faquir Taylor, Anke Van Keulen, Petra Wagner, Leslie Williams, Ellen Wolpert, Sheli Wortis, and Louise's Crossroads colleagues.

We also feel deep gratitude to the many people who read the original manuscript at various stages, gave us supportive yet honest critical feedback, and provided us with compelling stories and examples. They include (in alphabetical order) Lynne Brill, Catherine Goins, Janet Gonsolez-Mena, Eric Hoffman, Suzanne Jones, Mary Pat Martin, Debbie Revaçon, Marilyn Segal, and Meg Thomas. In addition, a special word of appreciation to Julie Olsen Edwards, whose insightful assistance was invaluable in revising the first and second editions of our book, and to Jane Schall, who helped us solve some of the tricky organizational challenges while writing the original book.

A special thank-you to Mount Holyoke College for the time and financial support to Patty to work on both our first and second editions. Patty was on sabbatical both times, and Mount Holyoke College also provided a small grant for Jane Schall to help with the original book.

We also acknowledge with great appreciation the many teachers throughout the country who have taught us what anti-bias/multicultural work means in practice. A special thanks to the wonderful teachers at Gorse Child Study Center at Mount Holyoke: Barbara Sweeney, Janna Aldrich, Valerie Sawka, Sandy Johnson, and Sukey Heard, whose wisdom and stories are woven into many of our examples.

Susan Liddicoat, former acquisitions editor at Teachers College Press, first got us started on this book. She has been our friend and editor for many years on other books as well. We had the great good luck to have Susan again as development editor of this Second Edition. Both of us benefit enormously from her honest and supportive feedback, her creativity, and her commitment to bring out the best in our ideas and writing. We also thank Marie Ellen Larcada, our current acquisitions editor at Teachers College Press, for her caring, encouragement, and constructive support.

Finally, of course, we thank our families for their support and willingness to plan their lives around our work. I (Patty) thank my sons, Daniel and Alejandro, whose identity struggles have underscored the urgent need to create a more just world where young people do not have to straddle ever-widening racial, ethnic, and economic divides. To Fred Moseley, my wonderful partner and co-parent, thank you for your care, wisdom, and unflagging support! I (Louise) thank my son and daughter, Douglass and Holly, for all their love and encouragement. In the end, it is for them that I do this work. My eternal thankfulness to Bill, my partner in life and in anti-bias education work, for understanding from the beginning what I was doing and why.

Introduction:
Identity, Diversity,
and Fairness Still Matter

> What we've already achieved gives us hope for what we can and must achieve tomorrow.
>
> —President Obama, Grant Park, Chicago,
> election night address, November 4, 2008

"What if all the kids are White?" has been one of the most frequently asked questions in our workshops and discussions with early childhood teachers over the past 3 decades. Usually posed by White teachers, it reflected an assumption that the absence of obvious racial diversity in their classrooms meant that young children were not forming ideas about being White or about People of Color. It also reflected a narrow definition of diversity, ignoring the many kinds of differences that exist even within racially homogeneous groups.

More recently, teachers' questions reflect two additional, quite different perspectives. One echoes the idea that we are living in a post-racial society, and that, consequently, anti-bias/multicultural (AB/MC) education is no longer necessary. The second perspective reflects teachers' views that AB/MC education continues to be very relevant and necessary. They know that working for social justice will benefit all people, and requires people in all groups, including White persons, to join the long-term struggle. However, they are not sure *how* to engage White children in learning about differences and social justice. They may still be working with all-White groups of children, or as is becoming more common, their early childhood programs may reflect the new reality of racial/ethnic diversity in previously White cities and states.

Many activists and theorists engaged in the movement for social justice, here and abroad, believe it is necessary to identify the specific dynamics of "Whiteness" and the role of White people in challenging racism.

They argue that racism is a systemic, institutionalized force that advantages persons defined as White and disadvantages those defined as not White. Understanding that racism is not just a matter of individual prejudice and discrimination opens up new avenues for defining the roles and responsibilities of White people.

So, too, does the meaning of *anti-racism* work and *anti-racist*. *Anti-racism* refers to the ongoing dismantling of racism. The ultimate goal of anti-racism work is a racism-free society—what people often mean when they use the term *non-racist* or *non-racial*. While "this vision needs to be always before us" (Barndt, 2007, p. 224), it does not become an all-embracing reality until the people and institutions of a society are truly transformed. An anti-racist person is on a life-long journey that includes forming new understanding of and ways to live her or his racial identity and then increasing commitment to and engagement in anti-racism actions (Barndt, 2007).

This framework creates a new context for thinking about the engagement of White children, families, and teachers in AB/MC education. It is not enough for White people to accept and respect People of Color or to tweak the current system. Rather, White individuals need to undergo a profound shift from viewing the world through a lens of dominance, however unrecognized, to making a commitment to equitably sharing power and resources. In this process, they will also recognize that the end of systemic and individual racism will humanize and liberate everyone.

AN ALTERNATIVE VISION OF WHITE IDENTITY

Forty years ago, Robert Terry (1970) proposed the following image of a "new White consciousness":

> The *new* in the label points to fresh possibilities. We are not totally limited by our past. *White* is a constant reminder that we are not racially neutral, and also a reminder that we still participate in racist institutions and culture. *Consciousness* continually reminds us that we need to reconstruct totally our understanding of who we are and what we ought to do. (p. 20)

Terry ended his book with a hopeful and motivating call to White people:

> *The new White committed to justice and working to rid this nation of its racism can be a major force for social justice*. The time is right. *It is up to us to seize that time to turn our legacy of old White privilege into new White possibility*. (p. 97; emphasis in original)

At the time, this work received little notice, but now these ideas have gained momentum. Since the late 1990s many authors (e.g., Barndt, 2007; Brown, 2002; Howard, 1999; Kincheloe, Steinberg, Rodriguez, & Chennault, 1998; Kivel, 2002; Rothenberg, 2002; Wise, 2009) have focused on how White people perpetuate racism and how they can overcome their personal histories and engage in anti-bias work.

This paradigm shift calls on educators and families to nurture White children's early identity and social-emotional development in new ways. It is not enough to teach them to embrace racial and cultural diversity. We must also help children develop individual and group identities that recognize and resist the false notions of racial superiority and racial entitlement and realize how they would benefit from a society free of systemic and individual racism. To participate in this work, those of us who are White must develop our own new White consciousness.

DO WE STILL NEED A BOOK
ABOUT WHITE CHILDREN AND DIVERSITY?

Since the publication of the first edition of this book, a major milestone in U.S. history occurred. The election of Barack Obama took our country a major step forward on the path to a racially equitable society, forever changing the composite portrait of American presidents. It now includes one African American man as the 44th President, alongside 43 White male presidents.

Celebration

The night of President Obama's election was momentous and profoundly moving for millions of Americans—as well as for millions around the world. We were among those celebrating a victory we had not thought possible in our lifetimes. Two social justice activists and authors, one African American and one White American, reflected many people's feelings about that night. On a personal level, Fred McKissack (2009) wrote:

> I called my parents. I could tell my father was beaming. Through Obama, he could see the future for his grandsons and their peers—a collective sense of inclusion that has eluded the race for so long. My mother cried . . . and then, as folks would say, the spirit hit her. "Yes, we can," she yelled, "Yes we can. Yes we can. Yes-we-can." It was an unforgettable moment. (p. 32)

Tim Wise (2009) spoke to the political meaning of the presidential campaign and outcome:

The level of cross-racial collaboration (especially among youth) that made Obama's victory possible was something rarely seen in American politics, or history, . . . they demonstrated that "when a person of color has the opportunity to make his case day after day, for at least a year and a half" . . . he is fully capable of demonstrating to the satisfaction of millions of Whites (if still not most), his intelligence, wisdom and leadership capabilities. (Wise, 2009, pp. 19, 20)

Racism Is Still with Us

Despite what many people may have hoped, however, President Obama's election did not usher in a post-racial era in the United States. As author and activist Fred McKissack (2009) further wrote in his election-night reflections:

Exactly how can we be in post-racial America when nearly 40 percent of black children under the age of five live at or below the poverty line? . . . When the level of school segregation for Latinos is the highest in 40 years? . . . When the gaps in wealth, income, education and health care have widened over the last eight years . . . and the pain of poverty is disproportionately cracking the backs of minorities? (p. 32)

Racism continues to affect all of our institutions, our interpersonal interactions, and our thinking. As Tim Wise (2009) explains,

Abolishing racism . . . will require that we engage White Americans in an exploration of how, both historically and today, racial-interest thinking often stands in the way of true progress for all, regardless of color . . . . how it [racism] has substituted the false promise of racial supremacy for something greater, something more lasting and meaningful—an economically supportive, culturally diverse society. (p. 145)

Many social justice activists agree with McKissack's and Wise's assessments of the significance of President Obama's election. "Now is not the time to avert our eyes from the prize. . . . Indeed, the nation needs to refocus its attention on tearing down the walls that keep us from living in a truly post-racial America" (McKissack, 2009, p. 32). To not act "is to squander whatever progress we take Barack Obama's election to herald, and to ensure that the change so many have hoped for will likely never materialize" (Wise, 2009, p. 148).

Racism Revealed

In fact, while many celebrated Obama's election, others responded with fury, revealing the extent to which intransigent and vitriolic racism still lives in our country. Forms of this racism include a rise in hate groups and armed anti-government militia groups, threats and acts of violence directed at political opponents, racism directed at President Obama, and individual acts of racism.

Hate Groups and Armed Anti-Government Militia Groups. The Southern Poverty Law Center (SPLC) Intelligence Project, which keeps track of hate groups and anti-government militia groups in the United States, disturbingly reports "an astonishing increase in the number of anti-government 'Patriot' groups . . . from 149 groups in 2008 to 512 groups in 2009," a growth of 244% (SPLC, 2010a, p. 1). In addition, 309 nativist (anti-immigration) groups are active, a surge of nearly 80%, and Neo-Nazi and other hate groups are at a record number of 32. The SPLC maintains that one of the factors fueling this increase is members' anger over demographic changes that reflect a significant increase in the number of People of Color in the United States. The election of the country's first African American president has become the symbol of what some Whites see as a "take-over" of the country by People of Color.

Violence. The SPLC Report (2010b) further reminds us that "The people associated with the Patriot [militia groups] movement during its 1990s heyday produced an enormous amount of violence, most dramatically the Oklahoma city bombing that left 168 people dead" (p. 1). Since President Obama's inauguration, arrests of several individuals connected to hate groups in alleged assassination plots have taken place.

At least as disturbing, racial hatred, along with tactics of violence, now appear in mainstream political discourse and behavior. Threats of physical violence are commonplace at rallies opposing President Obama and at political events, such as the Town meetings held to debate the health care legislation. "Armed men have come to Obama speeches bearing signs suggesting that the 'tree of liberty' needs to be 'watered' with 'the blood of tyrants'" (Potok, Spring 2010). Others have held threatening signs, such as "We came unarmed [this time]" (Dees, 2010, p. 1). Some talk-show radio and TV commentators fan the flames of racial hatred.

This climate of hate normalizes offensive, disrespectful behavior toward democratically elected officials. Millions of Americans, as well as many people overseas, saw Congressional Representative Joe Wilson rudely interrupt Obama's 2009 State of the Union speech to a joint House and Senate gathering in the halls of Congress by yelling, "You are a liar!" During the 2010 Congressional vote on the Health Care Bill, protesters yelled racial slurs at Representative John Lewis and spat on Representative Emanuel Cleaver, both of whom are African American. They also hurled homophobic slurs at Representative Barney Frank, an openly gay congressman. In general, political analysts and commentators dismissed and minimized these events as merely the behaviors of a few extreme individuals or denied that the incidents even took place.

The rise in the number, membership, and activities of hate groups, White nationalist groups, and White militia groups poses a real threat to our democracy and undermines everyone's civil rights, the cornerstone of any democratic society. Everyone—White people as well as People of Color—are hurt when racism goes on the rampage.

Racial Bigotry Directed at President Obama. A disturbingly large number of Americans simply refuse to accept the possibility that an African American can be President. A website devoted to praying for the death of President Obama reports having a million members (Cohen, 2010). Many White Americans insist that Obama is not eligible to be President because he is not a legal American citizen, despite legally documented evidence to the contrary (www.nytimes.cpm/2010/04/15/us/politics).

Although all Presidents are ridiculed by cartoonists and political pundits, a flood of racist visual and verbal images directed at President Obama depict him as less than human, following a long-standing theme of racial bigotry. In multiple media outlets and in images and speeches of groups such as the Tea Party, stereotypes abound as the President is depicted as a chimpanzee, a savage witch doctor, a starving African child with a beer can, a Neanderthal man, and a pimp (Sauer, 2009).

Individual Acts of Racial Bigotry. Overt expressions of racial bigotry are increasingly affecting ordinary people. One form is violence directed at Muslim people.

- In New York City, a cab driver was stabbed and slashed after a passenger asked if he were Muslim.
- In the same city, a man urinated on prayer rugs at a mosque while shouting anti-Muslim slurs.
- In Jacksonville, Florida, a pipe bomb exploded in an Islamic center occupied by 60 worshippers. (Cohen, 2010)

Other forms of prejudice and discrimination against Arab Americans and Muslim Americans are also a serious component of current racism.

According to a report from the American Arab Anti-Discrimination Committee (ADC), "Arab Americans continue to face higher rates of employment discrimination than in the pre-9/11 period, in both public and private sectors. Arab-American students continue to face significant problems with discrimination and harassment in schools around the country. Defamation in popular culture and the media remains a serious problem facing the Arab-American community" (Ibish, 2008, p. 3).

I (Louise) recently heard about several disturbing incidents from colleagues and friends of color. A Mexican American colleague, a faculty member at a college in Southern California, reported the following incident:

Eating dinner with my husband at a restaurant patronized by many Latino families, I overheard four White people—two men and two women—loudly declaring the following: "All Mexican immigrants are lazy. They just come here to use what belongs to us. . . . They should all go back where they come from. They make me sick." I went over to their table and asked them to lower their voices. They did so, but, as they left the restaurant soon afterward, one of the men stopped at my table, saying, again in a loud voice, "You know, everything I said is true. I guess you can't take the truth."

We know that the majority of White Americans do not participate in the extreme acts of overt racism, but their increasing occurrence is disturbing evidence that we are far from being a post-racial society.

What Are Children Learning?

In this environment of great hope, yet virulent anger, we need to ask ourselves: What are children learning about their world? As Kenneth Clark (1963) pointed out many years ago, a key influence on children's ideas about others comes from the ideas and messages surrounding them in the larger society, as well as those they absorb from their families. Either these influences teach racism and other divisive beliefs, or they support connection and social justice for all.

Aside from whether we agree with President Obama's agenda, we need to ask ourselves what happens when young children see racist images and messages about President Obama. Do they generalize these hurtful ideas to other people with a similar appearance or racial identity? What is the effect on African American and other children of color? On White children?

What are children learning from the vitriolic language, threats, and acts of violence that now permeate political discourse? When children are angry at one another, do we allow them to use racial and other kinds of name-calling or to spit on one another? Do we allow them to threaten or use physical aggression? What are these adult behaviors teaching children about how to constructively deal with differences of ideas and background? What are they teaching children about respectful ways to disagree with democratically elected government members?

The 2008 presidential election is evidence that a multi-racial/ethnic coalition of people can prevail over racial bigotry. Yet racism is far from over—either individually or systemically—as shown in the current resurgence of racial polarization and discrimination. In this promising yet perilous time, we invite you to join in the conversation about how to raise and educate White children to become part of building a more just society and world for all. As you engage in this process, we hope you gain a deeper and stronger sense of self and of purpose as a teacher for all children or adults.

WHAT TO EXPECT IN THIS SECOND EDITION

What If All the Kids Are White? spotlights one aspect of anti-bias/multicultural education work. It is not a substitute for books that discuss the multiple aspects of AB/MC curriculum for children of all racial/ethnic backgrounds (e.g., Derman-Sparks & A.B.C. Task Force, 1989; Derman-Sparks & Edwards, 2010; Ramsey, 2004) or books that focus on the specific developmental and educational needs of children of color. Rather, we write for readers who are familiar with AB/MC work but wish to explore the theoretical and practical ramifications of Whiteness in more depth.

Furthermore, the focus on White children in no way implies that their needs and interests should be the center of AB/MC education. We write this book, not to detract from programs and curricula that support children and families of color, but rather to increase the possibilities that White children will grow up to join them in the ongoing struggles for social justice. As Lewis (2001) says, "We must ask ourselves, can much change if the educational experiences of White middle-class children do not undergo some transformations?" (p. 805).

As you may have noticed, we are using the term *anti-bias/multicultural* to describe our work. Multicultural education, which had its roots in the racial inequities that fueled the civil rights movement, has gone through many phases since its inception in the 1970s. It has broadened its scope and has evolved from a focus on cultural pluralism to the critical analysis of all areas of diversity and inequity. In the early childhood field, the publication of *Anti-Bias Curriculum: Tools for Empowering*

Young Children in 1989 (Derman-Sparks & A.B.C. Task Force) was pivotal in shifting the focus of early childhood multicultural education from "appreciating diversity" to working toward social justice (see the 2010 revised edition, *Anti-Bias Education for Young Children & Ourselves*, Derman-Sparks & Edwards). In this current book, we use the term *anti-bias/multicultural education* (AB/MC) to embrace the history of both of these movements and their contributions to the struggle toward social, economic, and cultural equity.

Since both of us live and work in the United States, this book is about the dynamics of racism and anti-racism work in the United States. However, writers and teachers in other countries have also discussed and addressed these issues. Despite historical and political differences between countries, many power and personal dynamics are similar. Therefore, we do include some research and examples from other countries and hope that the international exchange of ideas will continue to grow.

The conceptual framework and learning themes of this book are relevant for White children and families in all or primarily White settings, as well as for White children and families in racially/ethnically diverse settings, although specific approaches and activities vary across programs. We hope that White teachers will gain new and deeper insights into their identities, ideas, and practices and that teachers of color will add to their knowledge about the dynamics of Whiteness and working with White children. Our ultimate aim is to open up new conversations that enhance the likelihood that White children will grow up to resist and challenge racism in its many forms.

Core Learning Themes

We propose seven core learning themes for working with White children. They derive from the four anti-bias education (ABE) goals, listed at the end of this chapter in Figure I.1 (Derman-Sparks & Edwards, 2010) and reflect our understanding of the construction of "Whiteness" in our society. Through numerous opportunities to engage in learning experiences related to the core learning themes, White children will

1. Develop authentic identities based on personal abilities and interests, family history and culture, rather than on White superiority. (ABE Goal 1)
2. Know, respect, and value the range of the diversity of physical and social attributes among White people. (ABE Goal 1)
3. Build the capacity for caring, cooperative, and equitable relationships with others. (ABE Goal 2)

4. Understand, appreciate, and respect differences and similarities beyond their immediate family, neighborhood center/classroom, and racial group. (ABE Goal 2)
5. Learn to identify and challenge stereotypes, prejudice, and discriminatory practices among themselves and in the immediate environment. (ABE Goals 2 and 3)
6. Commit to the ideal that all people have the right to a secure, healthy, comfortable, and sustainable life and that everyone must equitably share the resources of the earth and collaboratively care for them. (ABE Goals 3 and 4)
7. Build identities that include anti-bias ideals and possibilities and acquire skills and confidence to work together for social justice in their own classrooms and communities and in the larger society. (ABE Goal 4)

Book Organization

This revision retains the basic structure of the first edition. Chapter 1 continues our introduction to the issues this book explores with a particular focus on early childhood practice. The rest of the book consists of two parts. Part I (Chapters 2, 3, 4, and 5) focuses on the construction of Whiteness, White identity, and learning experiences that support development of children who can thrive in a diverse world. Part II (Chapters 6, 7, 8, and 9) focuses on expanding and deepening the sense of connection among the human family and the capacity for critical thinking and activism. Both Parts have a parallel construction: first, a chapter describing the historical roots of the main themes; second, a chapter reviewing relevant research on children's development; third, a chapter illustrating how this information can be applied to working with children; fourth, a chapter on ways to engage adults in these issues. While activities in the curriculum chapters (4, 5, 8, and 9) spotlight identity and attitude development among White children, they can be adapted to use with all children in settings that include White children and children of color.

In this second edition, we updated content to reflect the latest research as well as current societal dynamics. In Chapters 2 and 6, we added discussions about the dynamics of racism and anti-racism since the election of President Obama. We included current research about how young children form and enact identities and attitudes in Chapters 3 and 7. In the chapters that focus on teaching strategies—4, 5, 8, and 9—we added ideas for working in programs in which White children are the majority, rather than the sole population.

To help you see the connections between this material and your own work with children and families, look for "Reflection Questions" at the end of Chapters 1–3 and 6–7. In addition, Parts I and II conclude with "A Tale of Two Centers," illustrating how teachers have implemented specific learning themes in two different early childhood programs. (If stories help you understand conceptual issues, you may want to peek at these first. However, you will better understand them after reading through the previous chapters.)

Lastly, we updated material in the three appendices. Appendix A offers guidelines for selecting children's books in an AB/MC classroom and useful websites for finding these books. To help readers begin to learn more about anti-racist movements in the United States, we have included a list of current organizations and websites in Appendix B, and a chart of 20th-century White anti-racist activists in Appendix C.

In your eagerness to learn how to implement the ideas in this book, you may be tempted to skip the history and research chapters (2, 3, 6, and 7). We *strongly* urge you to resist doing that. Anti-bias/multicultural teaching is not a matter of simply carrying out a collection of activities. It is a complex of large and small decisions that reflect our life histories, beliefs, and knowledge about children and the contexts of their lives. Often the best curriculum arises from a spontaneous event such as a child's question, a community issue, or a family's concern. Generating curriculum that is responsive to current issues and appropriate for a particular group of children requires a deep understanding of how the learning themes and children's development reflect the larger social-political dynamics.

It is crucial to take the time to reflect about the broad social and economic context, as well as your specific community, your own life, and the families with whom you work. In particular, knowledge about the history of the social-political construct of "Whiteness" makes clear that absorbing the power codes of racism is not the "fault" of individual children or adults, but an inevitable outcome of growing up in a racist society. Conversely, an appreciation of the history of White anti-racism activism can inspire teachers, children, and families to push past their fears and practical concerns and join with people who are working for a society where the right to pursue of life, liberty, and happiness is truly shared by all people.

To conclude our description of the book's organization, we want to clarify our terminology. Terms used to name *race* and *racial identity* vary in usage, and we will discuss the origins and meaning of the concept of race in Chapter 2. We choose to use the term *White people* to refer to all people of European descent who receive advantages from the system of racism in the United States, although this category includes several different ethnicities and nationalities (countries of origin of ancestors or of oneself) (see Chapter 2). We use the term *People of Color* to refer to groups that experience systemic disadvantages from racism, including (in alphabetical order) African Americans, American Indians, Arab Americans, Asian Americans, Mexican and other Latino Americans, and Pacific Islander Americans. The term *People of Color* therefore encompasses a range of different specific ethnicities and cultures.

OUR OWN BACKGROUNDS

In the spirit of self-reflection, we will tell you a little about ourselves, since all authors' life experiences deeply influence their thinking and writing. We first connected 30 years ago and have since then collaborated on many projects. As two White women, we continually work to come to terms with our roles as anti-bias, anti-racist, multicultural educators in a White-dominated society. We believe that, although it is not possible to undo history, it *is* possible to learn from it and to create a new future.

Louise

I have been a teacher for 40 years, first of preschool children and then of adults. I grew up in a White, Jewish American, working-class, activist family in Brooklyn and Manhattan, New York. I was very lucky to have parents who believed in working for social change. I learned about activism from an early age, by observing and listening and by accompanying my parents on some of their community activism work.

I went to public schools, from kindergarten through college. In elementary and junior high school, a few very good teachers illuminated the possibilities of caring and meaningful education. I was fortunate to attend the High School of Music and Art, which we would now call a public "magnet" school. In a high school more diverse than most in New York City at that time, I found my voice and began becoming an activist in my own right.

Over the many years of doing social justice and anti-bias work, I have had to deepen my understanding of the multiple parts of my identity. My parents taught me that I had a responsibility to work with others to end racism, but our Whiteness was not a topic of conversation, other than that we were not to engage in racist behaviors. But then the growing Black Power/Black Liberation movement raised profound and sometimes disturbing questions about the roles and behaviors of White people in the Civil Rights Movement. Insights about these issues first came to me from

Robert Terry's *For Whites Only* (1970), which also proposed an action agenda for White people wanting to end racism.

At the same time, the several growing social/economic justice movements also challenged me to think about other facets of my identity. I had new questions about what it means to be Jewish. The lightning flashed when, in the mid-1970s, I read Albert Memmi's *The Colonizer and the Colonized* (1965), which argued that Jewish people have a foot in both worlds—that of the oppressor and that of the oppressed. I came to understand that Whiteness enabled Jewish people (specifically those with White skin) to gain benefits from systemic racism *and* that these privileges could be withdrawn at any time, making Jewish people the targets of oppression.

Figuring out my White identity also required analytically considering my class and gender identity. While the anti-racism movement challenged me to critically examine my role on the *advantaged* side of societal power, the women's movement challenged me, as a woman, to comprehend the *disadvantaged* side of societal power. In my family of origin, I was working class. Now I am college professor—a different socioeconomic status—but I continue to identify with my working-class roots. I am also the mother of two grown, adopted children, who each has a White birth mother and an African American birth father. While this does not change my own racial privilege, I suffer the anger and pain of seeing my children experience racism in their lives.

So, I am White and, as I said before, gain many privileges in this society. At the same time, the other facets of my identity make my reality more complex and affects my thinking about what it means to raise and teach White children.

Patty

Like Louise, I have benefited from the economic, educational, and political advantages of being White. However, I have additional layers of privilege and resistance to change and often wish that I had been raised in a politically activist family. My ancestors, representing different strands of Protestantism, came to the United States from England, Scotland, the Netherlands, and Germany, many during the 17th and 18th centuries. Although they were escaping poverty and, in some cases, religious and political persecution, they benefited from their status as White Anglo-Saxon Protestants once they arrived on these shores. Most of my ancestors were people of modest mean—small farmers, shopkeepers, carpenters, teachers, and ministers—but they were not victims of the racist ideologies that Italian, Irish, and Jewish immigrants faced. Across generations, my forebears benefited from the growing wealth in this country and became comfortably middle class.

My parents were good middle-class "liberals." They supported the civil rights movement, but they were not activists, and these issues never intruded on our daily lives. We lived only a few miles away from the turbulent desegregation of Boston schools in the 1970s, but in our virtually all-White suburb, buses were simply a way to get to school, not the targets of flying rocks.

Despite my privileged and unchallenged status, I also remember, from a very young age, feeling that something was wrong; that I was only seeing a thin slice of reality. As a good White person, however, I kept my silence and did not rock the boat with questions. The first time I spoke up was in high school, when I joined my Jewish classmates to protest several anti-Semitic practices. Not only had the administration dismissed my friends' discomfort about performing in a highly religious Christmas concert, but they also systematically excluded them from receiving certain awards.

I also grew up believing that I had "no culture." My life seemed very bland and ordinary in comparison to the vibrant holiday celebrations of my Jewish and Italian friends. Looking back I realize that, because my life fit the "invisible norms" of the White middle class, I could not see that I was immersed in particular cultural values. My yearning for more ethnic connections also blinded me to the power and privilege that I unconsciously absorbed and enjoyed.

With many lurches and missteps, I have spent most of my adult life trying to broaden my perspective, to uncover and challenge my assumptions and biases, and to resist injustice. Many experiences—working in Honduras, serving in VISTA (Volunteers in Service to America) volunteering in a Mexican American community in California, living in Mexico for 2 years as a parent of young children—have made me acutely aware of my cultural blinders and economic advantages. Most recently, parenting two young adult sons, both adopted from Chile, has laid bare my White middle-class assumptions about social and academic "success." I have been immersed in the painful reality of the pressures and invalidation that children of color experience even with well-intentioned and highly trained teachers and counselors.

Writing this book prompted me to revisit and reconsider my own racial and anti-bias identity. It led to my learning about several ancestors who were abolitionists, enabling me to connect with my family's history in new ways. At the same time, it has also made me painfully aware that I will never fully understand the lived experience of those who have been penalized by the same system that has elevated my family.

Figure I.1: Anti-Bias Education Goals

The following four goals are for *all* children: They interact with and build on one another. The specific activities and strategies for working toward these goals will depend on children's backgrounds, ages, and life experiences. The underlying intent of anti-bias education is to foster the development of children and adults who have the personal strength, critical-thinking ability, and activist skills to work with others to build caring, just, diverse communities and societies for all.

Goal 1: Each child will demonstrate self-awareness, confidence, family pride, and positive social identities. This goal calls on teachers to create the educational conditions in which all children are able to like who they are without needing to feel superior to anyone else. It also means enabling children to develop biculturally—to be able to interact effectively within their home culture and within the dominant culture.

Goal 2: Each child will express comfort and joy with human diversity; accurate language for human differences; and deep, caring human connections. This goal involves guiding children's development to respectfully and effectively learn about differences, comfortably negotiate and adapt to them, and cognitively understand and emotionally accept the common humanity that all people share.

Goal 3: Each child will increasingly recognize unfairness, have language to describe unfairness, and understand that unfairness hurts. This goal asks teachers to guide children's development of the cognitive skills to identify "unfair" and "untrue" images (stereotypes), comments (teasing, name-calling), and behaviors (discrimination) directed at one's own or others' identities (be they gender, race, ethnicity, disability, class, age, or weight) *and* having the emotional empathy to know that bias hurts.

Goal 4: Each child will demonstrate empowerment and the skills to act, with others or alone, against prejudice and/or discriminatory actions. This "activism" goal requires helping every child learn and practice a variety of ways to act when another child acts in a biased manner toward her/him, when a child acts in a biased manner toward another child, or when an adult acts in a biased manner. Goal 4 builds on and enhances the other three ABE goals.

Source: Derman-Sparks, L., & Edwards, J. O. (2010). *Anti-Bias Education for Young Children & Ourselves*. Washington, DC: NAEYC. Reprinted by permission of NAEYC.

TO OUR READERS

Since the publication of the first edition of *What If All the Kids are White?*, we have spoken with many teachers who are finding it useful in their work with children, families, and pre-service and in-service teachers. Perhaps the most moving feedback we have heard is their accounts of the impact of the book on their own sense of identity and self-esteem. Many have talked about a new, fuller, and positive understanding about themselves as a White person, similar to the idea of Robert Terry's (1970) "new White" person. We are greatly encouraged by these comments. When teachers feel this way about themselves, they are much better equipped to help young White children construct a positive sense of self that includes the emotional and cognitive capacity to thrive in and contribute to a diverse world. Indeed, they have the disposition and skills to become better teachers for all children and adults.

We invite you to join with us in the much needed project to "grow" White children who will strive for a society without racism and thrive in a just, equitable, peaceful, multicultural world. If you are reading the book for the first time, we look forward to your joining in the conversation about how to raise and educate White children to become part of building a more just society and world for all. If you are a returning reader, we hope the new material will give you further insights and tools for continuing your AB/MC education work.

We wrote this book in the spirit of humility, knowing that as White persons we will never be completely free of assumptions and actions that reflect our unearned privileges. However, we also write with hope that this book will encourage you to push through your fears and resistance, to examine your lives and assumptions more closely, and to consider how we might work together to change the way that children learn about the world.

1

Ideals to Practice:
The Journey

Something happens. You see a group of children laughing at a new class member who speaks with an accent. You listen in on three little girls (all White) playing in the costume corner, and one says, "I get to be princess 'cuz I've got blonde hair," and the other girls agree without comment. . . . And because you care about children, care about helping them live joyfully in a diverse world, can't bear to see children hurt or learning fear and bias, you feel that you have to do *something*.
—Louise Derman-Sparks and Julie Olsen Edwards,
Anti-Bias Education for Young Children & Ourselves

The vision that guides anti-bias/multicultural work with White children and families is a country and world where prejudice and discrimination no longer exist, and all children thrive. We construct the paths to this destination as we walk them; mistakes and insecurities are inevitable. Here are two examples of the feelings many teachers relate:

I loved your multicultural workshop; I felt inspired to come back to my center and work on these issues with the kids and families. But whenever I try something, it never goes the way that I had planned, and then I get anxious about saying or doing the wrong thing, and the whole thing falls kind of flat. (email to Patty)

"As I've been doing this work, I've found that most of the resistance I've met has been my own—feeling uncomfortable, feeling I wasn't ready. But I would go ahead, and for the most part, it would turn out fine. I'd be glad that I took the chance." (Barbara Yasui, quoted in Alvarado, Derman-Sparks, & Ramsey, 1999, p. 167)

Like all deeply important curriculum, AB/MC education requires self-scrutiny, preparation, constant tending, enthusiasm, and commitment. It also requires faith in the outcome, as Eric Hoffman, an experienced anti-bias early childhood educator, explains: "I try to provide experiences that will sow the seeds of change. Then, sooner or later, children will incorporate those experiences into their thinking. I've learned it takes concrete experience, time, and faith in their intelligence" (quoted in Alvarado et al., 1999, p. 89). Doing AB/MC education also has the possibility of great rewards as teachers gain confidence in their work. Beth Wallace speaks for many when she affirms, "for me, anti-bias work is about wholeness. It allows me to . . . keep intact the fabric of my convictions about children, equity, and social justice" (quoted in Alvarado et al., 1999, p. 155).

Unfortunately, for most White adults, neither their education nor their life experiences provide the knowledge, analysis, and critical thinking skills about racism and other "isms" to create a solid foundation for doing AB/MC work. They lack role models who openly and directly talk about race and racism (or other forms of diversity and inequalities) with other adults. Indeed, most White children experience silence on these topics as they grow up, with the tacit message that such conversations are inappropriate, impolite, and dangerous. In her work with White teachers, Thomas (2005) found that most felt "held back from the kind of questioning and experimenting that children need to do in order to understand a complex issue like race." One teacher said, "We don't talk about these things [race] in our family." Another teacher explained that her family's position was, "If they aren't in your life, what's there to talk about?" (p. 1). Moreover, insufficient professional training for doing AB/MC work stymies teachers. A few in-service workshops or add-on modules in a college class are not enough preparation to authentically raise and explore these issues with adults and children (Chang, Muckelroy, & Pulido-Tobiassen, 1996).

Thus, when children make comments that require direct responses, teachers often freeze—unable to use the knowledge and skills they do have, as illustrated by the following account:

> Darcy was talking with her kindergartners (90% White and 10% Asian American) about the many ways that people cook rice, which was part of a larger curriculum on food. Mei, Eileen's mother, a Chinese American woman, was in the classroom that day to do a cooking project with the children. As Darcy was showing the children photographs of families from different countries cooking and eating rice, one White girl asked in a loud voice, "Why do Chinese people have funny eyes?" Darcy felt her mouth go dry

and her stomach lurch. She glanced at Mei and saw that Mei and Eileen were both looking down. She knew that she should do something, but wasn't sure what to say and was afraid of making things worse. So she took a deep breath, went back to the topic of rice, and introduced the cooking activity that Mei was going to do. Afterward, talking to her supervisor, she realized how she often panicked when the subject of race and racial prejudice came up openly, especially if she was in the presence of people from different racial groups. She also worried that her discomfort had been obvious to the children and that in her rush to get to "safe ground" [the cooking project] she had probably reinforced the idea that Chinese people have "funny eyes."

Darcy and her supervisor talked about why she was so frightened about talking about race. They began to plan a series of staff discussion about the emotional challenges of talking openly and honestly about race as a critical aspect of effective AB/MC practice.

However, even well prepared and seasoned teachers still face events and comments that cause uncertainty. Teachers always take risks, as Hoffman describes,

> Anything I try will be unsatisfactory to someone, make someone uncomfortable, or cause a conflict. But if I try to meet every possible criticism before I take action, I will be paralyzed. So I've got to keep moving ahead with my best thinking, learn from the results, listen to the criticism, and try again. (quoted in Alvarado et al., 1999, p. 106)

EXPANDING AND DEEPENING YOUR SELF-KNOWLEDGE

Carrying out effective AB/MC education work with children and adults, be they colleagues, families, or adult students, begins with expanding and deepening awareness and knowledge about your own racial/ethnic identity and cultural values teaching. The process of self-reflection is necessary for all effective teaching. It has particular importance, however, when we are teaching material that requires us to grow and learn alongside the children and families to whom we are responsible. This work calls on us to look closely at our views, feelings, information, and behaviors in relation to the many issues of race, racial identity, and racism. Understanding the hallmarks of the anti-racism journey and the behaviors that either interfere with or support our growth is also part of the process.

In a society that has obscured and hidden the realities of White racial privilege and its effect on the rest of the world, all of us are finding new ways to think and act, learning as we go. We have all been affected by racial and racist thinking since our earliest social encounters (see Chapter 3). Thus, none of us are free from misinformation, discomforts, prejudices, or behaviors that reflect the power relationships of racism. At the same time, we all also have the potential to resist messages of racism and gain new knowledge and learn new behaviors that help build a society free of racism. To embark on the anti-racism journey, we need to truly accept that we all need to take it and that it will continue throughout our lives. We need to focus on the process, not the end point and pursue this work with honesty, persistence, and humility.

To get you started, here are a number of questions to consider. Some may be easier or more meaningful to you; others might make you angry or seem to be irrelevant to your life. All are important. The questions we resist or dismiss may be the ones that tap our deepest pain and fears and offer the most useful growth. The ones we are clearer about will lead the way. Deepen your self-reflection by talking with trusted friends and colleagues and/or keeping a journal.

About yourself:

- What are all my reference-group identities (race, ethnicity, national or regional origin of family ancestors, religion, gender, political affiliations, economic class, sexual orientation, ableness)? What does each mean to me? Which ones have most affected me at different points in my life?
- How central is race/ethnicity in my sense of myself? In what specific ways have I gained/lost societal benefits because of my racial/ethnic identity? (See McIntosh, 1995.) What experiences/lessons gave me the most insight about my racial/ethnic identity?
- What cultural rules (values and behaviors) and traditions did I learn growing up? How have these shaped my teaching goals and practices? (If you have trouble identifying your cultural rules, think about incidents in your childhood, perhaps a time you were punished or rewarded, and analyze the messages in those interactions. Then do the same for recent incidents in your work with children. How did your reactions reflect the cultural rules you learned as a child?)
- What are my current social and cultural contexts? What values, rules of behavior, and traditions guide my current decisions such as choice of friends/social groups, occupation, and spiritual, political, and leisure activities?

- What assumptions and comfort levels do I have about White people who are rich? Poor? Athletic? Disabled? Female? Male? Gay? Bisexual? Transgender? Straight? Who speak with an accent or dialect different from mine? Follow a different religion? How do these assumptions and comfort levels influence my interactions with specific individuals?
- How did the family in which I grew up define success? How do I now define success? By promotions and salary increases? Societal recognition? New acquisitions? Family relationships? Working with others? Contributing to the larger community? Being creative? Finding spiritual fulfillment? How have my race, culture, gender, religion, and family background influenced this orientation?
- What roles do competition and cooperation play in my identity? What lessons about them did I learn growing up? How do I react when someone is more or less "successful" than I am?
- In what ways is Whiteness "the invisible norm" in my life? My community? My workplace?
- What is my vision of a new White identity that is not based on racial advantage? What would it look like, feel like? What would my sense of self and my life experiences be like if advantage and disadvantage were not connected to race and racial identity? How do I think I can live at least parts of this identity in my current life?

About working with other people:

- Are there individuals I understand and empathize with more than with others? What accounts for these different responses? What roles do race, social class, culture, occupation, age, gender, sexual orientation, abilities, religion, or political views play in my responses to others?
- When I disagree with someone, how much do I try to understand his or her perspective and find common ground? How concerned am I about "winning" the argument? How do I react to people who disagree with me about lifestyles? Political views? Child-rearing values? Educational philosophies? Religion?
- How do I react when racial issues come up in conversations? Do I feel anxious? Defensive? Do I speak openly, or do I start censoring myself? How do my reactions differ if I am in a group in which everyone is the same race as I am versus one that is racially diverse?
- What are my hopes for and fears about opening up issues of race and racism with myself, with my family and friends, with colleagues? How can I work with and overcome these fears? Who are potential allies?

As you think about the self-reflection questions, treat these encounters as an exploration of where you are now and where you want to go on the anti-racism journey. You will find additional reflection questions at the end of Chapters 1–3 and 6–7. Use them to keep moving on your journey of self-awareness, deepening your knowledge and expanding your skills for doing AB/MC education with children and adults. You may also want to look at the "Stop and Think" questions in *Anti-Bias Education for Young Children & Ourselves* (Derman-Sparks & Edwards, 2010).

PHASES OF THE WHITE ANTI-RACIST JOURNEY

As you build your self-awareness and knowledge about doing AB/MC education, you may find that you experience unexpected feelings. Several educators and researchers have identified patterns and phases in how the anti-racist identity and action journey proceeds for Whites and People of Color (Derman-Sparks & Phillips, 1997; Helms, 1990; Tatum, 1992, 1994). Being aware of the main characteristics of these patterns and phases can be a useful resource for understanding and guiding your own growth, as well as that of other adults. While the research on anti-racism identity development reveals the challenges of this journey, it also offers hope and inspiration. It documents how people can grow in their self-understanding, learn to manage increasingly complex racial material, take active responsibility for challenging racism, heal the wounds of alienation and dehumanization that racism creates, and open up to the richness of human diversity in our country and world.

As you read the following description of common phases of White anti-racist identity development, keep in mind that the process is fluid and more like a spiral than a linear progression. Moreover, each person's journey is unique, and individuals often make detours and get stuck at certain points on the journey before moving ahead. So avoid pigeonholing yourself or others or expecting that you or anyone else will pass smoothly through these phases. To learn about the anti-racist identity journey of People of Color, start with the books mentioned in the previous paragraph.

Exploring Racism

The journey begins when you start exploring the reality and implications of your racial identity, Whiteness and the systemic advantages and disadvantages of racism. Doing this often requires overcoming fears of what might happen as you learn about racism—thus breaking silence and denial (Tatum, 1992). Many White individuals fear losing connections with family, colleagues, and friends when they start to learn and speak up about racism.

You may find that you have to overcome ideas that interfere with taking the initial steps of the anti-racism journey. You may tell yourself that racism is a thing of the past or that you have no responsibility for what happened before you were alive. You may claim that you are "color blind" and not personally prejudiced (Mazzei, 2008; Picower, 2009).

Stay open to learning about the realities of race and racism—including how racism works at an institutional level and how children are constructing their ideas about their own and others' racial identity from very young ages. Answer the self-reflection questions for yourself, then share them with supportive friends and colleagues and listen to their stories. Learn how children in your classroom think about people from various racial/ethnic groups. (Guidelines and strategies for this investigation are in Chapters 4 and 8.) Review children's storybooks and television programming, using the information about identifying stereotypes and misinformation (see Appendix A). Choose some of the selections in "For Further Reading" found at the end of Chapters 1–3 and 6–7, as well as novels and autobiographies that describe how many different people have experienced racism.

Experiencing Disequilibrium

As you open up your eyes and heart to the realities of racism, you may, as do many others, experience a sense of disequilibrium. Many people feel guilty, sad, angry, and overwhelmed. As you face uncomfortable realizations about racism and experience the discomforts of disequilibrium, you may say to yourself, "Who needs this?" You may look for rationales to stop participating in any further learning and discussions about racial issues (e.g., "There are so many racist people out there, what can I as one individual do to make a difference?").

Share your feelings with trusted friends or colleagues or write about them in your journal. Don't wallow or get stuck in them. Keep in mind that we all learned racism from a very early age but as adults, we do have the power to change our attitudes and behavior. Begin to explore ways that you can begin to make small changes at home and work. Talk with individuals who are doing AB/MC education. You might find them in your community or meet them at local, state and national early childhood conferences or in a diversity committee of your state AEYC affiliate. Participating in small anti-bias actions (e.g., writing to publishers or television producers about stereotypes or omissions in their materials and programs for children), will help you re-direct guilt and discomfort toward positive outcomes.

Reaching Out

If you keep moving forward, you will get to another phase of your anti-racist journey when you are ready to create or join a support group of other anti-bias/multicultural educators. Together, you can gain a deeper understanding of how racism operates, including its institutional dynamics and its impact on children's development and on your own life. With this support and deepened understanding, you will feel more empowered to explore how to integrate anti-bias/multicultural education into more and more aspects of your work.

Making connections between racism and other forms of systemic advantage and disadvantage (sexism, heterosexism, classism, and ableism) will also strengthen your understanding of the overall structure of inequities and what you can do about them. Reading the stories of other White persons who have struggled with their own racism and have participated in anti-racism movements can be a great source of encouragement and counsel. These accounts help reclaim the history of White dissent that has often been omitted or glossed over in history books and provide role models for the construction of a "new White" identity (see Chapter 6).

However, you also need to watch out for dynamics that will undermine your ongoing growth, as well your effectiveness working with other people. During this phase of the journey, some White individuals try to disconnect themselves from other Whites. They identify themselves as the "good Whites," to distinguish themselves from overtly racist White people (Hayes & Juárez, 2009). They may also seek out affirmations from People of Color to bolster their identities as "good Whites" (Derman-Sparks & Phillips, 1997). A support group will give you supportive yet honest feedback and brainstorm alternative ways of acting (see Chapter 9).

Engaging in AB/MC Work

By continuing on the anti-racist journey for the long haul and through many periods of doubt and discomfort, people gain a clear, positive racial identity within a social-political context, and accept their responsibility for working to end racism and build a more just society. Individuals in this phase recognize that their future is integrally connected to what happens to the rest of the human family. Actively doing AB/MC education and participating in other anti-racist, social justice movements feels normal. Many find that engaging in anti-racism work is a reflection of their core identity and integrity (Derman-Sparks & Phillips, 1997).

STRATEGIC PLANNING FOR CHILDREN

Another essential component of carrying out effective AB/MC work involves strategic planning for the learning environment and curriculum. We recommend the following six steps:

1. *Formulate a specific topic or central question* based on children's questions or incidents that have occurred in the classroom or community. Alternatively, the topic may rise from your own experiences, concerns, or those of parents or staff members. However, it must be relevant to children's current concerns and ideas. As you develop your focus, consider how it relates to the learning themes described in the Introduction.
2. *Gather and analyze relevant information.* Through observations and conversations, learn how children feel about this issue. How does it relate to family background and experiences and the community? How do families and staff members feel about the issue and what do they know about it?
3. *Use your analysis to generate clear, child-based inquiry questions* on which to build your curriculum.
4. *Collaborate with children and families to choose, create, and implement specific activities* for children, families, staff, or a combination of these.
5. *Observe how children and families respond to the activities and invite them to evaluate and offer suggestions* about how to develop the curriculum.
6. *Identify new or deeper ways to explore the current issue or choose a new focus,* based on what you learned in Step 5. The strategic planning cycle begins again, always building on the previous cycle.

In the following example, teachers in one all-White preschool classroom (3- and 4-year-olds) created a series of activities based on their observations that the children were avoiding dark colors in their artwork and making disparaging remarks about photographs of darker-skinned people. Working with the children, the teachers investigated this issue and created an integrated curriculum focusing on darkness and lightness in their many forms and expressions. Through these activities, they encouraged children to explore new perspectives and to challenge their racialized feelings about darkness and lightness. This project touched on learning themes four and five.

To learn more about why and how the children were avoiding dark colors, the teachers put out markers and paints of many different colors, including black, brown, and different skin tones, and closely observed which colors specific children selected and avoided. They also watched how much children played with the darker-skinned dolls versus the lighter-skinned ones. They provided books that depicted children of different racial groups. As much as they could, the teachers unobtrusively listened to children's conversations as they played with the dolls and leafed through the books. At times, they shared their observations with individual children or small groups of children and encouraged them to express their ideas about why they and their peers were making specific choices.

When they pooled their observations, the teachers felt that they had a comprehensive idea about how specific children were thinking and feeling about darkness and lightness as a physical phenomenon and how they related to children's early racial conceptions and attitudes.

The teachers knew that the families were not familiar with AB/MC work. Moreover, when teachers raised the topic at the initial family-school meeting, a few families expressed reservations. Thus, the teachers felt that talking about colors rather than race per se might provide a better entry point. As part of the information-gathering step, the children interviewed family members about their most and least favorite colors. Parents reported that some of these interviews evolved into interesting conversations about why people like certain colors and why they tend to dislike darker colors.

As the teachers began to sift through the information and make their plans, they reviewed, and when necessary, augmented the resources at the school—art supplies (there was *plenty* of black and brown paint and paper), lighting equipment to do experiments on light and dark, and books and photographs depicting lightness and darkness (including positive images of darkness) and people with different shades of skin color.

From the very beginning of the curriculum project, the teachers worked closely with the director of the school. She committed herself to supporting them and talked about which families might be receptive and which ones more resistant. She also advised them how to avoid some of the problems that had happened in the past. For example, one teacher had been very confrontational with parents, which had resulted in a backlash against all AB/MC activities for a while. The teachers also reported their experiences and discussed their ideas at the monthly staff meeting. Several colleagues were interested and offered a number of suggestions. The teachers also invited family members to join in a couple of late-afternoon meetings to brainstorm ideas.

The children often talked about how they found dark spaces and objects scary. So the teachers and children planned initial activities to explore and dispel this association. With the help and advice of children and several parents, they created activities using the colors brown and black—painting with light colors on brown and black paper, making black play dough, and experimenting with shadows. Children and parents brainstormed and provided positive images of darkness, such as black and brown puppies, stuffed animals, and the cool shade under a big tree. The teachers and children created a house out of a refrigerator box and painted the inside black and put in lots of soft pillows to make it a restful place.

Finally, teachers introduced activities and concepts; they observed and documented children's reactions carefully. They quickly discovered that the house was too frightening—the children either avoided it altogether or threatened to put each other into the "scary" house. One of the parents suggested punching a few small holes to let in a bit of light. From that point on, the house became a popular spot for children who needed time alone. It also provided opportunities for teachers to talk about how restful and peaceful darkness can be.

As the curriculum developed, the teachers shifted the focus from colors per se to skin colors and race. The children, having spent a lot of time working with black and many shades of brown, no longer had an automatic aversion to darker skin but were eager to learn more about why skin colors vary. When they discovered that a new box of markers did not include the colors black and brown (a common occurrence), the children dictated a letter to the manufacturer protesting this absence and its underlying message that black and brown are not appealing.

Doing AB/MC education means cherishing its hopeful possibilities and meeting its challenges. It requires that we engage in our own ongoing growth, and become skilled at observing how the children and adults with whom we work think about diversity and equity issues. It also requires learning about the ever-changing dynamics of the community and the larger society, and their influence on children and families. It requires our creativity as well as our knowledge.

Being an AB/MC educator means accepting that this work is a life journey of learning and growing, through which we must be persistent yet strategic, passionate yet thoughtful, proactive yet patient. Ultimately, it requires us to have faith that change can and will happen.

Reflection Questions

1. After reading this chapter, where do you see your strengths for doing AB/MC education? What are areas where you want to grow? What are some of the ways you can do so?
2. Did you recognize any of your own feelings and behaviors in the discussion of phases of the anti-racism journey? How might you use this information to further your own growth?
3. Reflecting on your work as a teacher, are there ways that you are already using the strategic planning process? How might you strengthen this approach?
4. What strengths, experiences, commitments, and understandings do you bring to this journey to help you continue and grow?

For Further Reading

Derman-Sparks, L., & Edwards, J. O. (2010). Becoming an anti-bias teacher: A developmental journey. In *Anti-bias education for young children & ourselves*. Washington, DC: NAEYC.

Derman-Sparks, L., & Phillips, C. B. (1997). *Teaching/learning anti-racism: A developmental approach*. New York: Teachers College Press.

IDENTITY AND RACISM

Part I (Chapters 2, 3, 4, and 5) turns the spotlight on White identity formation and characteristics. In Chapter 2 we look at the historic formation and evolution of Whiteness in the United States. In Chapter 3 we review research about how children develop White identities and learn racism's codes of power. In Chapter 4 we discuss how to implement the first three learning themes with children and in Chapter 5 how to engage families and staff. Part I concludes with Episode One of "A Tale of Two Centers," which illustrates how teachers might implement the ideas in Chapters 4 and 5 in two different early childhood programs.

2

Whiteness and Racism in the United States:
A Brief Overview

> Whiteness is a concept, an ideology, which holds tremendous power over our lives and, in turn, over the lives of People of Color.
> —Paul Kivel, *Uprooting Racism:*
> *How White People Can Work for Racial Justice*

Despite many decades of reform, systemic racism continues to be a reality in the United States that profoundly affects us all. Systemic racism includes any attitude, action, or practice by an individual or institution, backed up by societal power, that undermines human and legal rights, economic opportunities, and cultural expressions of people because of their racial or ethnic identity. Moreover, "interactive acts of individuals and systems inexorably reinforce and entrench pervasive racial power across institutions, sites, and events" (Vaught & Castagno, 2008, p. 96). Deeply rooted in our history, this system of advantage and disadvantage profoundly influences the official and informal ways people are classified and treated. It also determines children's lives, including their degree of access to wholesome and sufficient food, decent housing, quality medical care, education, and neighborhood and environmental safety.

In addition to affecting daily life, systemic racism also significantly shapes the developing racial identity of all children. White children's learning to be "White" is part of the maintenance of systemic racism, and "Whiteness" plays a significant role in the behavior of all White adults.

From childhood on, through both direct and indirect socialization and encounters with the many ways "race" plays out in the larger society, "Whiteness" is integrated into individuals' understanding and feelings about themselves and their role in society. Despite this, adults can make intentional choices about how they live their racial identity and how they teach children about being White people. While we recognize that changing individual beliefs and behaviors by itself will not end systemic racism, personal transformations can and do contribute to collective efforts to dismantle the system of racism and build a more just world.

ROOTS AND HISTORY OF RACISM

Racism requires the belief that within the human species, biological "racial" differences exist, and some racial groups are superior to others. This concept was deeply rooted in early European ideologies (e.g., the English view of the Irish as savages, the exclusion or restriction of Jewish people in many countries). When European colonizers came to the Americas, their assumptions about racial superiority enabled them to justify the genocide, enslavement, and removal of indigenous people and the kidnapping and enslavement of African people. Many "scientific" and popular writings in the 18th, 19th, and early 20th centuries supported this thinking and went to great lengths to "prove" that Europeans, particularly northern Europeans, were a superior race (Brown, 2002).

In the 20th century, scientific evidence increasingly made clear that there was no valid genetic basis for distinguishing racial groups. In fact, decades of genetic research and, most recently, the Human Genome Project, have shown that there is more within-race than between-race variability (Brown, 2002).

Regardless of scientific conclusions, race is, and has always been, a social-political construct masquerading as biological fact. Social, economic, and political forces define and redefine *race* (Omi & Winant, 1986) in ways that have reflected the interests and beliefs of those in power. Despite its lack of validity, this construct underlies a system of racial advantage and disadvantage and continues to influence the life prospects of all Americans—both those who are viewed as racially superior and those who are targets of racial discrimination.

The idea that racism is an intentionally created and maintained system that advantages European Americans is a difficult one for White people to swallow. Most would prefer to maintain the status quo and "help" the disadvantaged rather than recognize and challenge their own racial power and privilege (Tatum, 1997). Accepting this definition of racism requires White people to face the fact that eliminating racism does not mean simply unlearning individual prejudice. Rather, it requires transforming economic and political systems and structures, giving up power, and equitably sharing resources.

Racism and Entitlement

Many analyses of racism focus on People of Color, while ignoring the notion of Whiteness that is imbedded in racial hierarchies. However, assumptions about racial inferiority could not exist without the concept of superiority. "Ideological racism includes strongly positive images of the White self as well as strongly negative images of the racial 'others'" (Feagin, 2000, p. 33). These beliefs, in turn, engender a sense of entitlement, which is the core of the social-political construct of Whiteness.

> When people grow up in a society where, despite rhetoric about equal opportunity, they are given more access to power, status, goods and services, they will come to think that they or their group is superior and that they deserve more than others. And they may become upset, bitter, and resentful if they don't receive what they see as their due. In fact, when they are treated the same or like everyone else, because of their expectations they will perceive themselves to be victimized or to be at a disadvantage, simply because they have lost the unacknowledged advantage they had. (Kivel, 2002, p. 42)

This sense of entitlement reinforces the widespread belief that White people's financial and professional successes are the results of their own efforts, while denying the fact that they have also benefited from White racial advantage (Tatum, 1997). It also underlies the bitterness that many White people feel about affirmative action programs.

The Definitions and Contradictions of Whiteness

The earliest European settlers needed to define who was and was not White, in order to distinguish themselves from the "race" of enslaved Africans and their offspring. As Eric Dyson explains, "Only when black bodies—through slavery on to the present—have existed on American terrain has Whiteness been constituted as an idea and, indeed, an identity-based reality" (cited in Chennault, 1998, p. 300). Court cases and legislation attempted to clarify racial boundaries and to codify White powers and privileges not legally given to other "races." Furthermore, it was necessary to define which people were property and therefore not qualified to receive any of the legal benefits of the new United States (e.g., the right to their children, the right to vote). Thus, White indentured servants from Europe were able to earn their freedom and subsequently gain legal and economic advantages (e.g., owning and inheriting property, voting, getting an education, receiving legal protections of due process), whereas enslaved Africans could not.

The parameters of Whiteness, however, have not remained constant. Debates about which ethnic groups are White have erupted from time to time. The outcomes of these controversies were not simply academic; they affected the civil status, rights, and economic viability of each group. The determination of European Americans to maintain control often resulted in convoluted and contradictory legal reasoning. For example, in 1923 the U.S. Supreme Court denied citizenship to a Japanese resident because, notwithstanding his White skin, he did not have Caucasian features. Three months later the Court denied Indian immigrants citizenship because, although they had Caucasian features, they had dark skin (Foley, 2002).

Wealth and connections with the European American establishment also played a role in these legal proceedings. In California in the mid-1880s, Mexicans who were rich landowners and business partners with White people were legally designated as White, whereas poor Mexicans and Chinese laborers were categorized as non-White (Kivel, 2002).

The "Whitening" of European Immigrants

During the great waves of immigration from southern and eastern Europe in the late 19th century, scholars and politicians in the United States "discovered" that "Europe had inferior and superior races" (Brodkin, 2002, p. 36). Earlier, European immigrants from different countries had assimilated into Anglo-American communities. When 23 million immigrants arrived, however, they were too numerous to blend in, and cities had increasing numbers of distinct ethnic communities. Not surprisingly, wealthy White Protestants who had come from northwestern Europe felt threatened and regarded this influx as "race suicide" (p. 37).

Similar to the "scientific" justifications for slavery that had appeared in the 18th and 19th centuries, tests were created in the early 20th century to distinguish superior "Nordics" from inferior "Alpines," "Mediterraneans," and Jews. "By the 1920s, recognized scholars endorsed the notion that real Americans were White and real White people came from northwest Europe" (Brodkin, 2002, p. 38). However, even these categories embodied many contradictions. For example, the courts consistently ruled that Finns, who were ethnically Nordic, were not White people, because they occupied the lowest-paid and riskiest mining and lumbering jobs in the upper Midwest (Kivel, 2002).

New "non-White" European immigrants were scorned and marginalized and were often the target of racial violence (such as lynching and race riots). They quickly learned that to be American meant becoming "White" (Barrett & Roediger, 2002). European immigrants from various nationalities and ethnicities bought into the myth of White supremacy to legitimize their membership in the dominant group and their claims to economic privilege (Roediger, 2005). Becoming White, as Toni Morrison writes, required that "a hostile posture toward resident blacks must be struck at the Americanizing door before it will open" (cited in Foley, 2002, p. 55). Ignatiev (1995) describes how Irish immigrants, who experienced great discrimination from Anglo-Americans and initially identified with their Black coworkers, became hostile to Black people as they learned the advantages of being White people. Likewise, Brodkin (1998, 2002) and Guglielmo and Salerno (2003) trace the history of how Jewish and Italian people in the United States also became "White." This pressure to distinguish and distance oneself from African and Asian Americans sowed the seeds of intransigent racism that has undermined the unity and effectiveness of the labor movement and has deeply imbedded a racist ideology into our national psyche. Moreover, the choice to become "White" came at a personal cost: the significant loss of cultural and linguistic heritage and family history (Brodkin, 2002; Gossett, 1963; Ignatiev, 1995). Not surprisingly, many White Americans now express regret about "not having any culture."

Diversity Among White People

Although the umbrella of White advantage benefits all people allowed under it, White people are not homogeneous. Nor are the advantages of Whiteness equally distributed.

Historically, upper-class settlers emigrating from England in the 17th and 18th centuries became the most privileged group. "Boston Brahmins," New York merchants, and Southern plantation owners dominated the early cultural and political history of this country. Many of their descendents still hold sway in financial, political, and educational institutions. In contrast, poor English, Irish, and Scottish families who arrived at about the same time often settled in isolated communities in the Appalachian Mountains. Their descendants have been the targets of ridicule and discrimination for centuries, giving rise to derogatory remarks about "hillbillies" and "rednecks."

Today, the material advantages of being White are still not equally distributed. Lower-income White people do not experience the full benefits of White privilege accorded their more affluent counterparts. White families from a range of ethnic groups suffer chronic severe poverty. As with other racial groups, gender and age affect economic status; with women, children, and the elderly most often living in poverty. Yet even though they have less economic and political power than middle-class and wealthy White persons, the poorest White people do not suffer the added pressures of racial discrimination that shape the lives and prospects of People of Color. Their Whiteness functions as blinders that enable them to focus their resentment of their poverty on People of Color (Leonardo, 2007).

Within ethnic and social-class groups, individual White people respond to the realities of racism in different ways. Some dismiss the notion that they are privileged. Others feel powerless and resent programs that they perceive as unfairly advantaging People of Color. Some may be more secure in their livelihoods but choose to ignore or justify the plight of groups that suffer from racism. Still others may challenge the existing racially based power structure by engaging in multicultural and social justice work.

CONTEMPORARY WHITE RACISM

The end of legal segregation occurred during the 1950s and 1960s. Since that time, legislation designed to remedy the inequitable outcomes of two centuries of legal slavery and segregation has appreciably moved the United States toward the goal of becoming a "post-racial" society (Lipsitz, 2002). These changes came about because of the long-time efforts of many hundreds of thousands of people from all racial and ethnic backgrounds who participated in the civil rights movement. Too many among them gave their lives to the cause of ending racism.

Still, the United States is not a post-racial society. We have a long way to go to fulfilling the dream of ending all forms of institutional and individual racism.

The Impact of Racism on People's Lives

Economic and other quality-of-life statistics give clear evidence of how institutionalized racial advantage and disadvantage continue to reverberate in this country. Nowhere is this more apparent than in data about young children. According to the National Center for Children in Poverty (Wight & Chau, 2009), figures for 2008, the percentage of children under age 6 living in low-income families was 30% for White children, but 69% for American Indian children, 64% for African American children, and 64% for Hispanic children. Furthermore, economic inequities are increasing in the United States. A recent study revealed that the wealth gap between White and Black people had more than quadrupled in one generation (Cose, 2010). In 1984, the discrepancy between the accumulated wealth of White and Black Americans (excluding home equity) was $20,000; by 2007 it had grown to $95,000.

The economic meltdown that began in 2008 revealed how low-income people, who are disproportionately People of Color, are still victimized by financial practices such as subprime mortgages and predatory lending policies. Conversely, many of the CEOs and other higher ranking members of these financial institutions benefited from bailouts and retained their multimillion-dollar salaries and bonuses. As economic conditions continued to worsen, thousands of low- and middle-income individuals lost their jobs and homes. During the recession, low-income Black families (household incomes under $40,000) lost most of their savings, leaving them with financial reserves that would last less than a week if their incomes were reduced or lost altogether (Cose, 2010).

The gap between affluent and poor families directly affects children in a number of ways. Kozol (1991) described the "savage inequalities" between schools in wealthy and low-income neighborhoods that create unequal educational opportunities from the very beginning of children's lives. Economic disparities also have health consequences. Not only do poor people have less access to health care, they suffer more health risks because hazardous waste sites and highly polluting industrial facilities are likely to be located in their neighborhoods (Carr & Kutty, 2008; Wise, 2009). Unlike White affluent communities, poor communities lack the economic and political clout to protect themselves from these risks.

The effects of economic disparities also emerge across and within early childhood settings. The majority of early childhood programs are segregated by income and therefore often by race. Affluent families either employ nannies or send their children to expensive private schools; working-class and poor families use federally funded services such as Head Start or rely on family members or neighbors for childcare; and middle-class families struggle to find quality child care that they can afford. Racial hierarchies often exist within child-care centers and schools; the custodial and paraprofessional staff and at least some teachers are likely to be People of Color, whereas directors and principals are usually White.

However, despite their many advantages, most White people are paying the costs of racism, even though these costs may not be apparent to them. Tatum (1997) points out how racism undermines the whole economy:

> Whether one looks at productivity lowered by racial tensions in the workplace, or real estate equity lost through housing discrimination, or the tax revenue lost in underemployed communities of color, or the high cost of warehousing human talent in prison, the economic costs of racism are real and measurable. (p. 140)

In addition, the lower wages of People of Color have been and continue to be an available weapon to undermine the wages of White workers, a weapon that has been used repeatedly (Roediger, 1991).

Despite many legal efforts and the widespread perception that racism is a thing of the past, indicator after indicator demonstrate that White families enjoy higher incomes, longer life spans, better health care, more education, and better-serviced neighborhoods than do People of Color. Although some individual People of Color do have high incomes, they do not have the protective racial bubble that provides White people a sense of belonging and an assumption that they have the right to access resources as needed.

Current Beliefs about Race and Racism

With the official, legal ending of segregation laws affecting a range of public institutions, the notion of *color-blindness* began to dominate cultural discourse. While initially an argument against White bigotry and White supremacist ideology, the notion of color-blindness harbors serious flaws. Many White people use the claim that "color doesn't matter" to ignore the past and continued realities of the impact of systemic racism. Insisting "I don't know if my children are Black or White or green or purple" enables teachers to deny their own racial ideologies and to dismiss children's racial and cultural contexts and their families' experiences of racism (Derman-Sparks & Edwards, 2010). In fact, "Today, the color-blind ideology provides a veneer of liberality which covers up continuing racist thought and practice that is often less overt and more disguised" (Feagin, 2000, p. 93).

Recent studies have revealed disturbing evidence of racial bias in the behavior of early childhood teachers, who, for the most part, believed that they were color-blind. In a large-scale study of the quality of pre-K programs Barbarin and Crawford (2006) reported that trained observers documented case after case of teacher actions that stigmatized African American boys. These practices included isolating and excluding children, expressing hostility, and giving racially disparate punishment and rewards. A study of expulsion numbers of pre-K children revealed that the rate for African American children is twice the rate of White children (Gillian, 2005, as reported in Barbarin & Crawford, 2006). Mednick and Ramsey (2008) observed a consistent pattern of teachers favoring White 2nd graders for classroom privileges and academic recognition. Moreover, teachers often punished children of color based solely on the White children's reports of "misbehaviors."

A variant of the color-blind line of reasoning is the contention that because race is not a valid biological entity, eliminating the use of the term is a way to end racism. However, the dynamics of racism continue to powerfully influence the life prospects of America's children who all experience "either the societal advantages or disadvantages connected to . . . [their] racial identity" (Derman-Sparks & Edwards, 2010, p. 78). Not talking about race does not make the inequalities of racism go away. *Enlightened exceptionalism* is another way for White people to accommodate the success of individual People of Color, while still holding stereotypes and fears about the larger mass of Black and Brown Americans (Wise, 2009). For example, White individuals might vote for Barack Obama, while continuing to blame the majority of African Americans, and other People of Color, for their poverty, unemployment, and lack of health care (Wise, 2009).

Beginning with the ending of legal segregation, and further strengthened by the election of America's first African American president, many White people argue that White dominance and racism are a thing of the past. For example, the day after the election of President Obama, the *Wall Street Journal* editorial page stated, "One promise of his [Barack Obama's] victory is that perhaps we can put to rest the *myth of racism* [emphasis added] as a barrier to achievement in this splendid country" (quoted in Wise, 2009, p. 25).

Surveys over the past decade reveal that a majority of White Americans believe that racial discrimination is no longer a problem. However, People of Color disagree (Bush, 2004; Feagin, 2000; Wise, 2009). For example, significant differences were evident in three polls taken in summer 2008 (as reported in Wise, 2009, p. 31). In a survey for CNN and *Essence* magazine, "only one in nine Whites believe racial discrimination against Blacks is still a very serious problem, while nearly four times than that say it's not a serious problem at all." In contrast, in a *New York Times*/CBS poll, 7 in 10 African Americans said they had suffered specific discriminatory incidents. A Gallup/*USA Today* poll revealed that more than 75% of White respondents said that African Americans have "just as good a chance as White people" to get any job for which they qualify, a good education, and any housing they can afford. In contrast, less than 50% of African Americans agreed.

Given these data, it is not surprising that White people often claim that they are the victims of a "reverse racism" from affirmative action policies designed to begin to equalize opportunities in housing, jobs, and schools for People of Color (Lipsitz, 2002). However, there are no hard data to support the idea of "reverse racism." To the contrary, one study found that at least a third of all participating employers discriminated against job applicants of color. Another study found that White-owned firms received 92% of all municipal, state, and federal contracts (Wise, 2009).

Resurgence of White Bigotry: The Post-2008 Backlash

As we discussed in the Introduction, during and after the 2008 election, White nationalist/supremacist groups that openly advocate racial bigotry, hate, and violence resurfaced in both old and new forms with a significant rise in their membership (Potok, 2010). Some of these groups have roots in groups that appeared in the aftermath of Civil War (e.g., Ku Klux Klan); others are offshoots of groups formed in the post-legal segregation period to roll-back or prevent further integration of schools and services (e.g., White Councils, local groups that virulently and sometimes violently opposed all forms of racial integration). All of the White nationalist movements share the belief that "America's greatness derives from its racial character as an all-White nation . . . [and] that multiculturalism, immigration, and racial diversity fundamentally threaten America's future" (Levitas, 2010, p. 1).

It is not wise to dismiss these groups as "just a crazy fringe," given their numbers and their influence on mainstream Americans. For example, 18% of all people in the United States identify themselves as supporters of the Tea Party, which holds very libertarian positions on domestic and social policies and has concluded that "too much has been made of the problems facing Black people" (Zernike & Thee-Brenan, 2010, p. 2). Tea Party activists are largely White males who are over 45 years old and married.

Although people join the Tea Party for a number of reasons, racism is a key theme in their literature, as an analysis of their email newsletters for a 3-month period (May-July 2010) reveals. Stereotypic and caricature images of African Americans, frequently of President Obama and of Latinos, are one manifestation of their racism. Perhaps the most upsetting image appeared in an article entitled "Tea Party's Core Beliefs" (June 16, 2010). In an altered photograph, President Obama sits on a sidewalk in a run-down part of the city, two liquor bottles and what looks like a needle and vial in front of him, and an accordion in his hands. The caption on top of the image is "Obama goes fund raising" (p. 2).

A second manifestation of Tea Party racism, which has long-standing roots in overt racist ideology, equates African American men with thugs and gangsters. One issue of the Tea Party newsletter described the current administration as a "thug-ocracy" and "Obama Tyranny" (June 26, 2010).

Accusing the President of taking the nation down the socialist road is a third form of racism. Equating civil rights activists with communists has a long history in our country—a charge that was frequently leveled against Dr. Martin Luther King, Jr. Ironically, Tea Party emails (e.g., May 31, 2010) also equate Obama with Hitler, even though Hitler was the ultimate champion of White supremacy.

We believe that a preponderance of White Americans *do not* subscribe to the extreme racist views and violence of organized White nationalist hate groups. Tea Party members still represent a minority of the population. However, the ever-increasing levels of fear and anxiety most Whites feel about their safety since the tragedy of 9/11 and about their own economic survival because of the recession, create a climate vulnerable to the appeal of racial bigotry. Tragically, identifying the causes and finding solutions to economic and environmental challenges is sidetracked into anger at People of Color. As Archbishop Tutu of South Africa remarked during the early 1990s, another time of economic hardship in the United States, "Racism is becoming acceptable in western society because proponents are adept at playing on people's fears and anxiety at a time of economic difficulty. You have to stand up to be counted amongst those who oppose it" (*Jet*, 1/13/92).

Immigration and Nativist Movements

Immigration policies and the rights of migrants have long engendered controversy in the United States (and elsewhere). Ethnocentric and racist thinking is one consistent thread in a complicated knot made up of several different threads. Uncanny parallels exist between the arguments made against some European migrant groups in the 1900s and those made today against Mexican American and other Latino migrants.

In 1911, a Congressional Commission published a 42-volume report on the threats posed by large-scale migration from southern and eastern Europe. In a summary, two commission members wrote about their concerns that immigrants who failed to assimilate and learn English were displacing native-born workers, were illiterate, and caused limits on wage increases (Kaye, 2010).

During this period, the nativist movement took off. One well-known proponent, the chair of the New York Zoological Society, argued that "the 'Nordics' of northern and western Europe who settled America [were] a pure race of one of the most gifted and vigorous stocks on earth" (quoted in Kaye, 2010, p. 159). In contrast, new immigrants from southern and eastern Europe lowered and vulgarized the whole tone of American life—social, moral, and political (Kaye, 2010).

The nativist influence on the debate over immigration resulted in several Immigration Acts (1917, 1921, 1924), which established a literacy test, specifically barred some migrants (e.g., Asians), and defined national preferences and quotas that favored northern European immigrants. Then, supported by the rise of the Civil Rights Movement, Congress passed the Immigration and Nationality Act of 1965, abolishing the discriminatory system of assigning preferences based on national origins. Supporters of the law saw this as a milestone for racial equality (Kaye, 2010).

Skip to the 2000s, the debate over immigration policy and controls continues. According to the Southern Poverty Law Center:

> Since the late 1960s, the United States has experienced an explosive rise in nativism, or anti-immigrant sentiment, to a level of intensity not seen in nearly a century. This nativist backlash has been fueled by demographic changes, resulting largely from an influx of Latino immigrants and by projections that Whites will make up less than half the U.S. population by 2042. Hundreds of anti-immigrant groups have sprung up in all parts of the country, especially since 2005. (Beirich, 2010, p. 1)

In April 2010, a disquieting example of the impact of the nativist movement took place. Arizona passed a controversial immigration control law (SB 1070). Proponents argued that the purpose of the law is to identify, prosecute, and deport illegal immigrants. It requires police officers to detain people they suspect are in the country without authorization and to verify their status with federal officials. A stated reason for the Arizona law—a wave of crime brought about by undocumented migrants—is not backed by the state's official statistics. According to the U.S. Bureau of Justice Statistics, violent crime in Arizona fell from 531 to 447 people per 100,000 inhabitants over the 8 years ending in 2008. Nationwide, while the nation's illegal-immigrant population doubled from 1994 to 2004, the violent-crime rate declined 35% (Oppenheimer, 2010).

Opponents of the law argued that the law created an anti-civil and human rights environment. Carol Brunson Day, Executive Director of the National Black Child Development Institute, characterized the new Arizona immigration law as part of a long history of racially discriminatory legislation:

> From the time of the "three-fifths of a man" compromise inserted into the U.S. Constitution in the 1700s to the Jim Crow laws of the 1960s, Black men, women, and children have experienced the indignities of legislation designed to relegate our communities to the dangerous and disgraceful conditions of second-class citizenship. We are dismayed and outraged by these current governmental efforts to engage in these same practices with Latino and other ethnic communities, which we know have disastrous effects on children and on the parents and family members who care for them. (Personal communication, May 19, 2010)

Questions about the human-rights implications of the Arizona law reached beyond our country's borders. A group of United Nations experts on immigration, indigenous people, racism, and cultural rights warned, "A disturbing pattern of legislative activity hostile to ethnic minorities and immigrants has been established with the adoption of an immigration law that may allow for police action targeting individuals on the basis of their perceived ethnic origin." They questioned the "vague standards and seeping language" of the legislation, "which raise doubts about the law's compatibility with relevant international human rights treaties to which the United States is a party." The writers also stressed their concerns that people of Mexican, Latin American, or indigenous origin may be at heightened risks of being targeted (U.N. News Service, May 11, 2010, p. 1).

Instead of standing behind the curtain of illusion that the United States is now a post-racial society, it is vital to continue to challenge any form of racism. To do this, we need to understand how racism operates in all of its various faces and forms. One aspect of this work is how we foster the development of White children's identities and capacity for non-racist thriving in a diverse world. In the following chapter, we discuss how White children construct their racial identities and how racial categories, and their accompanying advantages and disadvantages, affect the course of development.

Reflection Questions

1. What do you know about your extended family's history that relates to the history of racism and Whiteness in the United States? What types of discrimination or privilege and economic advantages or disadvantages did they experience? How easily did they assimilate? What happened to their ethnic identity and cultural heritage in the process?
2. How do you think your extended family's history shaped your family's views about other groups? Your views growing up? Now?
3. How did you experience the "entitlement" and norm of Whiteness when you were growing up? Now?
4. In what ways do you think the White families and children with whom you work receive benefits or advantages from being White in our current society? In what ways do you and they experience the costs of racism?
5. Where do you stand regarding the current realities and differing beliefs about the continued existence of racial discrimination?

6.   What expressions or acts of racism have you witnessed, heard or read since the 2008 presidential election? How do you feel about the rise in racial hate groups and White nationalist groups, as documented by the Southern Poverty Law Center? What is your response to the Arizona law?

For Further Reading

Barndt, J. (2007). *Understanding and dismantling racism: The twenty-first century challenge to White America.* Minneapolis: Fortress Augsberg.

Kivel, P. (2002). *Uprooting racism: How White people can work for racial justice* (Rev. ed.). Gabriola Island, B.C., Canada: New Society.

Roediger, D. (2005). *Working toward Whiteness: How America's immigrants became White.* New York: Basic Books.

Tatum, B. D. (2007). *Can we talk about race? And other conversations in an era of school resegregation.* Boston: Beacon

Wise, T. (2009). *Between Barack and a hard place: Racism and White denial in the age of Obama.* San Francisco: City Lights Books.

3

How Children Form
and Enact White Identities

"Mommy, I'm really glad that I'm White," a 4-year-old child remarked to his mother, who was driving him home from his preschool, which maintains two separate programs, one for affluent, mostly White children, and a subsidized one for low-income children, mostly of color.
                              –H. Chang, personal communication, 2005

Renee (4, White) [is pulling] Lingmai (3, Asian) and Jocelyn (4.5, White) across the playground in a wagon. . . . [Renee gets tired] and drops the handle of the wagon. . . . Lingmai, eager to continue this game, jumps from the wagon and picks up the handle. As Lingmai begins to pull, Renee admonishes her, "No, No. You can't pull this wagon. Only White Americans can pull this wagon."
                              —D. Van Ausdale and J. R. Feagin,
                    The First R: How Children Learn Race and Racism

Contrary to adult assumptions that children do not notice race, a robust body of research starting in the 1950s (e.g., Clark, 1963; Goodman, 1952; Radke & Trager, 1950) tells us that children begin to construct their ideas about race and racism very early. Studies have shown that children notice racial cues during infancy and that, by the age of three or four, most children have a rudimentary concept of race (Katz, 1976, 2003; Katz & Kofkin, 1997; Kelly et al., 2007; Ramsey, 1991a, 1991b; 2004; Ramsey & Myers, 1990; Van Ausdale & Feagin, 2001). They notice, absorb, and enact the patterns of racial and economic privilege that permeate their environments, and as these quotations illustrate, young children create their own ideas about race that go beyond just parroting adult comments.

Racial identity is shaped from the outside, and constructed from the inside, beginning in early childhood. The social and political dynamics of the community and period in which children live, their family's attitudes, their teachers, and their individual life experiences all influence this development (Derman-Sparks & Edwards, 2010). Likewise, researchers have pointed out that children's racial identities are dynamic responses to experiences with adults and children, rather than fixed entities. Mac Naughton, Davis, and Smith pose the following questions about these interactive processes: "How do children enact and perform their racial identities? How do children enact racial privilege in their daily relationships? How does Whiteness operate in children's lives to produce dynamics of inclusion and exclusion?" (2009, p. 35).

In this chapter, we address these questions as we review research about how children develop White racial identities, develop attitudes toward other groups, and enact their beliefs.

DEVELOPING WHITE RACIAL-GROUP IDENTITY

Over the decades numerous studies have shown that young White children readily identify themselves as White and often see other groups as distant "others" (e.g., Clark & Clark, 1947; Goodman, 1952; Jordan & Hernandez-Reif, 2009; Katz, 1976; Mac Naughton & Davis, 2009; Porter, 1971; Ramsey, 1991b; Ramsey & Myers, 1990; Van Ausdale & Feagin, 2001). Van Ausdale and Feagin (2001) observed how children frequently affirmed the importance of being White. One White 4-year-old girl noticed that she was darker than her two White companions and asked worriedly, "Does that mean that I'm not White anymore?" (p. 48). She repeatedly sought reassurance that she was still White, apparently concerned about the consequences of being seen as not White.

Early studies found that European American children never expressed a wish to be Black, whereas African American children frequently expressed the wish to be White and to affiliate with White people (e.g., Clark & Clark, 1947; Morland, 1962; Radke & Trager, 1950). Unfortunately, these patterns have not changed. A recent study commissioned by CNN showed that White children continue to "have an overwhelming bias toward White, and that Black children also have a bias toward White, but not nearly as strong" (Spencer, 2010, cited in Kareem, 2010).

Researchers in the 1950s interpreted such findings as an indication of the negative effect of racism on Black children's sense of self. This finding was a primary argument in favor of integrating schools in *Brown v. Board of Education* in 1954. Interestingly, the recurring pattern of White children's strong preference for own-race people was not a concern, reflecting the widely held assumption that integration meant that Black people should adapt to White society, not vice versa. Now, however, researchers, theorists, and practitioners take a more critical view of White in-group preferences and see assumptions of racial superiority as obstacles to racial equity (e.g., Feagin, 2000; Kendall, 2006; Kivel, 2002).

Why is Whiteness so compelling for children? According to Social Identity Theory, individuals tend to identify with social groups they view as comparatively superior in order to enhance their own self-images. This identity in turn leads people to exaggerate their similarities with in-group members and to valorize that group's positive attributes, while seeking to distance themselves from out-group members that they define by negative stereotypes (Nesdale, 2008).

Cross and Cross (2008) offer an analysis of identity that is especially useful for understanding the impact of race and racism on children's development of their self-concept. Based on William Cross' earlier review and reinterpretation of the body of research about African American children's identity formation (1991), they discuss the important differences between personal identities (PI) and reference group orientation or Group Identity (GI) (Cross & Cross, 2008). Personal identity encompasses children's thinking/feelings about their personal abilities and self-worth; group identity reflects children's awareness, understanding, and feelings about their racial/ethnic group that are influenced by prevailing images and stereotypes. For example, the dominant culture's messages about being Black strongly affect African American preschooler's ideas about their group identity (Cross, 1991). Consequently, African American and other children of color may experience conflicts between their positive personal identities and negative societal messages about their group, resulting in ambivalence about their racial identity that they may express by wishing to be White.

Cross (1991) and Cross & Cross's work (2008) also provide a useful conceptual framework for thinking about White children's identity development. In contrast to their peers of color, White children receive a barrage of messages from society that reinforces their positive group identity. While individual children's personal identities vary according to their specific life experiences, the dynamics of systemic racial advantage and disadvantage provide fertile ground for all White children to highly value their Whiteness, and to develop a sense of racial superiority as seen in the recent CNN study (Kareem, 2010).

Learning About the Power Codes of Race

A sense of White superiority and knowledge of racial power codes appear to develop early in life. After observing preschoolers' conversations and play in a racially diverse preschool for a year, Van Ausdale and Feagin (2001) concluded:

Young children quickly learn the racial-ethnic identities and role performanc-es of the larger society. . . . As White children grow up they learn, develop, and perform the meanings associated with the White identity-role. Black children and other children of color must cope with the subordinating expectations imposed on them [by White children], expectations that they may accept or resist. (p. 182)

The authors cite a number of incidents to support their conclusion that White preschool children do incorporate a sense of White superiority in their early identities. For example, White 3-year-old Felicia refused to let Joseph, a 3-year-old Black classmate, on to a tire swing saying, "Black people are not allowed on the swing right now, especially Black boys" (p. 107). Children also construct their own versions of power codes (Mac Naughton, Davis, & Smith, 2009). For instance, Van Ausdale and Feagin (2001) report a long conversation in which a White girl repeatedly insisted that her Black classmate could not own a white rabbit.

Sometimes White children enact these power differentials by exclud-ing peers of color. Baker (2010) observed numerous examples of White children ignoring overtures from peers of color while responding to simi-lar ones from White peers. Other times the power assertions are more ex-plicit. In a study of a racially diverse 2nd-grade classroom, Mednick and Ramsey (2008) noted that White children frequently commanded and rep-rimanded children of color, often using threats and demeaning comments. However, in no observations did children reverse roles. As discussed in Chapter 2, some teachers reinforce these power differentials (Barbarin & Crawford, 2006; Mednick & Ramsey, 2008).

Prevailing messages that Whiteness is "normal" and that character-istics of other racial groups are inferior or deviant bolster this sense of superiority. Kivel (2002) describes children's reactions to a classmate's much-loved Black Barbie that she brought for show and tell: "They screwed up their faces and said, 'Yuck, That's not Barbie. She's ugly. . . . '" (p. 10). In one study, a White child said that all people who looked like her got their skin from God, but she did not know where brown people got their skin (Baker, 2010). Such ideas may be based on young children's incorrect theory-making, yet if they go unchallenged, they become part of the belief system that Whiteness is normal, natural, and superior.

Further, Van Ausdale and Feagin (2001) documented examples of White children equating Whiteness with being an American (e.g., two White girls told an Asian boy that he did not "look like an American" [p. 102]). Research in Australia found similar patterns. Glover (1996) de-scribed a White 5-year-old's insistence that an Aboriginal student teacher must come from another country because "you've got brown skin," despite the student teacher's explanation to the contrary (p. 4). Mac Naughton (2004) found that many of the Anglo-Australian preschoolers stoutly maintained that "being Australian," meant, "that you all have White skin" (p. 69). Moreover, several denied that Aboriginal people (who have lived on the Australian continent for 60,000 years) could be Australians.

Children absorb beliefs about White superiority from different sources, including intentional and unintentional messages about race from significant adults. They may sense their White parents' discomfort in neighborhoods of color and/or take for granted that only White people live on their street, are friends of their family, or attend their school. White adults describe the effects of growing up in racially and economically isolated communities, unaware of the existence and impact of racism. McKinney (2005) quotes one woman, "In my everyday normal life, I don't even think about being White . . . I could tell my life story without mentioning my race" (p. 1).

The Costs of Racial-Power Codes for White Children

Clearly racism has an enormous negative impact on People of Color in terms of mental and physical health, and educational and economic opportunities (Buhin & Vera, 2009). Yet, racism also harms White children's development.

Kivel (2002) notes that White children learn a distorted view of history and the current world, often laced with unrealistic fears of People of Color and a false sense of security about White individuals and White-run systems. Moreover, witnessing and sanctioning acts of discrimination damages moral integrity and leads to guilt, shame, and discomfort with individuals and communities of color. Clark (1963) argued that growing up in a world of contradictions between the professed goals of equality and democracy and the pressures to violate them by acting on racial prejudice, creates moral conflicts and guilt for White children. Furthermore, White children "are being given a distorted perception of reality and of themselves, and are being taught to gain personal status in unrealistic ways" (p. 81). Forty years later Kivel (2002) echoes these words, "Because racism makes a mockery of our ideals of democracy, justice, and equality, it leads us to be cynical and pessimistic about human integrity and about our future, producing apathy, blame, despair. . . ." (p. 47).

These contradictions may also lead children to mask their true feelings. Trager and Radke Yarrow (1952) observed that White 3rd graders already knew how to be polite about race relations even though they really thought otherwise. More than 5 decades later, Banaji, Baron, Dunham, and Olson (2008) found a similar pattern, noting that as children grow up, they explicitly express more tolerance toward different groups, while maintaining their implicit biased beliefs.

In short, basing their identities on a sense of racial superiority puts White children at risk for developing an overblown, yet fragile, identity, instead of developing a solid sense of self that is based on their interests, connections to people, and contributions to the community.

LEARNING ABOUT OTHER RACIAL GROUPS

Children construct their attitudes about people from socially prevailing beliefs as well as from direct, indirect, and vicarious experiences with racism (Quintana & McKown, 2008). They may hear racist comments (direct), learn about others' experiences of racist actions (indirect), or witness others such as teachers or other authority figures acting in biased ways (vicarious). In fact, many children form definite ideas about racial/ethnic groups in the absence of any direct contact. Often these perceptions embody a strong sense of "otherness," the view that unfamiliar people are inherently and permanently different from one's own group.

Most people assume that children's attitudes about groups other than their own are primarily learned at home. However, studies of correlations between children and parents' beliefs have not been conclusive (e.g., Aboud & Doyle, 1996b). In part, it is difficult to develop comparable and valid ways to measure both parents' and children's attitudes. Moreover, many adults have become adept at hiding their true feelings from researchers and even from themselves (Banaji et al., 2008). Thus, parents may consciously advocate cross-racial respect but unconsciously convey racist attitudes. For example, they may espouse the ideal of interracial friendships but have only White friends themselves, implying that in-race friendships are preferable or more viable. Teachers too may send double messages. They may have good intentions to teach children about racial and cultural diversity but then use a "tourist" approach that conveys the message that European Americans represent the norm, while "other" races and cultures are interesting but not part of the daily environment and curriculum (Derman-Sparks & A.B.C. Task Force, 1989; Derman-Sparks & Edwards, 2010).

Several studies suggest that adults' unconscious and implicit racism may have the most effect on children. In one of the few longitudinal studies of children's racial attitudes, Katz (2003) found that some parents, while looking at photographs with their children, spent more time talking about pictures of same-race individuals than different-race ones. Over time, their children expressed more negative bias toward other racial groups than those whose parents divided their time equally among the photographs. In an experimental study, children watched different video clips of a White adult talking to a Black adult. The findings showed that the White adult's nonverbal positive or negative behavior (e.g., gestures, posture) had a stronger impact than positive verbal statements on children's attitudes about the relationship between the two adults, about the Black adult, and about Black people in general (Castelli, De Dea, & Nesdale, 2008).

Finally, even when families and teachers intentionally provide children with accurate information and challenge prejudiced attitudes, children still absorb stereotypes and misinformation from their larger community (extended family, neighbors, peers, and the media). Indeed, both of us know the power of this influence from seeing its effects on our own children. The experience can be quite mortifying! These incidents also remind us of how it takes a great deal of persistence, patience, and persuasion to counteract the racist messages in the larger society.

Forming Categories and Attitudes

By the preschool years, children's comments reveal misinformation about other racial groups that they have learned in their homes, in their communities, and from the media (Bigler & Liben, 2007; Bigler, Jones, & Lobliner, 1997; Cristol & Gimbert, 2008; Katz, 2003; Monteiro, de França, & Rodrigues, 2009; Ramsey, 1991b; Ramsey & Myers, 1990; Tatum, 1997; Van Ausdale & Feagin, 2001). One common example is that children who have never had any direct contact with Native American people adamantly claim that all Indians live in tepees and shoot bows and arrows at people. A White 5-year-old at a progressive private school expressed another frequent stereotype. He insisted that his African American classmate must be the bad guy in a make-believe game, because the bad guys on TV are Black.

Cognitive Developmental Processes. Using their developmental intergroup theory, Bigler & Liben (2007) hypothesize that children use a range of cognitive-developmental processes to categorize people and attach meaning to specific groups. Based on several studies, they concluded that the following factors influence the content of those beliefs:

- Perceptual discriminability of particular groups (differences in appearance, language, and clothing)

- Proportional group size (equal or unequal numbers of particular group members in a classroom or neighborhood)
- Explicit labeling of groups (referring to students as "boys and girls," news reports about immigrants)
- Implicit function of groups (gender divisions in classrooms; racial segregation in jobs and neighborhoods)
- Explicit attributions (groups associated with excelling or failing at tasks, such as "boys are good at . . . ")
- Implicit attributions (over and under representation of particular groups in the high- and low-status positions) (p. 164)

For example, children attending a predominately-White school may notice that staff members of color usually occupy lower status jobs such as custodians and cafeteria workers. As children go about their neighborhoods, they may take for granted that virtually all their neighbors are White and that People of Color occupy service positions (house cleaners, gardeners). As they play with family members and peers, they may also hear particular groups referred to in derogatory terms. Or, they may hear racist attacks on President Obama directly or in the media and generalize them to other African American men. With these experiences, children learn to categorize different groups, to associate those with certain characteristics, and to form stereotypes.

Many White children begin to express negative biases toward People of Color during the preschool years. In a review of current studies, Cristol and Gimbert (2008) note that these biases may reflect, in part, children's cognitive level of development, which predisposes them to see everything in polarized ways. They note that young children tend to focus on differences between groups and cannot see individual variations among members of groups different from their own. As an example, one kindergarten teacher reported that the White children in her group quickly learned the names of their White classmates but repeatedly confused the two Asian girls. While this tendency does relate to cognitive stages, not "seeing" differences among People of Color is also one of the dynamics of racism.

In-Group vs. Out-Group. Cristol and Gimbert (2008) also note that young children consistently favor in-group members. Additionally, loyalty to the in-group may become self-perpetuating as seen in one study that showed that young White Italian children favored peers who preferred members of their own group and excluded out-group members (Castelli, De Amicis, & Sherman, 2007).

For children of all ages, out-group prejudice increases when they have stronger in-group identification and perceive the out-group as a threat

(Cristol & Gimbert, 2008; Nesdale, Durkin et al., 2005; Nesdale, Maass et al., 2005). Teichman and Bar-Tal (2008) found that prolonged inter-group conflict gives rise to in-group beliefs and symbols about the rivals that are polarized, intense, and aggressive. Using the Arab-Israeli conflict, the authors show how these beliefs become more rigid and widely disseminated through formal and informal social channels. They note that under these conditions, children as young as 2 years old develop negative feelings about the "enemy." Even when they have developed cognitive skills to see others' perspectives and become more tolerant, they maintain these views. These findings may have implications for White American children who are growing up in the current atmosphere of heightened racial bigotry and hatred (see the Introduction and Chapter 2).

Social Environment. As children cognitively mature during middle childhood, overt prejudice often declines. They shift from emphasizing inter-group differences to recognizing commonalities with different groups and individual differences within them (Aboud & Amato, 2001; Aboud & Doyle, 1995). However, this increased cognitive capacity to see both similarities and differences does not *automatically* or *necessarily* result in a decrease in prejudiced or discriminatory behaviors. As pointed out earlier, recent research suggests that children learn to avoid making explicitly biased statements and choices, especially in the presence of adults. However, their implicit bias remains unchanged, and may even increase (Banaji et al., 2008; Monteiro, de França, & Rodrigues, 2009). In other words, as they get older, children learn to feign more tolerance than they actually feel. The commonly noted rise in children's use of racial slurs during elementary school suggests that, at least in some settings, children are learning to be more, rather than less, biased.

Whether children become more or less racially biased may depend in large part on their social environment including the amount and type of contact they have with people from other racial groups and the racial attitudes of the family and community. According to Tropp and Prenovost (2008) several decades of research suggest that children are more likely to develop positive inter-group attitudes when they attend schools where they have ongoing interactions with members of other groups and the school structure and atmosphere exemplify the principles of Allport's (1979) contact hypothesis. Those principles include equal status between groups, which implies equal numbers and equal access to resources; support of institutional authorities for inter-group contact; and common goals and opportunities to work cooperatively.

Unfortunately, very few schools meet these criteria. Many public schools are racially homogenous or are predominately White, Black,

Asian, and/or Latino due to economic and political forces that have re-segregated schools back to the 1970s levels (Brown, 2008). Racially and economically segregated preschool programs also result from differences in funding sources (e.g., privately or federally funded). Even in the same school or classroom, the impact of racial discrimination and economic disparities on children result in unequal footing among the children, further hampering collaborative efforts. Nevertheless, even in less than ideal circumstances, teachers have found ways to create equitable classrooms and teach from an AB/MC perspective.

Individual Differences. For various reasons, some individual children are more likely than others to develop and maintain racial stereotypes. In Van Ausdale and Feagin's (2001) observations, a few White children consistently made explicitly negative racial comments about their Black peers. One White girl informed a Black classmate that she could no longer go to swimming lessons because she would make the water dirty. Another time she told the same child, "You're the same color as rabbit poop. . . . You have to leave [the sandbox]. We don't allow s_____ in the sandbox" (p. 109). In a study examining children's preferences for fictional classmates and neighbors, Lee (2004) found that most of the White kindergartners showed a small but consistent preference for White children and families. However, a couple of children adamantly refused even to consider being friends or neighbors with People of Color.

Differences in the ways that children process information may account, in part, for why some children are more vulnerable to stereotypes and negative reactions. Bigler and Liben (1993) found that White children, ages 4 to 9, who had more rigid classification systems in general formed stronger stereotyped images of African Americans and had greater difficulty remembering counter stereotyped stories than did their peers with more flexible classification systems. In a later study, children who learned to make multiple and flexible categorizations of both social and nonsocial items improved their recall for counter stereotyped information (Bigler, Jones, & Lobliner, 1997). This study suggests that training children to think more openly and flexibly may be one strategy to help them to be less driven by stereotypes.

Race and Children's Friendships

You might be inclined to say at this point (and you wouldn't be alone), "Okay, kids sound as though they are prejudiced, but they really aren't because they play with classmates from other groups." While many young children have cross-racial friends, 4 decades of research show that White children consistently show stronger same-race preferences and cross-race aversion than do their African American classmates (e.g., Fox & Jordan, 1973; Katz, 2003; Newman, Liss, & Sherman, 1983; Ramsey & Myers, 1990; Rosenfield & Stephan, 1981; Stabler, Zeig, & Johnson, 1982; Van Ausdale & Feagin, 2001).

Even while playing with cross-racial friends, White children often express racist views, seemingly unperturbed by the obvious contradictions. The following dialogue between a 3-year-old Black girl (C) and a 4-year-old White girl (T) illustrates this paradox:

> C cuddles a Black doll and says, "This is my baby." T replies: "I don't like it, it's funny. I like this one (holding a White doll), it's my favorite. I don't like this one (pointing to the Black doll). Because you see I like Sarah, and I like White. You're my best friend, though you're brown." (B. Brown, 1998, p. 16)

Although such contradictions are common to young children's thinking, they also bear much similarity to the position of "exceptionalism" that we discussed in Chapter 2. It is a more subtle form of bigotry but still keeps the power dynamics of racism intact.

Furthermore, when White children play with cross-race peers, the racial power differentials that they are absorbing may influence their play in subtle ways, as seen in an observation of three 4-year-old Australian girls, two Black and one White, who were playing house. Their teacher saw this cross-racial interaction as a positive development. However, when Mac Naughton (cited in B. Brown, 1998) more closely observed their play, she noticed the unequal power relationships, which reflected the realities of Australian society.

> The two Black children (N & T) made various attempts to be "mum" but were always firmly told by S (the White child) that she was "mum" and that they were the babies, whom she proceeded to tell what to do and when to do it . . . dictating, in a commanding tone of voice, the storyline they were to follow. At one point, obeying S's direction to put the baby to sleep, T chooses a Black doll. S quickly responds, "No, not that way, you always play with that one, no the other baby," and points to a White doll. (B. Brown, 1998, p. 20)

Thus, teachers and other observers need to scrutinize their perceptions of playmate patterns to be sure that they are not over-reporting cross-race friendships and under-reporting children's enactments of racial assumptions and power differentials. By closely observing children's interactions, we will learn much needed information about the beliefs and assumptions underlying their cross-racial/cultural behaviors.

LEARNING ABOUT ECONOMIC CLASS

Children's evolving awareness and understanding of economic class is another aspect of development that needs more study. However, what we know suggests that economic advantages and disadvantages do affect children's view of the world and themselves. Economic disparities among racial groups also bolster a developing sense of racial superiority and inferiority.

Economics and Race

As we discussed in Chapter 2, White people have enormous economic advantage compared with People of Color. Thus, as children grow up, they daily witness how economic status aligns with race. Furthermore, as with racial ideologies, serious contradictions exist between the White dominant cultural ideal of equal economic opportunity and the reality of racial discrimination. At the core of these contradictions is the myth that *all* people who work hard will have access to well-paying jobs and financial abundance and that those who fail to achieve these advantages are lazy (Levy, Karafantis, & Ramirez, 2008). Yet a web of national policies and institutional structures consistently favors the wealthy over the poor (e.g., tax codes, banking and bankruptcy laws, extravagant bonuses for CEOs, low minimum wages for hourly workers).

How and what children learn about economic class differences and their own economic status and prospects is influenced by these prevailing societal beliefs and the relative affluence of their families. Many children of White upper-middle-class and wealthy families have nannies, who often are women of color and, in many cases, recent immigrants. Such children experience the confluence of race, wealth, and power every moment of their early lives. When they get older and enter the wider world, these same children see people who look and talk like them occupying positions of wealth and power and those who look different working in subordinate positions. As they hear adults talk and begin to experience the rewards of achievement in school, they may also begin to expect that they will have unlimited access to resources and opportunities.

White children who live in low-income families absorb the messages of wealth and entitlement from a different perspective. Although they physically look like the children of White wealthy families they see in the media, they learn early on that their families cannot buy the latest constantly advertised toys or name-brand clothes. They may encounter teasing and shaming by wealthier children and rarely see families like theirs on television or in children's books. Consequently, White children from lower-income families are at risk for developing a sense of failure and shame about their families and, by extension, about themselves. These feelings may evolve into resentment, later predisposing them to buy into the overtly racist ideologies that blame People of Color for the poverty of White people, rather than prompting them to look to the economic system itself.

Ideas and attitudes about race and social class are further entangled by television shows and movies (geared to teens but frequently watched by younger children) that display the opulent lifestyles of sports and popular music stars. The stories often depict affluent People of Color, who represent only a tiny fraction of people in their racial/ethnic groups. These images obscure the economic disadvantages of People of Color, often-leading children to assume that, as one White child put it, "Black people have all the fancy houses and cool cars." These distortions also potentially contribute to White adults' conclusions that economic discrimination along racial lines does not exist (see Chapter 2).

Children's understanding of economic class changes as they grow up (Leahy, 1983). Young elementary school children are likely to both describe and explain poverty and wealth in observable concrete terms, such as number of possessions and type of residence. When they are around 10 years of age, children begin to refer to psychological traits, such as motivation, in their explanations of why people are in different circumstances. During childhood and adolescence, children increasingly make the connection between having a job and getting money; and they are more aware of the status and financial benefits associated with specific occupations (Furnham & Stacey, 1991). Finally, adolescents are capable of seeing the role of the social and economic structure in the unequal distribution of wealth (Leahy, 1983).

However, even as they are learning about the economic system, children also experience the underlying contradiction between the ideal of equality versus the realities of discrimination, competitiveness, and individualism that lead to inequality. When they are young, children have a strong sense of fairness and notice inequities (Damon, 1980). Often preschoolers say that it is not fair that some people have more money than others do, and the rich should share with poor people (Ramsey, 1991c). Leahy (1983) and Chafel and Neitzel (2005) found that elementary school children also advocated equalizing the wealth between rich and poor. However, older children and adolescents, who have a more comprehensive awareness of the economy, are more likely to justify inequalities by claiming that poor people get what they deserve ("They didn't work hard enough") (Chafel, 1997; Leahy, 1990). Children and adolescents from working poor families may succumb to the power of that myth and feel confused and disturbed about their families, who work very hard and yet still have little income. This contradiction serves to obscure the systemic inequities that create income disparities.

The Effects of Consumerism

The explosive growth of consumerism in the past 3 decades aggravates the effects of economic disparities. Because of media deregulation in the 1980s, messages equating happiness with buying new toys, clothes, and junk food saturate children's worlds. Overt and covert commercials inundate television programs, movies, and child-oriented websites. Marketers use child development research and sophisticated technology to "hook" children on to particular shows and products (Linn, 2004; Schor, 2004). These marketing efforts have been wildly successful. American children have become a $42 billion market in terms of what their families spend for them and a $700 billion dollar market when we factor in their influence on parent spending (e.g., responding to child-directed ads about which clothes and cars to buy or where to vacation) (Media Education Foundation, 2009).

Consumerism affects children's priorities in ways that undermine the development of authentic identity and the ability to connect with other people (Kline, 1993). First, children learn to relate to physical objects, especially toys and clothes, in terms of *getting* and *having* instead of *using* and *enjoying*. Second, children learn to identify themselves as consumers and owners, not as creators or contributing members of a family or group. Third, children quickly learn to judge themselves and others by the desirability and quantity of toys that they own, often setting off competitive comparisons among peers and reinforcing economic class superiority. Moreover, satisfying the desire to own new items overwhelms other considerations, such as caring for other people, environmental sustainability, or equitable distribution of resources. Furthermore, since many of these desired toys are highly technological products (e.g., video games; dolls that are programmed to speak, eat, and cry; building sets that can only be used with one particular, pre-determined design), they reduce children's options to play socially and creatively and to express their own feelings and ideas (Linn, 2009).

As children hanker after more and more expensive toys and clothes, the pressures intensify for families of little or modest means. Even people who have sufficient food and shelter often "feel poor," which affects their psychological functioning (McLoyd & Ceballo, 1998), and can lead to shame and, in some cases, violence (Vorrasi & Gabarino, 2000). Ironically, affluent families do not fare much better. Even when they have the means, consuming does not bring contentment to children, but rather stimulates new desires (Linn, 2009). In a study of school-aged children Schor (2004) found that high levels of consumerism was associated with depression, anxiety, lower self-esteem in peer and family relationships, and poorer family relationships. Other studies reveal that children in affluent families tend to be less happy and more at risk for drug and alcohol abuse than their working class peers (Csikszentmihalyi, 1999; Csikszentmihalyi & Schneider, 2000; Luthar & Becker, 2002).

Thus, as children develop their earliest identities and relationships, they observe many facets of the economic system. One disturbing developmental trend is that young children say that the unequal distribution is unfair but, as they get older, they come to accept it and to blame poor people for their poverty. Competitive consumerism exacerbates economic and racial advantage and disadvantage because it valorizes wealthy people and, by implication, demeans people who do not have the same resources. Because of the alignment of race and economic class, this view potentially supports assumptions of White racial superiority. Finally, as children's identity and self-esteem become more dependent on their purchasing power, their ability and motivation to imagine and advocate for more equitable systems may decline.

In sum, many years of research document that young children are not color blind, as so many White adults wish to believe. Young children also have sophisticated understandings of how "racial" categories link to social status and power (Mac Naughton & Davis, 2001, 2009), and White children begin to enact assumptions of White superiority and entitlement at an early age. Children are continually learning these implicit and explicit messages from their families, the community, and the media. However, they do not merely imitate adults; they "actively reshape, blend, and synthesize elements of the preexisting patterns found around them—in families, other social settings, and the mass media" (Van Ausdale & Feagin, 2001, p. 20). Most White adults do not "see" this process. Indeed, many live out their lives unaware of what is happening to their children and never question their own racist views and racial and economic privilege. There is, however, an alternative. In Chapters 4 and 5, we describe strategies for working with both children and adults to help them develop authentic and caring identities, the first step in the journey toward anti-racist awareness, identity, and action.

Reflection Questions

1. What are your earliest recollections of people from different racial groups? What were some of your questions and assumptions?

2. What are your earliest recollections/images about relationships among different racial groups? How did they reflect power differentials?
3. What childhood recollections do you have about adults' reactions to racial, ethnic, and economic class differences?
4. What questions and comments about racial differences do you hear from the children you teach? What do you notice about interactions within and across racial and economic groups? Are there preferences and power differences?
5. What do you observe about other adults' (e.g., fellow teachers, parents) conversations with children regarding racial identity, racial prejudice, and discrimination? What is said? Not said?
6. How do you feel about talking with young children about such topics? Do you avoid or engage in them?
7. How do the children you teach relate to consumerism? What messages about economic class and consumerism do you see in the media and children's books?
8. How do economic-class issues influence your day-to-day interactions with colleagues, staff, and families?

For Further Reading

Clark, K. (1963). The White child and race prejudice. In *Prejudice and your child* (pp. 66–84). Boston: Beacon Press.

Mac Naughton, G., & Davis, K. (Eds.). (2009). *Race and early childhood education: An international approach to identity, politics and pedagogy.* New York: Palgrave Macmillan.

Tatum, B. D. (1997). The development of White identity. In *Why are all the Black kids sitting together in the cafeteria? And other conversations about race* (pp. 93–113). New York: Basic Books.

Van Ausdale, D., & Feagin, J. R. (2001). *The first R: How children learn race and racism.* Lanham, MD: Rowan & Littlefield.

4

Fostering Children's Identities

"As I learn to like all the differences in me, I learn to like the differences in you."

—Bill Martin Jr., *I Am Freedom's Child*

In this chapter, we discuss ways to implement learning themes one, two, and three. These are the beginning building blocks for nurturing White children's construction of individual and group identities that can also resist racism. (In Part II, we address the last four learning themes.)

For White children to develop authentic identities based on their personal abilities and interests rather than on White superiority, they need to learn about the differences among White people, and that differences are enjoyable and worthy of respect. This is the first step to learning to understand and respect diversity in the larger society and world. If your classroom includes children from more than one racial background, White children still need to do this work, while you also explore and teach respect for the individual similarities and differences among *all* the children and their families.

In the following sections, we discuss the meaning of each learning theme and how to gather relevant information about your children's ideas and feelings. Then we describe guidelines and examples for implementation. These activities are not a prescribed curriculum but rather a roadmap to help you explore and build on topics and approaches that work for *your* children.

LEARNING THEMES

These first three learning themes spotlight children's White identity and interpersonal skills. Consistent with basic early childhood theory and practice, we begin with children's sense of self as the foundation for learning about others.

Theme One: Develop authentic identities based on personal abilities and interests, family history, and culture, rather than on White superiority. Authentic identities incorporate both a strong sense of oneself as an individual and the motivation and capacity to care about others. As we saw in Chapter 3, White children often develop identities that rest, at least in part, on internalized White racial superiority. This message often comes in the guise of Whiteness-as-the-norm—the sense that the definition of being human is to be White. This is absorbed from countless experiences and images in our society.

As children are drawn into a culture that prizes individual achievement, possessions, and competitiveness over connections with others, children may become invested in being "special," a self-esteem theme that has been overdone in many early childhood settings (Katz & McClellan, 1998). This approach potentially sets up children to feel entitled to unlimited resources and accolades. We need to support children in constructing authentic identities that embrace their uniqueness, competence, and their inter-connections with others.

Theme Two: Know, respect, and value the range of the diversity of physical and social attributes among White people. As children see how familiar people (such as classmates) vary on many dimensions, they can learn to appreciate their own attributes as distinct and empowering but not as better or worse than those of others. Learning theme two serves as a bridge to learning to value the differences and commonalities of people beyond one's own racial group.

Overemphasizing the differences between groups and, conversely, ignoring the differences within groups is one way that racism polarizes people. For White children, recognizing and respecting the range of similarities and differences among White people are the first steps to understanding and respecting all people. At this point, the emphasis should be on dimensions of diversity other than race so that children first learn about the variety within their own group. In racially/ethnically diverse classrooms, learning will be about *all* the children's similarities and differences. As you work on this learning theme, *never spotlight the child who is different in some way from the majority of the children.*

Theme Three: Build the capacity for caring, cooperative, and equitable interactions with others. Connecting with other human beings rests on core social-emotional dispositions and skills: empathizing with others, communicating effectively, initiating and maintaining social interactions, playing cooperatively, and resolving conflicts (Ramsey, 2004). These skills enable children to experience the pleasures of positive social engagements, to expand their range of relationships and understanding of people, and to deepen their capacity to care for others.

LEARNING ABOUT YOUR CHILDREN

A critical first step is to learn more about how children think and feel about their identities, about similarities and differences among familiar people, and about their capacity to connect to others. You can gather this information through regular observation and careful listening. Fortunately, many young children express themselves freely in play, informal conversations, peer interactions, and responses to teacher-directed activities. When you are collecting information, do not intervene. You want children to feel comfortable to express their true views, not what they think you want to hear or see. Remember that you will subsequently use their ideas to plan for materials and activities to correct and expand their ideas and foster comfortable, positive feelings with diversity.

Here are suggestions to help you learn more about the children you work with each day:

- *Make time for close and frequent observations of how children are identifying themselves.* Listening closely to children can provide rich data. For example, as children play, talk, draw, and paint pictures they often reveal how they see themselves (as superheroes, mothers, baby kitties, shoppers, bosses) and how they see roles in their families (who takes care of the baby, goes to work, cooks dinner).
- *Note children's feelings about their race and ethnicity and other aspects of identity as they play and interact with peers and adults.* Children may indirectly express their feelings through their choices of playmates, toys, images, and books. Try to notice if their preferences and aversions follow any pattern, and in particular if they accept or reject peers or objects (such as dolls) based on race, gender, ability/ disability, family composition, socioeconomic class, interests, or skills ("I only want to play with the doll with pink skin," "Boys don't play with dolls," "You can't play because you can't walk," "You can't have two mommies," "Only kids with [name-brand] clothes can play here").
- *Use photographs and books to generate conversations about economic class, gender roles, and other differences.* Read books that show how people differ in terms of occupations, access to resources, rural or urban location, and type of home, traditional and nontraditional

gender roles, abilities and disabilities. Engage the children in discussions about the stories and pictures. To begin, use images and stories that include people that are racially similar to members of the class. Ask them to create stories about where they might live, go to school, and what they would like to do. Through their comments you may learn how children react to people who are similar to and different from them along several dimensions—even if they share the same racial identity.

- *Listen closely for any sense of superiority and entitlement.* As you watch children and talk with them, listen closely for pervasive competitiveness. For instance, children may regularly brag about new possessions ("Look at my new shoes!" "My bike is better than yours because it's new!") Or boast about how they can outdo one another ("Your picture is ugly!" "I can run faster than you!"). A strong focus on material things and a need to be the best can undermine the development of healthy, reality-based identities and the motivation to care about other people.

- *Decipher social patterns.* Watch for ways that children divide themselves—by race, gender, economic class, interests, abilities, or neighborhood. Try to identify the personal and contextual factors that seem to be contributing to any segregation you see (e.g., play styles, activity preferences, after-school activities, neighborhood gatherings, friendships among parents). As you observe, think about the following questions: Which children seek out a wide range of peers? Which ones limit themselves to small groups or stay with a single partner? Which children spend a lot of time alone? Engage in many conflicts? Play leadership roles? These observations can provide crucial information about individuals' social skills and orientations and the group dynamics of your classroom as a whole.

- *Observe the overall social tone of your classroom.* Do children express empathy and caring for one another? How often do children engage in conflicts? How much do they show verbal or physical aggression? How do they resolve conflicts and manage aggression? Are children generally content and eager to try new things, or do they spend a lot of time complaining or angling for the teacher's attention?

After you have begun to develop your knowledge base of children's behaviors, attitudes, and ideas, you can begin to design activities that will help them recognize and expand their identities, their roles in the group, and their appreciation of differences as well as similarities among class-mates and members of their communities.

STRATEGIES FOR WORKING WITH CHILDREN

Some of the learning experiences we describe below are similar to those activities used to promote young children's self-concept and social-emotional development. However, they do not *stop* with the uniqueness of each child. Learning experiences also pay attention to children's group identities and promote cooperative interactions and respect for the diversity among people in their own racial group and in their immediate world.

Implementing Learning Themes One and Two

We address these two themes together because children learn about themselves in tandem with learning about the other people in their immediate environment. The same activities serve both purposes. These strategies focus on exploring similarities and differences among the children and families in the group and then expanding this awareness to other people with the same racial identity and then those with other racial identities.

Whether your class is all White, predominantly White, or includes some children of color, the strategies in this section still apply. You may need to do some adaptations to ensure that your activities, materials, and environment are equally inclusive of all the children as you explore the similarities and differences among them. Avoid the mistake of treating the children of color as the only individuals who bring diversity to your group. Always keep in mind that a range of diverse characteristics exists within all groups of children.

Learning About Our Own and Others' Families

Family is the context in which authentic identity begins to develop. Learning about family backgrounds provides concrete, meaningful ways for children both to learn about themselves and to consider their similarities and differences with others.

Provide materials (story books, posters, puzzles, dramatic play props, music) that give equal visibility to all the children's families, not just those children whose families reflect dominant-culture characteristics. Then, expand your materials to reflect family diversity among Whites beyond that in your group. Unfortunately, teaching materials still tend to mainly depict White families that reflect the dominant cultural norm (middle or upper class, nuclear, heterosexual families). Many White families are made invisible (working class, single parent, Jewish, gay or lesbian families, families in which there is someone with a disability). However, you can provide images of diversity among Whites through careful selection of available materials, supplemented by materials you make with families. (See suggestions in Appendix A and organizations and websites in Appendix B.)

In addition to purchased materials, make your own to ensure that all of your children's families and daily lives are equally visible throughout the environment and classroom activities. Take photographs of each child and his or her family and post them in your room. Provide materials for children and their families to make posters that portray family members in their daily activities. Ask family members to share stories about their lives throughout the year in the classroom using print and electronic media. Make every effort to equalize opportunities to participate. Provide materials and be flexible about the timing of visits to accommodate the financial constraints and work schedules of each family.

Monitor your own responses and be sure that you are respectful and responsive to different family cultural styles, incomes, and individual needs. Even if all your families are White, they may have different values. For example, in some families, children are allowed to express themselves freely to adult members; in other families, that is considered "talking back" and disrespectful. If you expect your children to speak out in your program, you need to know how families feel about this behavior and help children learn to express their ideas and feelings in ways that are respectful to their families.

Create admission forms that provide for different family structures. Instead of offering only the traditional spaces for *mother* and *father*, make spaces for the names and roles of a wider range of family members, thus accommodating two moms or dads, grandparents as primary caretakers, blended families, and foster parents.

Be aware of and respect the religious traditions and rules in each family. Carrying out this strategy involves more than celebrating additional holidays. Different religious rules may also require adaptations in daily life routines. For example, many Jewish children do not eat leavened products during Passover. Alerting parents may prevent awkward situations, such as a classmate bringing in leavened cupcakes to share. Jehovah's Witness families do not celebrate holidays or birthdays, and their children require supportive adaptations in the classroom.

Explore the range of families within your group and talk about how every family does similar "family" things in different ways. Emphasize the many ways that all families love and take care of their children. Invite families to share their favorite bedtime stories, type the stories into a computer file, and turn the file into a big book to share with your children. Have a teddy bear or doll that "visits" each child's home for a weekend and returns with a new entry (a photo and a short description of the weekend, an activity, or a meal) in the bear's "journal." Consider sending along a disposable camera and a digital or small tape recorder so the families can take photos and record their entries. The class can listen to their families' entries, and if you have the staff to help transcribe, you can turn these narratives into a book for the classroom. The main point is to make sure that all families can participate. As children hear or read the entries, they may spontaneously notice and talk about similarities and differences in favorite foods, bedtime rituals, religious traditions, and leisure activities.

Invite family members to come to school to be interviewed by the children about their lives. Help the children develop the questions they want to ask family members. Then use the information from the interviews in the curriculum activities.

Use "Family Homework" to engage families in the curriculum and to explore the similarities and differences among them. Eric Hoffman, preschool director and author, describes how he uses "family homework" assignments throughout the year (personal communication, April 2005):

> Once a month, my staff and I sent home a fun, voluntary activity for families to work on together. We would use the results to create bulletin board and table displays, circle time presentations, charts, and books. . . . While the family homework topics have covered all areas of my curriculum, many of the assignments were designed to stimulate discussion about how the children and their families are the same and how they are different. Some examples:
> - What are your family's three favorite foods? (We made a recipe book from the responses.)
> - Bring in something red that represents your family. (We set up a color display table that changed color every week.)
> - Draw a family portrait. (Parents borrowed markers and created a bulletin board display.)
> - Find a book in our lending library that your family loves to read, take it home, and do a family "book report" about it. (Some families drew pictures; some took dictation from the child; one family created a skit for circle time!)
> - Write about a time when someone in the family saw something that was unfair and helped make it fair. (The responses made a very popular book).

- Ask adult family members to share: What games did you like to play when you were young? Tell us about a mistake you made and how you corrected it. (More books!)

We made a few mistakes in choosing assignments. When we asked everyone to take pictures of their front doors, it brought up issues of economic competition for several parents, and it angered a family who had been homeless. An assignment about pets left out several children who didn't have any, and was upsetting to a family whose child couldn't have a pet because of his sister's allergies. But these mistakes proved valuable because they stimulated important discussions about family differences among the adults that were concrete and personal.

Be sensitive to the particular needs of transracial and transnational adoptees. While growing up in a White and culturally European American context, these children need to learn about their origins, as well as learning to live within the dominant culture. The children and family members also need to learn how to cope with racial prejudice. It is vital that the classroom materials (posters, books) make visible multiracial/ethnic families.

Explore how the women and men in the children's families play a wide range of roles (some that fit gender stereotypes and others that contradict them). Ask families to take photographs of the various roles they play, with emphasis on those that counter stereotypes (men cook, women fix cars, men are nurses, women drive trucks). Put the photos in a book or a wall chart and discuss them with the children.

Pay attention to economic class. "Identifying economic class is confusing in our society. Many people live in mixed class backgrounds. There are no hard lines between the moment when one calls oneself working poor or working class or middle class. But the lived realities are markedly different" (Julie Olsen Edwards, personal communication, 2004). Help children learn that everybody does important work—both inside and outside the home. Ask families to contribute to a class display about all the work it takes to keep a family functioning within the home (laundry, food preparation, cleaning). Then have them briefly describe the work they do outside the home and how it helps others. Make a book or chart based on what they say. If family members are unemployed or retired, ask about the activities they currently do for others in their extended family or neighborhood. If a family member is incarcerated, ask about his or her work in prison that contributes to people in that environment or in the larger society. Make a group storyboard about how each child's family contributes to our community well-being.

Ensure that children from different income levels experience equal visibility and respect from staff and other children. Among children, differences in family income and situations reveal themselves in many ways. For example, not all children have families who can afford name-brand clothes, so it is important to emphasize how all clothes serve the same purpose and downplay competition about the latest fashions. Children from lower-income homes may need to keep their clothes clean and intact. Providing smocks and having sewing material to mend torn clothing can meet this need. Some programs install their own washing machines to wash clothes as necessary before children go home.

Find ways to create equitable conditions for children from families with limited resources. If children live in families without access to reliable health care, and the adults are not able to stay at home with ill children without losing their jobs, look for programs or community solutions to meet these families' needs. Some families do not have homes, and their children may come to school undernourished and without access to daily baths and clean clothing. In addition to immediately intervening in any teasing or rejection by other children, create respectful, private ways for children to get clean, clothed, and fed.

Challenge behaviors reflecting societal messages that equate material acquisitions with self-worth. Interrupt bragging about toys and keep show-and-tell about new toys to a minimum (or, preferably, do not permit them at all). Similarly, if children are using their material possessions as a way to make and keep friends, encourage them to find other ways of connecting.

Create ways to recognize national holidays and children's birthdays without playing into societal messages equating material acquisition with reward and family love. Some families can afford to give their children lavish birthdays; others cannot. Consider implementing a policy that ensures equitable celebrations at school (make birthday snacks at school or limit the amount and kind of snacks brought by families), and work with families on alternative ways to observe their children's birthdays at home.

Exploring Individual Similarities and Differences

We now turn to engaging children in investigating the physical similarities and differences among their classmates.

Document how all children have a range of physical characteristics and abilities. Make a mural of everyone's faces using photographs and then list ways children are the same and different. Make a collage or graph of everyone's eyes. Then count up the sum of each color. Discuss and make a book about what children are good at and are also learning how to do. (Susie is a fast runner but wants to learn how to build a car out of Legos; Diego is very good with scissors and hopes to make it to the top of the climber soon; Matt, while sitting in his wheel chair, can throw the ball very far and is learning how to make origami figures.)

If children in your group have disabilities that require adaptations of activities, engage the group in learning what the children need to fully participate in the program. For example, if a child uses sign language, then teach everyone how to sign words and phrases in daily use. Ensure that children recognize all the abilities of a child with a disability and find ways to make daily management activities (such as getting snacks ready) inclusive. Throughout all these activities, stress that abilities and disabilities are on a continuum and that everyone has things they can and cannot do physically.

Demystify the tools used by children with disabilities by explaining how each is used. When appropriate, rent equipment for children to try (or check second hand stores). If there are no children with identified disabilities in your program, then provide books to open up children's questions, counter their misinformation and fears, and build their knowledge about the strengths of children with disabilities. If possible invite people with disabilities to visit your classroom to talk with children, answer their questions, and teach them respectful ways to interact with people who need assistance with some tasks. This approach works best if people can visit more than once and participate in ongoing activities such as reading books to children or singing together.

Encourage children to learn about how they have similarities and differences in preferences and interests. Make a book together that illustrates children's preferences (Mary and Peter like spaghetti, but Mary likes hamburgers, and Peter likes chicken; both enjoy chase games, but Peter likes the swings, and Mary likes the trikes). Suggest that older children "interview" one another about their preferences and draw pictures to show the answers. Help the group graph the similarities and differences.

Encourage children to see that similarities and differences can coexist and that people can connect with one another even if they are different in some ways. Ask children to list two or three ways that they are the same as one of their friends or a family member and five ways that they are different. Note and address tensions or discomfort that emerge when differences come up among the children (for example, when a child laughs at or makes a negative comment about another child).

Be alert for instances of exclusionary play (both obvious and subtle rejections). Help children explore the source of their discomfort and see beyond their initial reactions to new ways of connecting with classmates.

Explore and support the range and variety of gender roles in the classroom. Make a chart of all the different activities the girls like to do and those the boys like to do, and note how similarities and differences exist both within each gender and between genders.

Support children in developing all aspects of their personalities and in expressing the range of human feelings. Help children learn how they and their peers express common emotions (pain sadness, anger, joy, fear) in different and similar ways. Support girls to show their anger directly; boys to express feelings of sadness.

Explore diversity among White people in the larger community. After laying a strong foundation about valuing differences and exploring the similarities and differences among the children and the families in your group, it is time to introduce additional areas of diversity among Whites. The methods for doing this are like those for introducing any form of diversity that is not present in your class. Books, posters, stories, and classroom visitors expand children's awareness of the great range of diversity among same-race people. As you explore these differences, always make connections between your children and unfamiliar people. Remember, one of your goals is to build their awareness, empathy, and comfort with people beyond their immediate environment. It is not necessary to cover every dimension of diversity that exists among White people. In fact, it is more effective to explore a few aspects in depth.

Implementing Learning Theme Three

These strategies focus on children's development of the dispositions and skills for caring, connection, and cooperation. They encourage children to develop authentic identities that balance their self-knowledge and specific interests with their connections to others. Learning these dispositions and skills within their own group then becomes the bridge to developing caring and equitable relationships with people beyond their immediate environment. The activities we suggest can also be used in both homogeneous and heterogeneous classrooms—always remembering to engage *all* of the children.

Encourage children to appreciate how their specific skills and interests can help them connect with others. Invite children to talk about the many activities that they do with family members and friends, especially ones that show caring and love ("I play games with my sister," "I help my dad wash the car," "When I make silly faces, my baby sister stops crying," "I play ball with my friends").

Nurture children's empathy by encouraging them to recognize the emotional similarities (pain, joy, fear, sadness) among people and the different ways people express the same emotions. Begin with the children and families in your group and then extend the reach to people beyond the children's immediate environment. When reading books about the experiences of people from a variety of cultural, economic class, and family backgrounds, ask children to imagine how they would feel if they were in that situation, and point out similarities between their responses and those of the characters in the story.

Nurture children's sense of competency and connection based on the many ways they contribute to the group. Identify and acknowledge actions such as helping one another get dressed for outside, cooperatively moving tables or large pieces of equipment, and helping one another solve conflicts. Involve children in observing and learning to "read" the needs of classroom pets and plants and responding sensitively to them.

Make a book together about the many ways each child expresses caring for others and contributes to the group. ("I take turns being the mother with my friends," "I helped Josh tie his shoes," "Susanne [who is partially blind] and I are putting out snack together.") Keep this book and others created by children and families in your book areas, so that children can browse through them whenever they like. Avoid emphasizing the message that individual children are *special*. Instead, help children to see that they are *unique* (this does not carry the same tone of entitlement as special) and that everyone is competent in his or her own way.

Provide regular opportunities for children to practice cooperating. Provide a balance of individual and cooperative ways to engage in ongoing activities. Many typically individual activities that are a daily part of early childhood programs can be turned into cooperative activities, such as group art and construction projects, and collective classroom "maintenance" activities. For example, in "cooperative tag" each tagged child joins hands with "it." The children run as a group and learn to adjust their pace and direction to the other runners. (For activity ideas, see Hill, 2001; Kirchner, 2000; Orlick, 1978, 1982.)

Encourage children to expand their friendships to include the range of diversity within your group. Involve children in cooperative activities with the children with whom they rarely play, to help them see beyond their initial likes and dislikes.

Address the hyperindividualism and sex stereotypes of superhero play in ways that help children value their real power and the value of cooperation to enhance what they can do. Hoffman (2004) advocates community service activities that encourage children to connect with others. For example, children and their families might plant flowers for a person who loves flowers but is physically unable to plant them. Alternatively, they might clean up an elderly neighborhood's yard or a local park.

Develop strategies to help children become comfortable with a range of verbal and nonverbal communication styles. Support children who are reluctant to speak or have trouble entering conversations. At group time, create practices that enable all children to have a fair chance to participate. For example, slow down conversations and help all children feel comfortable with silence as they wait for classmates who need more time to gather and express their thoughts. Conversely, encourage children who always jump into discussions to wait their turn without forgetting what they want to say. Interrupt any teasing directed at children who have trouble communicating for whatever reason.

Pay attention to and address behaviors that reflect the hierarchies of power in our society and help children learn alternative responses. Children who are used to having their own room and supply of toys may need to "unlearn" their expectations of having absolute control over materials. Children who have absorbed expectations of gender or economic class entitlement may expect their desires to dominate the group. Conversely, teachers can support children who give in whenever a conflict occurs to identify their needs and develop effective negotiation strategies.

When guiding children through conflict resolution, be alert to family differences in how children learn to handle conflict. When your beliefs and strategies differ from those of a family, discuss these differences with the parents or guardians. Let them know the school's approach to conflict resolution and try to reach an agreement. If necessary, help the child understand that it is fine to use different methods at school and at home. Help children negotiate equitable solutions despite different communication styles or expectations of entitlement.

Help children explore a wide range of feelings and interpersonal behaviors and do problem solving about common life experiences and incidents of bias by storytelling with persona dolls. Persona dolls can depict a range of human diversity. Unlike regular dolls, children do not play with the persona dolls whenever and however they want. Instead, the teacher brings the dolls out during group time and introduces each doll to the children by creating and describing his or her life story. Over time, children regard these dolls as members of the classroom, and the teacher creates ongoing stories about the dolls to introduce, personalize, and explore aspects of diversity. These stories are grounded in the principles of exploring similarities and differences along several continua, first through the diversity among children in the class (even when all the children are White), and then bridging to more diversity. Thus, in all-White classrooms, teachers might create stories that address differences and related teasing among the children in the class (e.g., height, freckles, eyeglasses, and different family constellations) before introducing dolls of color. In classrooms with children of color, always begin by focusing on issues that all the children share across racial and ethnic backgrounds (e.g., grandparents, cousins, family get-togethers). Then you have a foundation for exploring skin color, hair texture, eye shape, and other racial attributes. At no time should the stories or activities imply that the children of color are the "different" ones or the ones "with color." Rather emphasize that we all have skin color, which is similar to or different from others on a continuum.

The activities in this chapter support White children's understanding of how they are the same and different from other Whites and People of Color in their immediate world. The approach supports awareness of themselves as contributing and caring members of their family and their classroom. They also lay a necessary foundation for developing empathic and equitable engagement with diversity beyond their racial identity group and immediate world—learning themes that we explore in Part II.

5

Exploring White Identities with Staff and Families

> It felt like I had this big closet to clean out, and I had taken everything out and was now trying to decide what stayed, what needed fixing, and what to throw out. It's a big job but it feels great. I know I am going to be more of the person I want to be.
>
> —Student, in L. Derman-Sparks and C. B. Phillips,
> *Teaching/Learning Anti-Racism: A Developmental Approach*

With patience, persistence, and practice, doing AB/MC work with adults is as rewarding as it is with children. What is more, your work with children will be more fruitful if there are caring and collaborative relationships among the staff and families. Yet many teachers find it considerably more difficult to raise anti-bias issues with adults than with children.

It is true that talking about issues of race and racism with adults can be uncomfortable, especially at first. However, natural bridges do exist. Families want their children to be good people. For many, that includes wanting their children to grow up without prejudice, although that may mean different things to different families. Early childhood teachers also want to do what is best for children's healthy development, even if they do not yet fully understand the role of race and racism in White children's lives. Keep these larger goals in mind as you hold ongoing conversations with your colleagues and families, share your ideals, and negotiate differences.

UNDERSTANDING DISAGREEMENT OR RESISTANCE

The more we understand about our own assumptions, views, and formative experiences, the better we are at opening up discussions about race, racial identity, and racism with other adults (see Chapter 1). The more we understand about the useful role of disagreements in dialogue, and the sources of resistance and of hope, the more we can find ways to make these conversations fruitful.

Mary Pat Martin, an experienced White anti-bias educator, explains that

Many of the issues come from the way White individuals have been unknowingly socialized about race—taught not to notice, ask openly, or discuss issues around racial diversity. Many people don't see any reason to talk about diversity with their children (e.g., "Why raise issues when there aren't any?" "Don't make waves."). Most lack knowledge about how children develop identity and prejudice, and, therefore, about what children's questions and statements mean developmentally. They do not know how and are not comfortable with handling children's questions and responses to racial and cultural diversity. They want to keep their children "protected" from having to know about prejudice and discrimination at such a young age—not recognizing that such obliviousness is itself a luxury of White privilege. Some worry that talking about race and racism will lead to the child's feeling guilty about being a White person. Even when White families have chosen an early childhood program that is diverse, that does not necessarily mean that they have considered all the issues of racism for themselves, their children, and society. (Personal communication, October 2004)

Many White adults vigorously maintain that young children do not notice racial or other kinds of differences and that talking with children about differences leads to prejudice. Many years of research about how young children absorb and enact race and racism make clear that the "color-blind" position is not accurate (see Chapters 3 and 7). It also serves to silence White children and adults and invalidate the ongoing racism experienced by People of Color. Some White families and teachers may believe that AB/MC education threatens their children, arguing that strategies used to redress the inequities of racism victimize White people.

Some White families and teachers may believe that AB/MC education threatens their children, arguing that it disrespects or unfairly targets White people. This perception often rests on the mistaken assumption that AB/MC education leaves out White people because it only addresses the contributions and life experiences of People of Color. As one White parent once asked Louise, "Where to my children fit in?" We hope that this book will provide useful content for countering the concern that White children will be "left out." Help White families learn about the benefits to White children of engaging in AB/MC education and provide opportunities for them to talk about their own identities and family histories. Another related assumption is that AB/MC education mistreats White culture. However,

AB/MC education does not disrespect the dominant culture. Rather, it asks that, instead of taking center stage, it share the stage with other groups of people who also helped create the United States and continue to contribute to its well-being. Moreover, accurately portraying White people's role in our country's history—both the positive and the negative—respects children and adults enough to teach complex realities rather than simplistic myths.

White families who struggle economically may resent what they see as special privileges being given to People of Color at White people's expense. It is particularly important to explore the realities of their lives and the many contributions working-class people have made and do make to our society. It is equally important to learn about the economic and social justice struggles of White working-class people and how both Whites and People of Color benefit when they work together for higher wages and better working conditions (Zinn, 1995). Furthermore, since most White people do not know about the role of White individuals in past and current anti-racism movements, exposing them to this information is another key way to counter the belief that Whites get left out of AB/MC education.

Another obstacle to openly discussing AB/MC issues is the culture of early childhood education, one that embodies gentleness, nurturance, and cohesiveness, and that often inhibits conflict. "The need to keep everyone happy or have harmony at any price is not compatible with the strong feelings and knotty issues raised by anti-bias curriculum" (Alvarado, Derman-Sparks, & Ramsey, 1999, p. 198). Passionate discussions sparked by differing perspectives about AB/ MC issues are inevitable. They produce growth for everyone when carried out in a spirit of shared learning. Experienced teachers agree that it is essential to embrace disagreement and criticism, rather than shying or running away from them.

Just as you are asking them to be open to your perspectives, respectfully listening and patiently seeking to understand families' and staff members' issues is essential. People are most likely to shift their thinking when they feel heard and acknowledged and when they are truly part of a dialogue. At the same time, do not let either the fear or the actuality of people's disagreements or resistance undermine your confidence and commitment. You need to forge ahead, yet be open, flexible, and creative in developing strategies; striking a balance between optimism and realistic expectations. Above all, have faith that all individuals can grow, although their pathways and timing will vary considerably.

LEARNING ABOUT YOUR CHILDREN'S FAMILIES

Involving families in your AB/MC work requires thoughtful preparation and strategic planning. For example, many teachers beginning their anti-bias work decide to modify how they handle holidays in their program. However, this change can easily become an emotional issue for some families and staff. If your program has a tradition of a big, well-attended Christmas party, it is not wise to *unilaterally* stop or replace it with an alternative celebration. Rather, learn how staff and families relate to Christmas. Engage them in examining the meaning of Christmas for them and the reality that Christmas is not a part of everyone's religious beliefs and traditions. Then, collaborate with staff members and families to make the December holiday period more inclusive for all members of the school.

During the first months of the school year, take time to learn about your children's immediate and extended families, their important traditions, roles, and experiences, and how families identify themselves. (A number of the activities described in Chapter 4 will help families provide this information.) This is one of the best ways to support families to feel they are valued members of your classroom community.

Some family members may consider themselves "just plain Americans" and deny that they have a culture. In fact, they may resent these questions or may feel envious of families who have retained some aspects of their ancestral culture. You can work with families to help them to see that they all have a complex of identities and values that they are imparting to their children even though it may not reflect a particular ethnic "culture." Ask them to think about the mosaic of rituals (such as Saturday-morning pancakes); roles ("Aunt Martha *always* brings that chocolate cake to *every* family party"); and favorite family stories that get told over and over again (that disastrous vacation trip where everything went wrong) that define their family's culture.

At enrollment time, include questions in your enrollment form to help you learn about each family's composition and parenting strategies that reflect their cultural values and beliefs. Examples of such questions include "Who lives in your household?" "Who else cares for your child?" "How can we validate and support your family's lifestyle here at the center?" "How do you handle sharing; messy play; gender roles?" "What are your child's responsibilities at home?" (York, 2003, pp. 112–113; see York, 2003, for the complete "Enrollment Form Questions").

Another element to examine is the relative status of different families in your program and how that affects your relationship with the families and their relationships with one another. Even within racially homogeneous programs, hierarchies and divisions exist. They usually reflect differences in economic class and occupations, which, in turn, influence access to resources, child-rearing expectations, and leisure activities. Thus, some parents who are "professionals" (doctors, lawyers, executives) may have the benefits of more money and greater prestige in the community. Their children in turn may have more advantages such as sports activities; art, dance, and gymnastics classes; and expensive family trips. Other families may not be able to afford these luxuries or may not view them as priorities.

Sometimes teachers focus more on the children of affluent families because their parents may be more outspoken than others and pressure teachers to devote more time and resources to their children. As a result, a teacher may unintentionally perpetuate the advantages of these children and shortchange the children from lower-income families. Divisions and power differentials among the families may exacerbate this inequity. Parents in professional occupations may dominate family discussion groups and silence others.

Gathering some basic demographic information about the communities in which your families live will also add to your understanding of their contexts. Through municipal and school documents, you can learn about community indicators, such as range and average of household incomes, levels of unemployment, percentages of people under the poverty line and on welfare, and the percentages of different racial and ethnic groups. By talking to people; visiting the homes of the children in your class; reading local newspapers; and attending community performances, celebrations, and meetings, you can also learn about local culture(s), concerns, and prevailing racially related images and assumptions.

LAYING THE FOUNDATION FOR WORKING WITH FAMILIES

Before you initiate work with families on the core learning themes, certain ongoing activities need to be already in progress. These create the supportive relationships among staff and with families that allow for discussions about the potentially sensitive topics raised by the learning themes.

Open up and encourage ongoing conversations among staff so they learn about one another's views and experiences on the issues related to the learning themes. Explore the self-reflection questions in this and other chapters in small-group conversations. These create opportunities for staff to learn about one another's views and background. They also contribute to building community among the staff. If you are working by yourself in a classroom, look for other teachers in your school or your local area who are interested in joining you for regular conversations about the AB/MC learning themes.

In your discussions, tell stories about your own background related to race, economic class, and culture. Share information you are gathering about your children's ideas about race and their White identities (see Chapters 3 and 4) and encourage your fellow group members to observe children in their classrooms. This topic allows people to talk about their common interest in children's development and creates the possibility for sharing ideas about implementing AB/MC curriculum in ways that are appropriate for their centers or classrooms.

As you have these conversations, you will learn which of your colleagues and administrators may become or already are allies and you can begin to build these relationships. You may also identify colleagues who do not wish to be involved. In these cases, respectfully agree to disagree, and create a mechanism to ensure that these differences do not blossom into insidious or overt conflicts (for example, agree to work on other projects together).

Build and strengthen mutually respectful communication and partnerships between staff and families, so that all feel welcomed, honored, and connected with the school's teachers and administrators. To create caring connections with families, teachers can use a combination of strategies.

- First, stay in touch through a variety of means, including informal conversations before and after school, phone calls, and, if computers are available to teachers and families, email.
- Plan and follow through with more formal contacts such as teacher-family conferences, home visits, and large- and small-group meetings.
- Keep parents up to date with a classroom newsletter that goes home once every 2 to 3 weeks. Describe ongoing AB/MC activities; include examples of children's comments and questions.
- Enable parents to feel part of the classroom by participating in "family homework projects" (as described in Chapter 4), school celebrations, and advisory committees that meet regularly with the teachers.
- Hold ongoing discussion groups and workshops about a range of child development and learning topics. One teacher encouraged informal discussions by inviting families and staff to read an article and then write their reactions on a sheet of easel paper placed on a wall near the door. Organize potluck dinners, and workdays or work weekends to deepen and expand the relationships among families and between staff and families. (For more suggestions, see Cadwell, 2003; Ramsey, 2004.)

Encourage families and teachers to learn about one another. If you jump in with difficult questions, participants may feel anxious and resistant. So spend the first few meetings building comfortable and safe relationships among teachers and family members. The following strategies can be adapted for your particular group:

- You might start your first meeting by asking participants to pair up with someone they do not know. The partners then interview each other and identify three ways they are similar and three ways they are different. Then they introduce one another to the larger group and mention some of the similarities and differences.
- Another opening activity is to ask family members to "introduce" their children to the other participants (by, for example, talking about which aspects of their children they find most/least enjoyable). Such introductions often open up further sharing as family members hear that others experience similar joys and concerns.
- You can then introduce a group portrait activity that came out of the La Raza community-organizing movement. Make a large grid on butcher paper, with columns for various questions (how many children are in your family? where were you born?) and a row for each family member. During the early part of the year, ask families to fill out these grids. As the chart is completed, family members, children, and teachers can learn more about one another and note commonalities and differences.
- Another introductory activity is to have parents write down values they want to pass on to their children, what they envision their child will be like at age 25, and what they hope that their children will learn from the program. These might be recorded on index cards and posted on a wall chart. These comments enable teachers and family members to see the range of philosophies and goals among the families in their classroom.

FACILITATING TIPS

We have found certain facilitating techniques to be helpful in creating safe, open, and honest spaces for AB/MC discussions. Co-facilitating with either colleagues or family members enables you to have more support and insights as you navigate discussions. Co-facilitators who are different from each other along one or more dimensions (e.g., race, ethnicity, gender, sexual orientation, physical abilities, economic class) provide the advantages of a wider range of life experience, and can serve as role models for interacting across various kinds of similarities and differences. If you are relatively new at this work or if you anticipate that the discussions will be difficult (tensions among individuals and groups, the likelihood that some participants will dominate and silence others) you might want to bring in trained facilitators in the beginning.

As you read the following guidelines and strategies for facilitating discussions, think about which tasks you could do now and which ones seem more challenging to you. (For more ideas, see Jacobson, 2003; McDonald, Mohr, Dichter, & McDonald, 2007.) Plan how you will get the training or support to do the more challenging tasks.

Create a safe environment that encourages honest reflections and communication. Set and enforce a few basic ground rules for everyone:

- Be respectful while listening to one another's stories. Ask questions for clarification, but do not ask questions that express doubt concerning a person's experiences or feelings.
- Maintain confidentiality. No speaking outside the meeting about what others have said.
- Give equal time to everyone who wants to speak. Assure people that you will hold everyone to the ground rules. Telling your own story first creates safety for others to speak and models that it is okay to talk about topics that people may not have talked about before.
- Do not confuse safety with always being comfortable. You can be supportive and still have honest conversations. Listen carefully to how people are speaking. If they seem to be avoiding or masking some feelings, encourage them to express what they truly feel and support them when they make difficult disclosures. Help everyone to accept and learn from tensions and uneasy silences that are inevitably part of these discussions.

Keep the discussion both focused and open by using the following strategies: Choose specific questions as catalysts for opening up issues and inviting participants to tell their stories; support each person's opportunity to tell her or his story or make her or his argument; ensure respectful listening; pay attention to themes that emerge from the composite of individual storytelling; and summarize key themes and show how they relate to the learning themes.

Use a variety of discussion formats, such as dyads, triads, groups of four or five, and whole groups. Smaller groups give everyone an opportunity to tell his or her stories. Moreover, some participants only talk when there is a small audience. Another advantage is that people are sometimes more honest with themselves and each other when the facilitator, who may be seen as an authority, is not present. So always have some break-out groups. People can then come back together to share insights from their conversations.

Support the range of speaking styles and ensure a fair division of speaking time. Some people take more time to share details about themselves. Others need more wait time; so be sure that people who jump in faster do not take more than their fair share of time. To ensure that everyone has a voice in the meeting, use methods such as allocating a specific amount of time for each person's story, using a timer to enforce those agreements, or adapting the Native American strategy of passing a talking stick (only the person holding the stick may talk).

Pay attention to power dynamics that reflect those in the larger society. Notice and, when necessary, interrupt patterns such as men talking more than women, or people from higher-income families taking more than their fair share of time. You may want to make a ground rule that a person may not talk a second time until everyone has had a first turn.

When facilitating racially diverse groups, be careful to maintain a balance between the issues and needs of all participants. Sometimes, White participants want to hear the stories of People of Color so that they can avoid examining their own issues. This strategy also forces People of Color into the all too familiar position of being responsible for educating White people. At the same time, the concerns of White participants should not dominate the discussion. It is often helpful for the participants to meet in racially separate groups and then come together to share each other's discussions.

Stay open to staff and family members who choose not to participate in AB/MC discussions. While you hope that everyone will want to participate in your AB/MC program, some may choose not to. It is useful to talk with them individually to find out their reasons and to explain your purposes in doing the work. These conversations may be enough to draw them in to the process. However, you will not win over everyone. Respect their decisions, and try not to get discouraged by or overly focused on those who are not interested.

Recognize and honor different paths in the overall journey. Growth does not usually happen in a simple straight ascending line. People might change in some ways but not in others; they may engage in some of the learning themes but resist others. Allow for individuals' differing paces and rhythms, while supporting them to continue the journey.

Hasten slowly. All of us are always in process. While the work and need for change is urgent, people need time to grow. Keep your expectations open and have faith that people can learn and change. Remember that you can plant the seeds, but you cannot force the harvest. Celebrate small victories!

STRATEGIES FOR IMPLEMENTING LEARNING THEMES

In the following section, we discuss how to open up productive conversations with families and staff on the first three learning themes. You can involve people in classroom activities, facilitate discussions about implementing the learning themes at home and in the classroom, and encourage people to examine their own racial identities and related attitudes. As with the children's activities, our suggestions are not prescriptive, but we hope that they give you ideas about how you might proceed. We focus on families; however, you can easily adapt these activities to use with staff.

Every group of families and teachers is unique. Make decisions about where to take the discussions and experiences in light of the group's composition, interests, preferred communication and learning styles, and experience with the topics of the first three learning themes. Once you open up the conversation, issues will emerge that are most pertinent to the participants. They can become topics for further exploration and help you set priorities about activities and discussion topics.

Before turning to specific strategies, we want to discuss the issue of *finding time*, which is frequently a major staff concern in regard to working with families.

Finding Time

You might wonder, "All this sounds great but how do we find the time to have all these discussions?" Indeed, finding sufficient time is one of the main impediments to having in-depth discussions among staff members or between staff and family members. Teachers, who often have their own children at home, are reluctant to spend more (unpaid!) hours at the school. Family members who work full time while raising children may feel that they cannot add a single thing to their schedule. Moreover, availability often reflects economic inequities. Family members who do not have to work or have jobs with flexible schedules are able to participate more than individuals who are managing long inflexible work hours. Lower-income families also may be hampered by lack of transportation and childcare and not able to attend meetings unless you find ways to address these needs.

Finding time to meet the challenges of diverse family pressures requires flexible and creative thinking. Make meeting times as convenient as possible. For example, provide child care and food, and have meetings when parents come to pick up their children. Some programs have increased participation by offering a "menu" of small group meetings on a range of issues that meet at different times and in different locations. You might experiment with early-morning or lunch meetings to see if those times work for families who cannot come later in the afternoon or evening. Other programs use an informal approach, making a teacher available to family members who bring their children to school and stay to chat over coffee or tea. Over time, the teacher introduces anti-bias education topics among other development issues. Email discussion groups are another way to encourage ongoing conversations among staff and family members. People can participate without having to leave their homes, and some people find that they are more open and honest using email than they are in face-to-face conversations. Earning credit at a local community college or university for participating in discussion groups might be an additional incentive for some family members and teachers.

Finding time for staff members to meet together is another perennial challenge and requires creative planning. Some staffs have bi-weekly pizza meetings right after the children leave; others have longer meetings 1 night a month. If there is a time in the year when the demand for child care is low, a center might close for 2 days and have an extended staff retreat. Some directors find ways for staff to meet during working hours by hiring substitutes to supervise naptime. Alternatively, substitutes could fill in for either lead teachers or assistant teachers so that those groups can meet.

Time is an issue for everyone. Nevertheless, many programs have discovered that, as the old saying goes, "Where there's a will, there's a way." If you plan discussions around topics that are especially important to your families, colleagues, and staff, people will be more likely to come and participate. Reaching every family on every issue is an unrealistic goal but try to ensure that each family engages in at least one discussion during the school year. Above all, do not let the lack of time serve as an excuse to avoid addressing AB/MC topics with families or staff. If you find yourself delaying or avoiding these discussions, take time to talk with supportive colleagues or friends about the sources of your anxieties and find ways to overcome them.

Implementing Learning Theme One

Applied to adults, learning theme one is about better understanding our own racial and cultural identity and expanding our ability to support children's authentic identity development.

Encourage family members to examine their own racial and cultural identities and socialization. Select relevant self-reflection questions from the lists in this and other chapters and organize people in dyads or triads to tell their stories. Encourage them to explore how they developed their own racial and cultural identities. People can also consider the impact of the history of Whiteness on their ethnic/cultural heritage as discussed in Chapter 2 (for example, if their ancestors were originally part of the dominant Anglo-American culture or if they had to abandon their ancestral culture to be accepted and successful). Remember that racial identity is socially and politically constructed; ethnic identity comes from one's family's countries of origin.

Facilitate discussions about supporting children's positive racial identity development. Since racial identity is not commonly discussed among most Whites (ironically, it is usually an overt subject only among people who hold White-supremacist beliefs), initiating conversations about it may be challenging. As a first step, find out how families racially identify their children. Many may say they don't, that their child is "just a person." Use material from Chapter 3 and your classroom observations to provide information about how young children do begin to construct their racial identities and to give a context for understanding the children's experiences and ideas. Invite family members to talk about their own early racial awareness and what racial identities they hope their children will form. These discussions may lead to clarifying goals and generating ideas about how to collaboratively support the development of positive racial identities.

Facilitate discussions about families' cultural heritage and what/how they teach values to their children. Help people understand that culture is always evolving and defines how people live their daily lives now. It is not just about coming from a particular country or ethnic group or carrying on intact traditions from the past. Invite family members to describe the cultural values, beliefs, and traditions that are most important to them and how they are conveying these to their children. At first, it may be hard for people to name specific strategies, because they do them unconsciously. You might relate a few stories about approaches you use in your home or that you experienced as a child to help people identify ones that they use. (For more suggestions, see Carter & Curtis, 1997; York, 2003.)

Involve family members in the activities you do with children. Many of the strategies described in Chapter 4 require participation from families. When teachers take the additional step and identify the activities as "family culture," they help participants recognize and gain vocabulary to describe who they are as a family. "Family homework" classroom visits and participation in activities, curriculum built upon family interviews (see Rogovin, 1998), newsletters and photo displays—all offer the opportunity for family members to share their lives and be recognized and honored.

Hold discussions about how families can support children's positive identity development related to gender, social class, abilities, and family configuration. Some programs find it helpful to start with a "safer" topic such as gender and then move on to racial identity at another meeting. Invite family members to talk about the messages they got about these aspects of identity when they were growing up and what they want their children to learn or not learn. Encourage them to describe their efforts to help their children feel good about their various identities. Exploring these aspects of identity can continue for several meetings; however, do not let them become a substitute for looking at racial identity.

Implementing Learning Theme Two

Learning about similarities and differences among families will happen naturally, as you implement learning theme one activities. Encourage participants to be open to a range of values and ways of life and to see that they can both agree and disagree with other individuals. For example, ask people to move to various areas in the room depending on their responses (agree, disagree, not sure) to a series of statements about child-rearing beliefs and practices ("I teach my children that boys are boys and girls are girls," or "I let my children decide how much food they want to eat"). After they assemble in their response groups, members can discuss why they chose their particular responses and then explain their position to the larger group. With each statement the compositions of the groups will change, enabling family members see how they share both similar and different views with other families.

Encourage families to expand their children's awareness of diversity among same-race people. Ask families to relate and then reflect on the experiences their children have had with people who are racially similar but different from them because of class, sexual orientation, abilities/disabilities, religion, ethnic background, or a combination of these. Encourage them to think about questions such as, "How do I want my child to approach people who are different in some way?" "What assumptions and comfort level do I want my child to have about people who are rich? Poor? Athletic? Disabled? Female? Male? Gay? Straight? Practice a different religion?" In the context of this discussion you can invite people to explore why some aspects of diversity are more difficult for them to talk about and consider if they want their children to feel the same discomfort. Brainstorm and practice strategies for responding more effectively to children's questions about those dimensions of diversity they find challenging. You might encourage families to review and discuss children's books that are particularly effective in raising these issues.

Implementing Learning Theme Three

For adults, this theme is about building cooperative relationships that include respecting and connecting across lines defined by social class, ethnicity, racial identity, religion, or family configuration. This theme applies to both all-White and racially/ethnically diverse groups.

Engage family members in cooperative projects to enhance your program. These can include building and installing a new piece of equipment, cleaning up the school environment, or working together to create a winter holiday celebration reflecting the range of traditions within the group.

Encourage families to strengthen their children's capacity for and experiences with cooperative interactions as a balance to competitiveness. In conversations, identify the competitive messages children learn from the media and the ways that teachers and family members may be unintentionally promoting children's competitiveness. Brainstorm strategies to make games and activities at home and school more cooperative.

Support family members to collaborate on projects to improve some aspect of community life. For example, families might work together to create community gardens or clean up and improve a local park (see the environmental projects described under learning theme six in Chapter 8), or to advocate for longer public library hours or the installation of a traffic light to make it safer to cross a busy street near the school or the neighborhood playground.

GOING DEEPER

With staff and family members who are ready to go further in their exploration of their White identity, facilitate a discussion about how each of them has benefited from being White. Kivel (2002) suggests starting these discussions by having each participant respond yes or no to statements, such as the following:

- "I live in or attended school in a district where more money is spent on the schools that White children go to than those that children of color attend."
- "I lived or went to school in a district where the textbooks and other classroom materials reflected my race as normal [and members of my race] as heroes and builders of the United States,

and where there was little mention of the contributions of People of Color to our society." (p. 33)

For the complete list of examples of White benefits, see Kivel (2002, p. 32). You can devise other statements relevant to your particular group. After individually responding to the questions, people share their answers in small groups and the whole group and identify the similarities and differences in how they experience White privilege. You may also want to use another list from Kivel (2002, p. 47) that examines the personal costs of racism for Whites.

Finally, some programs have ongoing study groups for family and staff members who want to continue their learning about White identity. The books listed in "For Further Reading" in Chapters 2 and 3 are appropriate for such groups.

The strategies in this chapter have the potential to open up meaningful discussions with staff and families about what it means to be White. These lay a foundation for moving to the learning themes in Part II that call upon staff and family members to consider their relation to the wider world of human diversity and strengthen their capacity for critical thinking and social activism. At the same time, the activities we suggest in this chapter are only one aspect of the larger task of educating ourselves to become anti-racist/anti-bias activists. To appreciate fully what it means to create a more just society intentionally, we also need to investigate the dynamics of Whiteness in the context of an economic, political, social, and cultural system of racial advantage (Tatum, 1992). In Chapter 9 we suggest ways to initiate these discussions with staff and family members who want to take the next steps.

A Tale of Two Centers
EPISODE ONE

To give you a sense of how the ideas we wrote about in Chapters 4 and 5 might come to life in a real early childhood setting, here are stories about how teachers in two different centers, Mother Jones and Louisa May Alcott, developed specific aspects of the first three learning themes.

THE MOTHER JONES CENTER

Mother Jones became a beloved union organizer when she was in her 50s and a grandmother. She worked with miners in Appalachia and with children working in Southern cotton mills.

A full-day, state-funded program for low-income families, the Mother Jones Center is located in a low-income neighborhood in a community highly segregated by income, ethnicity, and race. The center families are primarily White and include single parents, student families, and government-assistance families. Recently, a few children from new migrant families from El Salvador joined the center as well.

Liz and Charlie are the morning teachers. Liz grew up in the neighborhood, went to the local community college, and, eventually, at 32, earned her associate degree in early childhood education. Being a head teacher in the very center her children attended 12 years ago is a dream come true. Charlie is a university graduate with plans to become a psychologist someday, after taking a few years off to work directly with children. The afternoon teacher, Marina, taught elementary school in her native Mexico. She and her engineer husband came to the United States when he got a job with a large company in a nearby city. She is the only person of color on the staff. The three teachers have a strong commitment to respecting families and working with children to build their self-respect and self-esteem. They want the children *and* families to feel safe in the program.

They decided to be explicit about their goals and call the classroom a *caring community* (learning theme three). They made a sign for the door saying, "Welcome to our Caring Community—Everyone Is Respected and Safe Here." The teachers focused on encouraging children to help one another. Liz filled small plastic bottles with water to freeze for "owie bottles" that children could run and get if another child fell down and got hurt. At snack time, the teachers arranged for each child to have the opportunity to serve, and they helped all the others thank the "server who helps us have snack." When quarrels arose, the staff approached them as opportunities to learn how to live together. After putting words to children's feelings and helping them describe what was going on ("Mikey is crying and holding on to the block. Jesse is pulling on the block and shouting, 'Mine!'"), they would ask questions such as, "How many people are in this problem?" "Whose problem is this"? "What can we do so both of you are safe and okay?"

While all the teachers and families liked the goal of safety for all children, implementing them revealed some differences among the staff. Charlie found it particularly hard to let go of his own learned sense of fair play, which focused on the individual ("She had it first—it's hers"). However, he worked hard to support children to find solutions grounded in the children's relationship to one another, rather than on object ownership.

Another complicating factor came from the fact that several of the older 4s and 5s had younger siblings in the program, and intervened immediately on the side of a younger brother or sister when there was a problem. In talking with parents, the teachers came to understand that in many of the children's families, the older siblings had the important job of keeping their younger siblings safe in a truly unsafe neighborhood. Recognizing the older siblings' behavior as a sign of caring and protection helped the staff transform their interventions into thanking the older children for caring, while also suggesting alternative ways for helping their younger siblings.

The teachers started the year with a curriculum on "Who are our families?"—and almost instantly ran into trouble. Here is why: Teachers asked the families to bring in snapshots to contribute to a family collage that would hang on the wall. They also invited families to attend the morning circle and have an opportunity to talk about their home. Only some of the families participated.

Liz, who had been uneasy about this approach from the beginning, realized that many of the families did not have cameras. She also understood that some of the families might be embarrassed about the places where they lived. Instead of pictures, she suggested that they set up a family altar, a sacred place, where each family could display a few items that represented important aspects of their family. They would make a shelf, high enough that children could not get at the items unsupervised, but low enough for children to see. Teachers personally invited each family to have a week of display time. This approach seemed easier for families.

People brought in such things as a CD of favorite music, a bowling trophy, a wedding picture, the baby's handmade booties from Grandma, and a framed community college diploma. Two families, however, objected. "Altars," they explained, "are for religious items, sacred items—not for family stuff." "Besides," said one of the parents, "in my religion we do not show human images on an altar." Listening to this conversation (which took place in the entry hall of the school), another parent added, "We're not religious, and I don't want my child to partake in religious activities."

The staff, determined to honor the families' beliefs, but unwilling to give up an idea that seemed to be working, went into a huddle. They decided to rename the shelf "the family shelf." It was hard for Liz to give up her sense of wanting the space to be unique and sacred, but she agreed. To her delight, the very fact that the materials mattered to families created the special quality for which she was hoping.

The children loved the shelf, and conversations began about home activities. Children discovered that several of them had parents who loved to go bowling and that others had grandmothers who knit or crocheted. "Everyone has a family—our families are different" became a theme as children learned that some families had one mama and three children; others had a grandma, a grandpa, and two children; and still others had a mama, a daddy, an auntie, and two cousins. All are families. All of them take care of their children.

Charlie began a chart with the children about things families did together, and was delighted by the conversations that occurred about the differences and similarities in the families. He was startled, however, to hear Deirdre reply to the question, What does your mommy do? by saying, "Nothing. My mommy doesn't work." Deirdre's mother was, in fact, at home during the day caring for her new baby. In the evening, Deirdre's aunt came over, and Deirdre's mother took classes at the local college. The comment "My mommy doesn't work" bothered Charlie a lot. He started asking the children what kinds of things their parents did and was surprised to find out that all the caretaking, homemaking, and life management that their parents did was invisible to the children.

The three teachers decided to create a curriculum to address the many ways in which family members work to support one another and maintain family life. They thought it would be wonderful to have photographs of all the family members working to keep their family functioning. One problem surfaced immediately: where to get cameras so that all families could participate. Luckily, one of the parents worked at a local electronic store and was able to get a donated digital camera for the school that all families could use. Often as they shared the camera, they enjoyed looking at the pictures taken by other families in the school. Each family took photographs of the day-to-day work of each family member. These included pictures of their pre-school children also doing something helpful (putting away toys, playing with the baby, cleaning the cat box). After each family had the camera, the pictures were downloaded on the school computer and printed using an on-line discount service.

Liz, sensitive to the feelings of some of the lowest-income families, reminded everyone that photographs did not need to be inside the home, but could include buying groceries, taking the bus to deliver the child to school, or older children playing with younger children at the playground.

After printing the pictures, the teachers made a series of classroom books called "Everyone Works in My Family." The children loved the books, and the teachers helped them explore comparisons and similarities in the different ways people contributed to family life. Each child received a badge (made by Marina) labeled "Family Hero" that described a particular contribution that child made to family life (HENRY. Family Hero. Picks up toys and puts them away).

A few months into the school year, three new children arrived in the Mother Jones Center. Their families were new members of the community, coming from El Salvador to work at the canning factory on the outskirts of town. The children and their families brought some new dimensions of diversity to the center. They spoke Spanish, had brown skin and black hair, ate some different foods, and lived as three-generation families.

The teachers' first concern was to address the new children's language development. They spoke with a faculty member at their community college to learn more about the current thinking about bilingual education. The teachers decided on a dual-language approach. One, they would encourage the children's continued home language development in order to foster the children's healthy self-concept and connections to their families. Two, they would also help the children to learn English so that they could more fully participate in the classroom, as well as develop a skill they needed for all further schooling. In addition, the teachers made plans for fostering the White children's respect and comfort with a second language by teaching them the Spanish terms for English words and phrases commonly used in the daily life of the center. They planned to invite the Spanish-speaking families and children to help them decide on these words, as well as on the correct way to pronounce and spell them.

While Mariana was bilingual, she spoke a somewhat different version of Spanish than did the El Salvadorian families, so she also asked a few parents to help her translate for the children. The teachers remade all labels of classroom materials for each curriculum area and for food, water, and the bathroom, so that they were in both English and Spanish. They agreed to encourage the new children's inclusion in all activities and to help the rest of the children participate in making the new children part of the class.

Other families helped them make home language books, stories, and songs on tape. Staff members also found a community group who would help them translate forms, newsletters, or other ongoing written communications. They took photographs of the daily activities to show families what their children did at school. Finally, teachers encouraged families to continue to develop their child's home language, including reading to their child in their home language. They created a lending library of bilingual children's books, and introduced two of the families to people at the local adult literacy programs.

The teachers also helped the new children to make books about their families that could be added to the ones the other children had previously made. Family members helped them to make these books bilingual. When they read these new books to the children, they made sure to explore the similarities of the new children's families with those of the rest of the class as well as the ways that each family was different.

THE LOUISA MAY ALCOTT CENTER

Louisa May Alcott was the author of several books, including Little Women *and* Little Men. *She also worked for the abolition of slavery and women's right to vote.*

Brenda and Vera cotaught a class in the Louisa May Alcott Center, a private preschool that served middle- and upper-middle-class, predominately White families who lived in an affluent suburb. Most of the children lived in two-parent households. The children whose parents were divorced still spent a lot of time with each of their parents. Vera was from a White middle-class family and married to a local doctor. They had two children, both of whom had finished college. She had both a bachelor's and master's degree in early childhood education, and had taught at the school for 25 years. Brenda was from a working-class background and had worked in child care for many years before getting her bachelor's degree in psychology. She was married to a construction worker and had three children, all in high school. She had been teaching at the school for 10 years.

Both teachers were concerned about the competitiveness among the children in their 4- to 5-year-old group. No item was too small or situation too trivial to elicit boasts about having or being the best. The children constantly compared their work—drawings, clay structures, Lego constructions—announcing to the world that theirs was best and disparaging the efforts of others at the activity. School arrival often set off a barrage of comparisons and put-downs, when one child began regaling the others about the purchase of a new article of clothing, toy, or video game.

Brenda and Vera felt that the children's preoccupation with being "best" interfered with their learning and peer relationships. The teachers were also uncomfortable with the strong sense of entitlement and superiority that pervaded the children's comments. Although specific individuals were most likely to engage in this competitive talk, all the children engaged in it to varying degrees.

At a parent meeting and during individual conferences, Brenda and Vera raised these issues with the parents. Many responded that they, too, were concerned and did not understand why the children were so competitive, because they did not encourage that kind of conversation at home. At the same time, the parents also repeatedly asked about whether the curriculum at the school was academically challenging enough and wanted assurances that it would give their children an "edge" to get into a prestigious private school or to excel in the public school. In these conversations, the parents enumerated items from long lists of extracurricular activities that the children were doing to better position them for excelling in sports and the arts.

In short, while most parents were not explicitly promoting competition, their expectations that their children be superstars were permeating their family lives. The teachers surmised that the children were absorbing these values and expectations and expressing them in their own ways with their peers. A few parents, whose children were at the school on scholarships, talked about how isolated and humiliated they felt because they could not compete with the wealthier families. One mother tearfully described her son's embarrassment about his birthday party, which was modest compared to the lavish affairs thrown by his classmates. As Brenda listened to these stories, she thought about how often she too had felt diminished and angered when families talked about their exotic trips and extravagant purchases. She and her husband had worked very hard to make a good life for themselves and their children, but it seemed paltry compared to the glamorous lives that many of the families had.

Vera and Brenda decided to tackle the competition and entitlement issues by helping children see themselves more realistically and appreciate their own and one another's skills as gifts to the group (learning theme one), by exposing children to ways of life that were not embedded in privilege and entitlement (learning theme two), and by stressing cooperation over individual achievement (learning theme three). They also planned to engage the parents in these explorations and changes.

The teachers started by redesigning many of the activities so they would be collaborative rather than individual projects. For example, easel painting and blocks became cooperative activities. Needless to say, many children balked at these changes, and conflicts frequently arose. However, the teachers worked with the children on learning to see one another's perspectives and to communicate more effectively, and over time children became more skilled at working together. They even complimented one another on occasion. In a similar vein, the teachers also adapted several routines. For example, at circle time, instead of having children talk about what they themselves had done that day or over the weekend, the teachers had them interview one another and report what their partners had done. To underscore the message that each person contributed to the whole group, the teachers designed some class projects to which each child could contribute (one was a classroom quilt in which each child decorated one piece and all the pieces were sewn together).

Also to enhance children's knowledge of and appreciation for all of their classmates, the teachers set up a few activities in which the children worked with rotating partners to learn about one another's families and their likes and dislikes, giving the class a concrete way to see how people can be both alike and different. They also sent a stuffed animal (Kanga) home to each child's family for a few days along with a digital camera and journal. Family members then took pictures and wrote descriptions of things that Kanga did with the family (ate pizza, played with cousins, attended church). When Kanga returned to school after each visit, the teachers would show the pictures and read the journal entries to all the children. Children spontaneously mentioned many similarities and differences that they noticed among the families. To ensure that Kanga's stories did not become a source of competition for the most glamorous, exciting, and expensive outings, the teachers asked families to avoid including stories about activities that required money (such as shopping or a theme park).

To stretch the children's awareness beyond their immediate lives, Brenda and Vera used books to introduce the children to other ways of life and to show them that not all people lived with the same resources that they did. At this point, the teachers used mostly stories of White families so that the children would not immediately assume that difference in income meant difference in race.

The teachers also introduced Natalie, a White working-class persona doll whose father had recently lost his job. Through Natalie, Brenda and Vera told the children about the hardships that families face when they have few resources to begin with and then lose their income. To ensure that the children did not simply feel sorry for Natalie and her family, the teachers told stories that showed how Natalie and her family were strong and creative in the face of these challenges. The children listened attentively to the stories and often raised good questions. On occasion, they commented on how few resources a particular family had. The teachers used these comments as opportunities to encourage the children to talk about how they felt about their possessions and to think what really made them happy (playing with a friend or playing with a new toy).

Brenda and Vera involved the parents in their curriculum planning by inviting them to see the group projects and encouraging them to offer their ideas to reduce the competition among the children. Many of the parents had agreed with the teachers' initial concerns about the children's competitiveness. However, as the curriculum continued, others began to complain. At a parent meeting later in the year, a few parents dismissed the emphasis on cooperation as "feel-good" activities and argued, "These kids have got to learn to compete—otherwise they won't get ahead!" Their comments generated a lively discussion among the adults. After about half an hour, the parents began to polarize and repeat themselves. Brenda wanted to help participants find some common ground, so she asked the participants to write down their own definitions of a "good life" and three things they wanted to be remembered for when they died. All of a sudden, the room became very quiet; most of the parents looked thoughtful. After they finished writing down their ideas, Brenda had them meet in small groups to compare their responses and then report back to the whole group. Not surprisingly, most of the participants had written about loving their families, caring for others, and contributing to society, *not* about getting promotions or shopping for expensive items.

As a follow-up to this discussion, the teachers and a few parents organized a number of discussion groups that focused on the pressures that families feel to "get ahead" and raise "perfect children." To create a safe place in which parents could speak honestly, Brenda and Vera told humorous stories about their efforts to be "perfect teachers." They encouraged the parents to look at the stress that their expectations for perfect families and superstar children created for themselves and their children.

We will return to the stories of the Mother Jones and Louisa May Alcott Centers following Chapter 9.

MAKING CONNECTIONS AND BECOMING ACTIVISTS

Part II (Chapters 6, 7, 8, and 9) focuses on expanding children's connection to the human family and their capacity for critical thinking and activism. In Chapter 6 we sketch a picture of the history of White anti-racism activism. Chapter 7 looks at research on children's development of racial attitudes and children's responses to experiencing anti-bias education. Chapters 8 and 9 offer teaching guidelines, strategies, and examples for carrying out learning themes four, five, six, and seven. Episode Two of the "Tale of Two Centers" illustrates how to use the learning themes of Part II in actual early childhood programs.

6

A Short History of White Resistance to Racism in the United States

"I joined the 'other America'. . . . I've got this sense that I'm part of this long movement that's like a chain back into the past and will go on after I'm gone."

—Anne Braden, quoted in Brown,
Refusing Racism: White Allies and the Struggle for Civil Rights

Being an activist may seem beyond your experiences so far, contrary to your self-image, or in opposition to your family values and beliefs. However, social justice activism, including White resistance to racism, is a powerful theme throughout the history of the United States. Activists have come from all the diverse groups in our country, and their work has taken many forms. Members of your own extended family may have been activists, even if you do not know about them. Becoming an activist is not a departure, but rather, a way to link with generations of change makers of the past, present, and future.

Individuals and organizations have critiqued and resisted racial oppression from the institutionalization of the slavery of Africans during the colonial period. Each period of overt struggle by African Americans against racism created a recurring ideological crisis for White Americans (Feagin, 2000); and at every point, at least some White individuals took up the challenge of participating in the struggle for freedom and equality. This rich history illustrates how "human beings have a unique ability to reflect on their own circumstances and to create, in association with others, a collective consciousness that can lead to change" (Feagin, 2000, p. 34).

Unfortunately, few White Americans know about this aspect of their history. When asked to name three White anti-racists, most people draw a blank (Tatum, 1997). In this chapter, we hope to whet your appetite to learn more by highlighting a few themes of this significant story. At the same time, our focus on the role of White anti-racists in no way implies that they were the only or the primary participants in movements for social change. History clearly shows that the leaders of the long struggle to eradicate racism's many forms have been African Americans and other People of Color.

Aptheker (1993) and Thomas (1996) provide compelling histories of interracial efforts to overthrow slavery and subsequent forms of discrimination. Their volumes are the primary sources for the following brief history of the role of White anti-racists. As you read it, you might think about what (if any) of this history you learned in school.

ANTI-RACISM MOVEMENTS IN THE 17TH AND 18TH CENTURIES

As early as the mid-17th century, both Black and White people resisted the institution of slavery:

> There is no doubt that those who ruled the South were committed to the creation and preservation of a White supremacist South . . . [but] challenges to it were continuous and serious, and the history of the White South is not of a placidly existing White male supremacist society but rather of a society constantly facing challenge, protest, and dissent, both individual and collective. (Aptheker, 1993, p. 24)

The Quakers and other White religious groups were active in challenging slavery from early on in U.S. history. In the Germantown Protest of 1688, Quakers issued a call for the unequivocal abolition of slavery. They argued that it violated the Golden Rule, traded human beings who have immortal souls, separated families, encouraged adultery, and was, in short, based on thievery. Later, in 1746, John Woolman, a famous Quaker, said, "To consider mankind otherwise than as brethren, to think favours are peculiar to one nation and to exclude others, plainly supposes darkness in understanding" (Aptheker, 1993, p. 77). Foreshadowing the thinking of 20th-century psychologists such as Kenneth Clark, Robert Coles, and Beverly Tatum, Woolman also warned that slavery would be detrimental to the psychological and moral health of children of slave owners (Aptheker, 1993).

Because slave owners and traders defended their practices on the grounds that Africans were an inferior race and fit only for servitude, a number of White ministers and scholars took up the task of refuting these claims. They cited many examples of learned Africans in Europe and United States—writers, poets, preachers, and doctors—as proof that Africans had intellectual capabilities equal to those of European Americans (Aptheker, 1993). In her speeches, Lydia Maria Child frequently asked why, if slave owners believed their own propaganda about inferiority, they so vehemently forbade any learning for Black people (Aptheker, 1993). The abolitionists pointed out that subjugation, not inherent abilities, had reduced Africans to living lives of drudgery: "We first crush people to the earth and then claim the right of trampling on them forever, because they are prostrate" (Lydia Maria Child, quoted in Aptheker, 1993, p. 134).

In the 18th century, before, during, and after the American Revolution, many White politicians and writers vigorously pointed out the contradictions between the ideals expressed in the Declaration of Independence and the existence of slavery. The preamble to the constitution of the New York Manumission Society of 1785, drew on both religious and civic rationales for abolishing slavery:

> It is our duty, therefore, both as free Citizens and as Christians, not only to regard, with compassion, the Injustice done to those among us who are held as Slaves, but . . . to enable them to Share, equally with us, in that civil and religious Liberty with which our indulgent Providence has blessed these States, and to which these, our Brethren, are by nature, as much entitled as ourselves. (Aptheker, 1993, p. 92)

Ben Franklin, one of the authors of Constitution of the United States, thought that, "These blessings ought rightfully to be administered without distinction of color, to all descriptions of people" (Aptheker, 1993, p. 99). At the same time, many of the Founding Fathers embodied the fundamental contradiction between slavery and liberty. For example, Thomas Jefferson condemned slavery as "a perpetual exercise of . . . the most unremitting despotism on one part and degrading submission on the other" (Aptheker, 1993, p. 49), yet he owned enslaved Africans on his plantation.

THE ABOLITIONIST MOVEMENT AND THE CIVIL WAR

During the 19th century, the abolitionist movement gained momentum, and many White activists, including William Lloyd Garrison (editor of the abolitionist paper, *The Liberator*) joined Black abolitionists such as Frederick Douglass, Theodore S. Wright, and John S. Rock to call for the immediate end of slavery (Aptheker, 1993). The abolitionist movement had two thrusts: one was to end slavery; the other, more controversial one, was to integrate society racially. Many people, including Abraham Lincoln, were anti-slavery but not anti-racist. They envisioned a segregated post-slavery society with Black people continuing to do menial work, albeit under more humane conditions. As several Black abolitionists pointed out, many White abolitionists abhorred slavery but did not want to live and work with former slaves. Moreover, most of the White abolitionist leaders insisted on keeping leadership in their own hands (Aptheker, 1993). After many years of collaboratively fighting against slavery, Frederick Douglass broke with William Lloyd Garrison because the latter refused to support a Black-run newspaper (Thomas, 1996).

However, some White abolitionists, including Angelina and Sarah Grimke, Lucretia Mott, Lydia Maria Child, Samuel May, and Charles Olcutt, took a more anti-racist stand and believed that society should be racially integrated (Aptheker, 1993). Sarah Grimke argued that it was

> the duty of abolitionists to identify themselves with these oppressed Americans, by sitting with them in places of worship, by appearing with them in our streets, by giving them countenance in steamboats and stages [stage coaches], by visiting them at their homes and encouraging them to visit us, receiving them as we do our White fellow-citizens. (Aptheker, 1993, p. 138)

Her sister Angelina strained family relationships by having African Americans in her wedding party and among the guests at her marriage ceremony (Thomas, 1996). Many White anti-racists challenged social conventions by living in Black communities or openly participating in interracial gatherings, despite criticism from many quarters. A number of White people worked with Black men and women to establish and run schools for Black children. At the time, racial integration existed in only a few educational institutions, among them Oberlin College and some public schools in Ohio.

During the period leading up to the Civil War, enslaved people initiated more uprisings, and arrest records indicate that at least some White people participated (Aptheker, 1993). Many White families were involved in the Underground Railroad, often at considerable risk. White individuals caught participating in these activities were usually punished, although not nearly as harshly as were Black people who were arrested. The Fugitive Slave Law, passed in 1850, radicalized many White people because it required, as William Lyman, a Connecticut farmer, said, "all good citizens to be slave-catchers: Good citizens cannot be slave-catchers any more than light can be darkness" (Aptheker, 1993, p. 148). At this time, state legislatures, Congress, and newspapers hotly debated the questions of ending slavery and extending voting rights to Black Americans. Although most of these initiatives failed, the speeches and writings radiate with the passion and determination of both Black and White advocates.

Eventually, frustration with so many failed efforts led some Black and White abolitionists to advocate violence to end the oppressive system of slavery. John Brown, a White man, was one of the most famous. Driven by fervent religious beliefs that slavery was wrong, Brown participated in nonviolent abolitionist movements throughout his life. He set up schools, worked with the Underground Railroad, and gave impassioned speeches. Then, as his frustration grew, he began to advocate the overthrow of the slaveholding system, concluding that only physical fighting would stop slavery (as, in fact, it ultimately did, in the Civil War). After his capture at the uprising at Harpers Ferry (during which two of his sons were killed), Brown was tried and executed. From an anti-racist perspective, John Brown is a man to honor, giving his life both figuratively and literally to end the evil of slavery. However, mainstream history books and school texts portray John Brown as a crazy fanatic, if they mention him at all. So, while most White Americans scorn John Brown, people from all over the world and many African Americans visit his last home in Lake Placid, New York, to pay their respects to him and his sons.

ANTI-RACISM MOVEMENTS IN THE 20TH CENTURY

Since the Civil War, civil rights and anti-racist activism has continued, sometimes stronger, sometimes weaker, involving interracial cooperation and, at times, facing serious repression. The Civil Rights Movement of the late 1950s through the 1960s would not have occurred without the on-going grassroots community organizing and union-based, faith-based, legal, and educational movements of the preceding decades. Some of these strategies focused on civil rights—achieving basic rights, such as voting, for groups denied them. Others focused on profoundly changing existing economic and political systems in order to end racism, along with other forms of systemic advantages and disadvantages (e.g., sexism).

Brown (2002) describes the history of 20th-century interracial efforts and organizations that predated the Civil Rights Movement. We touch on a few salient examples. In 1909, the National Association for the Advancement of Colored People (NAACP) came into being with the involvement of White activists such as Jane Adams and John Dewey. The National Urban League followed in 1910, and during the 1920s, the American Communist Party began to participate actively in anti-racism work. In the 1930s, the Interracial Association of Southern Women for the Prevention of Lynching formed, with the purpose of eliminating that horrendous hate crime directed at African Americans. During this time, a union-based Civil Rights Movement began to emerge as Black workers joined unions affiliated with the Congress of Industrial Organizations (CIO). In contrast to many Whites-only labor unions, the CIO had a policy of racial equality.

In the late 1930s, the NAACP initiated a legal strategy to end segregation in the education system, which resulted in the pivotal 1954 Supreme Court *Topeka v. Brown* decision. Many White people supported the ensuing push for school desegregation, but others openly and violently resisted it. Likewise, the struggle for voting rights, one of the primary objectives of the Civil Rights Movement of the 1950s and 1960s, met with strong White resistance. At the same time, many White activists participated in this struggle. Indeed, some gave their lives.

Since the 1960s, organized efforts to end racism (as well as other institutionalized forms of prejudice and discrimination—sexism, heterosexism, and ableism) continued, waxing and waning depending on the political and economic climate. This work forged ahead on many fronts and included a range of educational, political, and legal strategies. Some people focused on individual change through education; others collaborated to transform the underlying structures of key social, economic, and political institutions; still others exposed the links between racism and the environmental degradation in poor communities or between racism and sexism or classism.

Just as it is essential that we learn the story of White participation in civil rights and anti-racism movements, it is vital to understand and learn from the recurring problems that plagued these efforts. One disturbing pattern, even before the abolitionist movement, is the persistent difficulty many White people have had in accepting leadership from colleagues of color and in scrutinizing and eliminating ways that they as Whites enact White privilege. The history of the NAACP, one of the most sustained interracial efforts (Thomas, 1996), reflects these tensions, as well as some ways to resolve them.

Originally, White members held most of the leadership positions in the NAACP. Over time, however, Black members became the leaders. According to Thomas, some White members, such as Mary Ovington and Joel Spingarn, were dedicated to the organization and willing to play any role that was required. Unlike other White donors, they financially supported the NAACP without trying to control it.

White supporters acting out their White privilege often disrupted the Civil Rights Movement despite their many contributions. As a result, some African American leaders demanded that White people organize in their own communities, rather than trying to dictate what communities of color should do. Those White activists who took up this challenge forged new analyses and strategies for doing anti-racism work with other White people as well as acting as anti-racist allies of People of Color. People Against Racism (PAR) is one such group that formed in the late 1960s. Although it was active for a relatively short time, its educational organizing work opened up new conversations about White privilege and racism as a system of unearned advantage for White people.

In response to the uprisings in many African American communities around the country in the 1960s, Congress created the Kerner Commission. In 1968, the Commission, a primarily White entity, issued a significant report, naming the existing system of White advantage and institutional racism, "moving toward two societies, one Black, and one White—separate and unequal," as the underlying cause for racism in the United States. Their report stated that "White racism is essentially responsible for the explosive mixture which has been accumulating in our cities since the end of World War II" (Feagin, 2000, p. 91). As the first governmental body to identify the role of White privilege, the Kerner Commission's report played a key role in educating White Americans about the realities of systemic racism and provided an impetus for institutional change.

Starting in the late 1960s, several scholars, Whites as well as People of Color, published critiques of systemic racism and its role in multiple social institutions (e.g., Knowles & Prewitt, 1969). They also analyzed the inadequacy of "color blindness"—the common individual and institutional response to race in the 1960s—and laid the responsibility for the existence and the elimination of racism squarely at the door of White people (Browser & Hunt, 1981; Terry, 1970; Wellman, 1977).

Also in the late 1960s Chicano high students organized a school walkout in Los Angeles that brought attention to the impact of racism on Mexican Americans. In 1970, many Latinos became involved in the Civil Rights Movement by joining the Chicano Moratorium, a national movement of Mexican Americans that advocated for the end of the Vietnam war and increased civil rights for Latinos in schools, the legal system, jobs, and housing (Acuña, 2011). In the 1980s civil rights work again expanded as the Japanese American movement for reparations for the unjust internment of Japanese Americans during World War II took flight and sparked anti-racism activities in several Asian American communities (Wu, 2002). Native American activism also became part of national consciousness, even though it too has had a long history, beginning when Europeans first began to invade and colonize native lands (Cobb, Cobb, & Fowler, 2007). White anti-racism activists participated and supported these movements as well.

The work of the anti-racism and other human rights movements of the 1960s–1990s have been a significant step forward for our country. They teach us that individual and societal change is possible. However, much work remains, and our charge is to continue to build these movements and to press forward toward equality and justice for all people.

ANTI-RACISM WORK TODAY

In this section, we highlight some of the ways people are continuing the movement to end racism. Some focus on education and dialogue, whereas others build on educational strategies to organize actions at local and national levels. We need a wide range of strategies, because "no one has all the answers on how to end racism. . . . All of us involved in the struggle to end racism, are making a path by walking in it" (Barndt, 2007, p. 221).

Educational Strategies

Whiteness Studies. Starting in the 1990s, the analysis of Whiteness and White anti-racism development has become an active arena of scholarly work. Compelling analyses of how White privilege operates both at the systemic and social-psychological levels have been provided by White authors, among them Joseph Barndt, Joe Feagin, Ruth Frankenberg, Gary Howard, Paul Kivel, Peter McLaren, Paula Rothenberg, Christine Sleeter, Becky Thompson, and Tim Wise (to name a few), and authors of color, such as Janet Helms, Toni Morrison, Beverley Tatum, and Cornell West (again, only a partial list).

Whiteness studies have become a strong focus of many academic institutions and organizations. Some professional groups and conferences are built around this topic, such as the National Association for Multicultural Education and the annual White Privilege Conference (see Appendix B for websites). A few mainstream academic conferences have also been addressing Whiteness. Recent annual meetings of the American Educational Research Association have had several sessions that present research on different aspects of White privilege and on programs designed to train teachers and transform schools to engage in more equitable education practices. The annual conference of the National Association for the Education of Young Children (NAEYC) sometimes offers sessions about Whiteness and White children as well as on issues affecting children of color.

As part of this growing interest, a number of books about the history of White anti-racism movements in the United States (e.g., Aptheker, 1993; Thomas, 1996, Zinn, 1995) and of the journey of White individuals in these movements (Brown, 2002; Curry, Browning, Burlage, & Patch, 2002; Warren, 2010) are available. These bring a balance to the pain and guilt that White individuals often feel when they begin to understand how their racial privilege has and continues to injure People of Color. These stories also offer a sense of hope by letting anti-racist activists know that they are not alone, but rather are a part of a long history of strong, moral, American women and men of all races working to build a more just country.

Public Discussions About Racism. More frank discussions about race and White privilege now sometimes appear beyond the academic world. Some popular television shows like *The Oprah Winfrey Show* have had forthright and challenging conversations about race. During his campaign, President Obama gave a searing speech about race relationships in the United States in which he pointed out the role of White prejudice and the devastating effects of ongoing racial discrimination. Broadcast on national news, his words strikingly contrasted with the color-blind, feel-good racial platitudes often mouthed by politicians An article in *Newsweek*, entitled "See Baby Discriminate" (Bronson & Merryman, 2009), popularized research on the racial awareness of very young children. In 2010, CNN's week-long reporting of its commissioned study on Black and White children's racial identity and attitudes (Kareem, 2010) sparked several lively debates on the network's website.

In communities around the country, opportunities for cross-racial/cultural/religious dialogue exist. Local anti-discrimination groups, churches, synagogues, mosques, and temples have initiated some of these dialogues. These conversations broaden and challenge people's perceptions and assumptions and sometimes lead to decisions to collaborate on specific racism-related issues.

Increased Resources. As more White people have become interested in and committed to anti-racist work, the number of resources in this area has grown. Books (e.g., the readings listed after Chapters 2, 3, 6, and 7) and websites (see Appendix B) on Whiteness and anti-racism provide information, analysis, and practical action ideas that help people engage in anti-racism activities. A number of national organizations provide training to recognize and challenge systemic racism. Increasingly, community colleges and 4-year colleges and universities offer courses about racism, White privilege, and anti-racism. Some educational institutions now have ongoing study groups for White faculty and staff who want to recognize and analyze their privilege and become better equipped to do anti-racism work.

Organizing Efforts

"Dismantling racism is an active verb that calls for intentional and collective organizing action" (Barndt, 2007, p. 223). As a first step, as we have emphasized, White anti-racist activists must honestly confront the impact of internalized racial superiority on their own understanding of racism and interactions with others. In addition, since anti-racism organizing is long-term work, activists need to find ways of sustaining themselves through spiritual connections and strong networks. Barndt (2007) incorporates these core premises in his five principles for building multiracial, antiracist activist groups:

1. Develop a common analysis
2. Undo internalized socialization
3. Learn to be accountable (for White people this especially means being accountable to People of Color, rather than paternalistic)
4. Maintain spiritual roots
5. Learn to organize

Around the country, anti-racism groups, both national and regional, are attempting to follow these principles in their anti-racism educating and organizing work (see Appendix B for names and websites of some of these groups).

Some groups use the strategy of White people coming together to learn, act, and support each other, while being in close connection with anti-racism groups led by People of Color (see White Anti-racist Community Action Network *and* White Privilege Conference websites in Appendix B). Other multiracial local and national anti-racism groups, both community and faith-based, focus on specific societal issues created by racism. These include working on reducing the inequities in the educational system, advocating for immigrant rights, ending police brutality, increasing voter registration among underrepresented groups, and opposing the Ku Klux Klan and other White nationalist/militia groups. White people (along with People of Color) in other social justice movements (labor unions, women's rights, disability rights, gay/lesbian/bisexual/transgender rights) are also trying to build equitable, multiracial/multicultural organizations that work toward the elimination of racism.

Some organizations, such as One Nation Working Together, are responding to the current pressure from right wing groups that are pushing for racist and anti-immigrant legislation. Several internet-based groups are gearing up to fight laws and policies that adversely affect immigrants, such as the Arizona legislation that we described in Chapter

2. They include Presente.org, MALDEF (Mexican American Legal Defense and Educational Fund), the American Civil Liberties Union, and the Leadership Conference on Civil and Human Rights (see descriptions in Appendix B).

White activists have a long history of involvement in anti-racist movements, from before the early days of abolition to the Civil Rights Movement in the 20th century and on to the current efforts to scrutinize and challenge White dominance. Despite missteps, White people are vital participants in the journey toward racial justice. Not only are they participating in current movements, they are teaching and nurturing the next generation of White activists. Ultimately, we need to keep reminding others and ourselves that "Racism dehumanizes us all—dismantling racism heals us all" (Crossroads home page, http://crossroadsantiracism.org/).

Reflection Questions

1. What information in this chapter was new to you? Did any of it surprise you? Why do you think you never learned this history?
2. What stories about activism against racism and other social injustices does your extended family tell?
3. Have you ever thought of yourself as an activist? If not, what prevented you? If yes, what supports you? Given the discussion about the many forms activism takes, do you think you might choose to become an activist now or in the future? If so, what specific issues and activities do you find most compelling?

For Further Reading

Brown, C. S. (2002). *Refusing racism: White allies and the struggle for civil rights.* New York: Teachers College Press.

Curry, C., Browning, J., Burlage, D. D., & Patch, P. (2002). *Deep in our hearts: Nine White women in the freedom movement.* Athens: University of Georgia Press.

Parker, R., & Smith Chambers, P. (2005). *The anti-racist cookbook: A recipe guide for conversations about race that goes beyond covered dishes and "Kum-Bah-Ya."* Roselle, NJ: Crandall, Dostie & Douglas Books.

Tochluk, S. (2010). *Witnessing Whiteness: The need to talk about race and how to do it.* Latham, MD: Roman & Littlefield Education.

Zinn, H. (1995). *A people's history of the United States: 1492–present* (Rev. ed.). New York: HarperPerennial.

7

How Children Learn About Racism and Enact Anti-Racism

"Don't say 'no way Jose'; it will hurt Jose's feelings," one 4-year-old explains to a classmate.

—Louise Derman-Sparks & Julie Olsen Edwards,
Anti-Bias Education for Young Children and Ourselves

After learning about one of the young heroines of the Civil Rights Movement, a 6-year-old declares, "Ruby Bridges showed that kids can do something to change things."

—S. Walters, "Fairness First,"
In A. Pelo, *Rethinking Early Childhood Education*

Young children have the capacity to grasp that racial prejudice is wrong, to care about others, challenge assumptions, and take action to remedy injustice in their own worlds. While the social-political dynamics of our society socialize White children to form identities based on entitlement and own-race preferences (see Chapter 3), family and teachers can provide a balance to this pressure by nurturing pro-diversity and pro-justice identities and behavior.

A new line of research on children's perceptions of discrimination (Bigler, Arthur, Hughes, & Patterson, 2008; Brown, 2008) has shown that between the ages of 5 and 10 children become more aware of discrimination and how it affects individuals and the larger society (e.g., who is elected president of the United States). While these studies have not included preschoolers, the authors note that the underpinnings of this awareness are present by the age of 5 or 6 (Bigler et al., 2008).

However, we have to make a conscious effort to draw White children's attention to the reality of racial discrimination and its effects. As Brown (2008) points out, White children, especially those in predominately White schools, have difficulty learning these lessons because they are unlikely to experience discrimination themselves or hear about it from their parents and peers. On the other hand, as we discuss in following sections, recent studies of AB/MC approaches provide a compelling glimpse of how children begin to develop a social justice orientation when their teachers nurture this development.

LEARNING TO CARE

Caring about others is critical to connecting with individuals and groups and working toward equity. Three dynamics shape White children's avoidance and disregard of People of Color. One is messages, both explicit and implicit, that People of Color are not safe. A second is the interplay of White racial superiority and economic entitlement, which is aggravated by competitive consumerism. Third, children absorb misinformation that both causes and reinforces the previous attitudes. Together, they undermine children's capacity to empathize with others. As Clark (1963) pointed out, children who learn prejudice "establish their own identity as persons and as members of a group through hatred and rejection of others" (p. 81). At the same time, we know that young children have the capacity to care about the feelings of others, even if they cannot always accurately assess them. This capacity is a potential "handle" for helping children to overcome barriers and feel connected with unfamiliar people, and to understand the effects of discrimination.

The social-emotional dispositions and skills that underlie AB/MC work are already established parts of early childhood practice and include "empathizing with others, communicating effectively, initiating and maintaining social interactions with peers, playing cooperatively, and resolving conflicts" (Ramsey, 2004, p. 54). Sharp (2006) uses the term "caring thinking" (p. 151) to describe this emotional responsiveness and capacity to see others' perspectives and worldviews.

Empathy, the ability to understand and care about how others feel, is essential to forming both interpersonal and intergroup relationships. Human infants appear to be born with an innate ability to resonate with the emotional states of others. For example, they reactively cry when they hear other babies cry (M. Hoffman, 2000). During the early childhood years, children become more astute readers of others' emotions and begin to learn how their own actions affect others and how to communicate effectively.

One study in Canada found a marked increase in social inclusion and authentic communication and a decrease in bullying in elementary schools that implemented a "Roots of Empathy" Program (Gordon, 2006).

This approach engaged children in multidisciplinary activities that fostered self-awareness, problem solving, and consensus building. Empathy may also inhibit aggressive responses to unfamiliar others. Nesdale, Miller, Duffy, and Griffiths (2009) observed that more empathic children were less likely to express direct-aggression intentions toward out-group members, even when the in-group endorsed aggression.

Many early childhood teachers encourage children to express their ideas and feelings both verbally and nonverbally and, most important, to listen to, observe others, and learn how to interpret what others are feeling and thinking. Caring for classroom pets and plants is another way to heighten sensitivity and responsiveness. However, peer relationships provide the most compelling context for children to learn how to read and respond to others' feelings and needs. As children experience the pleasures and challenges of friendships, they become motivated to understand and get along with a wider range of people.

Children growing up with a sense of entitlement and superiority may have difficulty sharing space and materials, resolving conflicts, and connecting with peers. They may expect to be center stage and receive all available attention and always be the best at any activity. For these entitled children, learning how to develop mutually caring and equitable relationships with a wide range of children is a particular priority. Cooperative play and collaborative projects promote these goals because they require children to respond to others' needs, negotiate conflicts, and share power, all of which underlie AB/MC work. Moreover, many studies have shown that cooperative activities and structures are among the most successful strategies for fostering friendships between children from diverse groups (Johnson & Johnson, 2000; Slavin, 1995).

Caring for others is a critical element of AB/MC work. It can be an effective antidote to messages that promote entitlement and a sense of superiority, and is key to fostering emotional connections with individuals and groups across the boundaries of race, ethnicity, culture, language, economic class, abilities, and family way of life. We can most effectively tap and nurture this potential by engaging children in meaningful relationships with peers, adults, and all living beings.

BROADENING PERSPECTIVES AND WIDENING CONNECTIONS

Teachers can counteract children's internalizations of the visible and invisible norm of Whiteness by proactively challenging White children's assumptions that everyone looks and lives as they do and/or that people who look different are bad or frightening.

Assessing Approaches to Diversity Curriculum

One popular "multicultural education" strategy is to provide activities, images, and objects that depict diversity among human appearances and ways of living (e.g., Barrera, 2005; Swiniarski, 2006). For example, teachers use dolls that represent different racial groups, props and clothing from a range of cultures, and stories and songs in a variety of languages. In relatively homogeneous classrooms, such activities may be the primary way to expose children to the idea that people look, speak, and live different in different ways. Many commercial multicultural products support this approach.

Teachers, however, need to select and use these materials wisely. Stereotypical or inaccurate materials reinforce misinformation that the children may already be learning. Too often, teachers use historical images of children in other countries, instead of providing accurate and current information about the lives of diverse groups living in the United States. Also if materials—even good ones—are simply placed in the classroom, the activities can easily slip into a "tourist" curriculum that is unconnected to the daily life experiences and underlying values of children in the program and people in the larger community. Day (1995) and Lee and Lee (2001) observed young children's reactions to multicultural dolls, props, clothing, and food items. Although the children (especially the girls) played enthusiastically with the items, it was the novelty of the materials that attracted them. They did not connect the items with different cultures or other multicultural themes.

In contrast, a respectful AB/MC approach explores the range of ways people are both different and the same. In this context, materials that reflect cultural diversity, along with teacher-initiated activities, provide opportunities for children to explore their ideas, assumptions, and fears about differences and to begin to construct more realistic and individualized images of people who are not part of their classroom or community.

Authentic, accurate stories and images serve as mirrors for children to see themselves and their families, and as windows to learn about the rest of the world (Mendoza & Reese, 2001). However, if information is incorrect or incomplete, then books for children teach and reinforce stereotypes rather than challenge them. Mendoza and Reese (2001) note that even some award-winning picture books that have been hailed as multicultural have misappropriated and misrepresented material from marginalized groups. These authors also point out that publishers often overlook authors and illustrators from underrepresented groups and rely on well-known ones who may have only superficial information about the groups they are portraying (see Appendix A for criteria for selecting children's books).

To counter misinformation, Boutte (2002) urges teachers to scrutinize books for their implicit and explicit agendas and to encourage children to be critically aware of underlying messages and perspectives. Derman-Sparks and Edwards (2010) stress that when using books to introduce children to an unfamiliar group, teachers should "offer a variety of stories about that group to prevent children from forming stereotypes" (p. 46). They also urge teachers to first explore differences among the children within their classroom as a bridge to learning about diversity not present.

"What do children learn when they see images depicting human similarities and differences?" After reviewing several studies done in the 1970s, Aboud and Levy (2000) found that simply exposing children to books and televised images about other groups did not change their views. The authors concluded that, *to reduce prejudice, teachers cannot simply provide materials but also need to discuss and model alternative attitudes* (emphasis added).

Another cautionary note comes from studies suggesting that, when differences are emphasized by teachers, the potential for out-group stereotyping and in-group bias increases (Bigler & Hughes, 2009; Bigler & Liben, 2007; Patterson & Bigler, 2007). These findings imply that minimizing or blurring differences might be a better strategy than exposing children to them. In fact, many educators uphold the ideal of "color blindness," ignore differences, and deny their significance. However, as amply illustrated in Chapter 3, we know that young children notice and act on racial and cultural differences, so pretending they do not exist does not make sense.

These two perspectives (minimizing differences versus exploring them) are not necessarily irreconcilable. Teachers can include images of a wide range of people but also emphasize that similarities and differences are continua, not polarities, and that we all share a combination of common and unique traits and experiences. For example, children can learn that most people have the same senses (e.g., sight, hearing) and feel similar emotions but that faces vary by skin color and physiognomy and that individuals may express feelings in diverse ways. Stories about different life experiences can stretch young children's awareness, even as young as infants and toddlers (Quintero, 2004).

Effective Approaches to Diversity Curriculum

Encouragingly, one of the very few large-scale systematic studies of curriculum designed to broaden children's perspectives and encourage cross-group acceptance found more beneficial results (Connolly, Fitzpatrick, Gallagher, & Harris, 2006; Connolly & Hosken, 2006). The systematic evaluation of comprehensive programs developed in Northern Ireland revealed that dramatic video presentations and follow-up activities using large puppets, art activities, and simulations had a positive effect on young children's attitudes. Compared to the control groups, those who participated in the activities increased their recognition of social exclusion, their willingness to include others, and their awareness of commonalities they shared with unfamiliar children.

Likewise, many teachers describe their success in using dramatic stories with persona dolls to work with anti-bias goals. These stories can help children explore diversity among themselves; encourage them to think and care about individuals from unfamiliar backgrounds and life experiences; stimulate thinking critically and empathically about prejudice and discrimination; and explore ways to solve unfair situations (Brown, 2001, 2008; Derman-Sparks & A.B.C. Task Force, 1989; Pelo & Davidson, 2000; Whitney, 1999).

Another way to emphasize connections among all people is to provide concrete examples of how we all live on the same planet, breathe the same air, drink the same water, and share an interest in conserving our resources. Many time-honored early childhood practices of observing nature and growing plants can be expanded to incorporate this awareness. Nimmo and Hallett (2008) report how working in the school garden helped children to learn about different cultural practices and environmental issues and to connect with individuals of different ages and abilities. Likewise, Satterlee and Cormons (2008) describe how a family-based nature program in a low-income rural community heightened children's awareness of environmental issues and enhanced children's learning and family participation in the school.

Children are able to expand their perspectives and feel connected to unfamiliar people, even members of groups that they have learned to fear or dislike. However, this outcome requires thoughtful planning to promote in-depth learning and to avoid pitfalls that can derail the best of intentions. As we consider various materials and approaches, we need to carefully observe children's current knowledge and feelings and their interpretations of new information. Specific strategies will be discussed in Chapter 8.

LEARNING TO CHALLENGE ASSUMPTIONS AND INEQUITIES

Challenging prevailing views and inequities in society at large may be developmentally beyond young children. At the same time, they are able to identify injustices in their immediate world, as is evident in their vociferous claims of "That's not fair!" With support and guidance, they can extend their concern for fairness to recognizing stereotyped messages in books, materials, and electronic media; and school and community policies and practices that are unfair and/or environmentally destructive (Pelo, 2008; Pelo & Davidson, 2000; Vasquez, 2007; Walters, 2008). Hirschfeld (2008) notes that, given the prevailing prejudiced views in our society, children have to make an effort to resist learning and enacting biases, the motivation for which often comes from a sense of fairness. Juggling racist and anti-racist beliefs is complex, and children, like adults, often express contradictory feelings, as evident in the following account of how Sam, a White 2nd grader,

> grapple[d] with what it meant to be White and to try on different positions and perspectives as a White person. We heard him step into White talk that affirms there is no racism today (e.g., "Martin Luther King Jr. changed everything"), we heard him reproduce White privilege (e.g., "sitting on the back of the bus is better than walking"), we heard him assert his Whiteness (e.g., "If I were White, and I am, I would apologize"), and we heard him say if he were White . . . back then, he would have apologized for mistreatment and fought for the African American people who were escaping from slavery. Sam embodies the contradictions of what it means to be White in our racist society. However, we also hear the emergence of an understanding of the deeply rooted nature of racism and resistance to the privileges associated with Whiteness. . . . The question for educators . . . is "How can we support the development of a White racial identity that . . . [enables] White children . . . [to] practice a type of Whiteness where race and privilege are acknowledged and systematically resisted?" (Rogers & Mosley, 2006, p. 464)

Children's readiness to challenge assumptions and recognize inequities varies across individuals and situations. Mac Naughton and Davis (2001) noted that, although many of the Anglo-Australian children they interviewed had superficial and stereotyped concepts of Aboriginal people, others had perspectives that are more critical and were aware of how colonialism and oppression continue to affect many Indigenous Australians. At the same time, they pointed out that teachers play a key role in creating circumstances that are conducive to these insights by recognizing and deliberately addressing children's nascent attitudes and misinformation. After observing several teacher-child conversations, Skattebol (2003) concluded that teachers cannot simply respond to children's comments in a neutral way but need to challenge explicitly assumptions about different groups and relative positions of power. De Marquez (2002) described discussion groups, in which the children raised and challenged each other about social justice issues, demonstrating that, under appropriate conditions, young children can understand and discuss complex concerns. In several detailed observations, Rogers and Mosley (2006) showed how White children engaged in thoughtful conversations about race and racism. Yet, they also illustrated how easily the children slipped back into color-blind and privileged assumptions. The authors noted that teachers have to be alert to these shifts and continually encourage children to challenge their assumptions.

Several studies have described specific activities that appear to foster kindergarten and school-age children's capacity to identify and challenge inequities. Marsh (1992) documented how the children in her racially diverse kindergarten participated in a number of anti-bias activities and, as a result, became more aware of injustices and began to take actions (e.g., protesting the lack of African American crossing guards at the school). In a study designed to pinpoint the effects of specific multicultural activities, Lee, Ramsey, and Sweeney (2008) found that some activities, particularly games and simulations, encouraged kindergartners to engage in thoughtful discussions about racial and economic misinformation and inequities. Quintero (2004) illustrated how a problem-posing method engaged young children in critical discussions about their lives and the world around them. Chafel, Flint, Hammel, and Pomeroy (2007) used books to encourage children to engage in meaningful conversations about issues such as poverty and inter-group antagonisms. They noted that when children wove their own experiences into classroom discussions, they more actively engaged and generated ideas about how to challenge inequities.

Many children have a strong sense of fairness. Often it is most evident when they feel that others have taken advantage of them, but with encouragement, it also can extend to recognizing and challenging biased beliefs and actions. Teachers can use situations that arise in the classroom or community, or dilemmas that emerge in children's books or persona doll stories to draw children's attention to unfair situations. As children express and explore their ideas, they also can learn to question prevailing assumptions and their own sense of entitlement.

LEARNING TO BE SOCIAL ACTIVISTS

Experience has shown that teachers can effectively engage children as young as age 4 in activism if the projects emerge from real incidents or issues in their lives; are simple and direct; have a clear, tangible focus; and are geared to the children's experiences rather than achieving a particular outcome. These activities should not be about changing the world from an adult perspective, but rather about children making their own worlds a little fairer (Cowhey, 2006; Hoffman, 2004; Pelo & Davidson, 2000). As a first step, children need to believe that they have the efficacy and skills to make a difference. One teacher found that, after a series of stories and discussions about Ruby Bridges, her first graders realized that kids like themselves could participate in social justice movements (Walters, 2008).

Teachers can encourage children to identify issues and take the lead in proposing and making changes. In one case, a class of preschoolers noticed the lack of diversity in the images of children in a new calendar, and after much discussion, wrote a letter to the company about how the pictures did not represent them. When they did not get a response, they circulated a petition and sent that to the company as well (Derman-Sparks & A.B.C. Task Force, 1989). Vasquez (2007) reported that her kindergartners identified, protested, and changed several discriminatory school policies (e.g., the kindergartners were excluded from a bookmark contest; the food at the school barbecue did not include any vegetarian dishes). Pelo and Davidson (2000) offer many detailed examples of young children identifying issues in their everyday worlds (e.g., gender stereotyped assumptions about peers, vandalized trees in a local park, local people who are homeless, racist images in books). The authors also vividly depict how teachers worked with the children and families to learn more about these issues and to take actions to address them. Lalley (2008) describes how one Seattle program developed an activist culture in which all children, families, and teachers participate in efforts to gain resources for their program and other local services. They also collaborate with other organizations to work toward national and global equity and environmentally sustainable practices.

These accounts illustrate that young children can engage in meaningful activities that address unfairness, and gain a sense of power and efficacy through doing so, when adults thoughtfully guide them. To be effective, adults must be sure that issues and outcomes are relevant to the children's lives and perceptions of their worlds.

In Their Own Words

The following examples illustrate how children recognize and think about inequities and, in some cases, want to take action. These accounts also show how adults, by listening and observing closely, can support children as they re-think their assumptions and consider possible strategies.

Hoffman (2004) found that eliciting and exploring children's ideas about what is and is not fair was one way to make "fairness part of their classroom's everyday vocabulary." He goes on to say, "By modeling sympathetic listening skills, teachers can help children listen to each other and develop a more complete and mature definition of justice" (p. 153).

Examples of his preschoolers' responses during a discussion about "What is fair?" and "What is unfair?" illustrate their budding sense of equity and compassion (pp. 153–154):

- "Everybody should get to talk (3-year-old)"
- "One person doesn't get to be the boss all the time (4-year-old)"
- "If somebody gets too much. That's not fair (4-year-old)"
- "You have to be sure everybody knows not to be mean (4-year-old)"

Whitney (1999) recounts conversations about anti-bias issues she introduced through persona dolls in her classroom. For example, 4- and 5-year-olds heard a story about a persona doll with glasses (Rachel) whom some of the other dolls called "bug eyes." When asked how they thought Rachel felt, the children responded with empathy: "I bet that hurt her feelings," "I'd feel really, really sad," "Yeah, I'd feel like crying." When asked what they could do to support Rachel, the children replied, "I'd tell Rachel I like her glasses," "I'd play with her!" "I'd tell her [the child who was teasing Rachel] she hurt Rachel's feelings," "I'd tell her we all want to be safe in our school and calling names makes us feel not safe" (all quotes are from p. x).

In another persona doll story, one of the White dolls (Brad) tells an African American doll (Ianthe), "You can't play here. Only White kids are allowed in this fort." After hearing what the children thought about how Ianthe might feel ("hurt," "sad," "furious," "embarrassed"), the teacher asked what Ianthe could do and how she could get help if she wanted it. The children offered several suggestions: "[She could say] don't exclude," "African Americans can [play] too." "How would he like it [being excluded]?" "I'd give her a hug." "Me too. [I would say] 'Don't listen to Brad, he's wrong.'" (Whitney, 1999, pp. 143–144.)

Children display the capacity to use critical thinking to be aware of and change their own behavior. For example, I (Louise) recall my young son's evolving awareness about Native Americans:

Our family was camping and met a Native American family using the neighboring campsite. One evening we shared stories about ourselves. When the father related that they were Chumash Indians, my son blurted out, "No, you are not, where are your feathers?" I was quite embarrassed.

When we returned home, I decided to get some books with accurate images and stories about Native Americans and to ask a colleague of Native American heritage to tell my son about herself and her family. As I showed my son the materials, I also pointed out information that contradicted common stereotypes. A few months later, my son started to do an alleged Indian dance, then stopped himself and said, "I wonder if this is really how they dance?" Then, a month later, after going on the carousel in a San Francisco park, he announced, "This merry-go-round is bad," pointing to the decorations with stereotypic images decorating the inner drum. I was both surprised and pleased at how much he had learned.

Accounts from parents and teachers provide evidence that children are also able to take the next step—applying anti-bias principles of fairness in their social interactions. Andrea, a teacher of 3- and 4-year-old children in a predominately White middle-class school, related one example to Patty. She was chatting with children and parents at the beginning of the day, when Lauren, Lisa's mother, pulled her aside and told her the following story:

Last night at dinner, Owen (Lisa's 8-year-old brother) said, "Black people have ugly fat lips." Lisa immediately said, "That is not true! Everyone has their own special face, and no one is 'ugly' and it is mean to say things like that!" At first, we [Lauren and her husband] were speechless, both at Owen's comment and at Lisa's response. However, once we caught our breath, we said that Lisa was right and asked Owen what he meant and where he had heard it. We tried not to jump on him, but rather to find out what he was thinking and feeling. We then had a good conversation about how people have different faces and that sometimes people make fun of each other because of their differences but that all people deserve respect and a good life. . . . To see Lisa, my little 4-year-old, stand up to her older brother and to speak with more honesty and clarity than most adults, well, I feel so proud, hopeful, and grateful for the work that you are doing!

A parent in another preschool told me (Louise) the following anecdote related to him by his son's teacher:

My son [C] was playing with another White classmate. When a Mexican American child tried to join in the play of the two White children, C's friend insisted, "You can't play here. Your skin is too dark." C immediately argued back, "Yes, he can. All kids can play here." His teacher asked C how he knew that. C replied, "My dad tells me civil rights stories."

When I asked about these stories, the father explained that he had been a civil rights activist in his college years and turned his experiences into adventurous bedtime stories, which his son asked to hear repeatedly.

Looking Forward to Adulthood

Why do some White people become active anti-racists? What distinguishes them from people who either ignore racism or express anti-discrimination views but fail to take an active role in subverting racism?

Many anti-racists are optimistic, energetic, and creative and have a history of being observant and outspoken, often wading into conflicts and challenging the status quo even as children (Brown, 2002). They recognize that they are not doomed to repeat the past, but are committed to changing the future. They believe that not acting is no longer a choice for them: it becomes an integral part of their identity and sense of integrity (Derman-Sparks & Phillips, 1997). Moreover, by acting according to their principles, White people find allies and make connections that support them and replace those that they may lose by following an anti-racist path (Brown, 2002; O'Brien, 2001). Krejci (2008) interviewed 13 White men who are engaged in anti-racism work and found that they shared the following experiences: 1. an early sense of justice and fairness; 2. exposure to racial diversity, particularly friends of color, and the opportunity to learn about racism from People of Color; 3. personal experience of being oppressed in some way; 4. exposure to an anti-oppression culture; 5. participation in anti-racist training.

Another common theme that runs through biographies and stories of White anti-racists is moral courage, the ability to see through the delusion of White racial superiority and to align one's identity with moral principle (Brown, 2002; Curry et al., 2000). This code of honor keeps people going in the face of obstacles such as harassment and loss of livelihood. How people develop this moral courage varies: Some anti-racists have strong ties to religion; others adhere to more secular democratic values. Common to all is the refusal to accept the status quo and to ignore injustice.

Finally, the personal theme of anti-racism work as humanizing and liberating repeatedly appears.

> In untying the knot [of racism and other isms], you're unraveling the web of lies that each of us has inevitably experienced . . . [and] that have taken their dehumanizing toll. . . . in unraveling even a bit of the whole, we feel tremendously excited. We have only to unravel more of it to reclaim ourselves more completely. (early childhood teacher quoted in Derman-Sparks & Phillips, 1997, p. 137)

Knowing that children and adults can and do demonstrate empathic and respectful connections to the human family and the capacity to engage in anti-racist, social justice activism, we now turn to guidelines and strategies for nurturing these dispositions and skills. In the following two chapters, we explore learning themes four, five, six, and seven, and suggest a range of activities for implementing them in early childhood programs.

Reflection Questions

1. As a child, what types of unfairness did you notice? Were you concerned? Were you aware of racism? What did you do in the face of unfairness? What happened when you tried to act?
2. What comments and behaviors do you observe in children that indicate their capacity for caring and fairness?
3. As an adult, what specific incidents of racial prejudice or discrimination have you witnessed? Did you act? What motivated or supported you? If you kept silent, what stopped you from acting?

For Further Reading

Hoffman, E. (2004). *Magic capes, amazing powers: Transforming superhero play in the classroom.* St. Paul, MN: Redleaf Press.

Pelo, A. (Ed). (2008). *Rethinking early childhood education.* Milwaukee, WI: Rethinking Schools.

8

Fostering Children's Caring and Activism

Fair is when everybody gets everything, but nobody gets everything they want. Unfair is when somebody gets left out.
— Jenna, 5-year-old, quoted in E. Hoffman,
Magic Capes, Amazing Powers:
Transforming Superhero Play in the Classroom

We now turn to learning themes four, five, six, and seven. Since they build on the themes one, two, and three, we strongly urge you to spend time first on implementing them (see Chapter 4) before moving on to the curriculum in this chapter. Caring for others and acting for change rest on an authentic sense of individual and group identity.

As described in Chapter 7, young children have the potential to understand and feel connected to people and circumstances beyond their immediate worlds. They also have the potential to develop a courageous commitment to fairness and a sense of possibility that rest, not on dreams of individual entitlement, but on the desire to make the world a better place for everyone.

LEARNING THEMES

This set of learning themes is about nurturing children's capacity to think of themselves as coequal members of the human family and to feel connection with people who are racially, culturally, and economically different from them. These learning themes are also about enabling children to begin see themselves as agents of change toward a fair, equitable world where all children can thrive.

Theme Four: Understand, appreciate, and respect differences and similarities beyond their immediate family, neighborhood center/classroom, and racial group. As we saw in Chapter 7, White children in our society learn about People of Color from an early age and what they absorb is often incorrect, negative information that lays a foundation for prejudice and discrimination. However, teachers and families can promote accurate, positive understandings and attitudes about People of Color before the misinformation becomes too strongly rooted in children's minds. Through concrete examples, children can learn to see that every human being has differences and similarities with other human beings. The balance between the two varies: Sometimes the similarities are greater than the differences and sometimes the differences are greater than the similarities. By embracing these tenets, children can learn to reach out and connect authentically with people as equals, not simply to be nice to groups that they regard, perhaps unconsciously, as inferior. When children begin to feel connected to people different from themselves, they are more likely to recognize the harm caused by prejudiced behaviors and feel motivated to act in more just ways.

Theme Five: Learn to identify and challenge stereotypes, prejudice, and discriminatory practices among themselves and in the immediate environment. As Chapter 3 illustrates, many young White children come to early childhood education programs already holding ideas about White superiority and so-called "normalcy;" and negative, stereotyped attitudes toward People of Color that they have absorbed from images and messages all around them (books, television, video games, holiday decorations, greeting cards, and toys). Because of their level of cognitive development and their ongoing exposure to such misinformation, it is impossible to eradicate all of their stereotypical ideas. However, the experience of early childhood AB/MC educators tells us that we can help them develop their capacities to think critically and flexibly. Young children can profit from learning opportunities that encourage them to contrast accurate images and information with incorrect and stereotypical ones, and to learn that their way of life is not the only or right one.

Theme Six: Commit to the ideal that all people have the right to a secure, healthy, comfortable, and sustainable life and that everyone must equitably share the resources of the earth and collaboratively care for them. The United States currently consumes the lion's share of the world's resources. When people go shopping, they rarely think about the real costs of their purchases in terms of labor practices (outsourcing jobs overseas; unsafe factories in poor countries) or the impact on the environment. Moreover, most parents delight in making their children happy and may not consider the deleterious effects of showering them with toys and clothes that then become hallmarks of their children's sense of self. Consumerist attitudes and behaviors reinforce young children's belief that what they want is theirs by right, and, in turn, can undermine children's abilities to care about and connect with others.

Family, economic class, cultural contexts, and life experiences affect the degree to which children feel this entitlement. For White children in lower-income families, life realities temper expectations about consumerism. For White children growing up in economically privileged families, budding beliefs in personal and group entitlement (Coles, 1977) converge with and support assumptions about racial and class superiority. Economic class may also influence attitudes about environmental concerns. Wealthy people often focus on preserving pristine wilderness areas, which is a worthy cause. However, they often ignore struggles to stop environmental degradation in poor communities (e.g., waste-processing plants in low-income urban communities, mountain top removal in Appalachia, nuclear waste sites on Native American lands). Many scientists push for environmental regulations to mitigate climate change and protect land and waterways, but working-class people often resent these efforts because corporations use them as excuses for eliminating or outsourcing jobs.

Despite the saturation of children's environments with consumerist messages, teachers and families can promote counter-consumerist messages and behaviors. They can nurture a broad sense of responsibility in children, one that embraces all beings with whom they cohabit the earth.

Theme Seven: Build identities that include AB/MC ideals and possibilities and acquire skills and confidence to work together for social justice in their own classrooms and communities and in the larger society. As children develop more authentic identities and differentiated views of the world, learning to take a stand for fairness for oneself and for others is the next step on their developmental journey. Young children care deeply about fairness as it applies to themselves. By participating in learning opportunities respectful of their developmental needs (see Chapter 7), they can also learn to apply ideas about fairness to others and learn behaviors that promote fairness in their classroom and immediate community.

Children love tales of adventure and courage. Stories about the challenges and victories of anti-racists—White people and People of Color—are appealing to children. As with adults, children need role models of courageous anti-racists.

LEARNING ABOUT YOUR CHILDREN'S IDEAS

As we stated in Chapter 4, regularly observing, listening to, and informally talking with your children are essential to implementing relevant AB/MC curriculum. You can get a sense of the range of ideas that your children are developing, which, in turn, will help you to design meaningful activities for them.

The techniques for learning how children feel about different groups of people are similar to those we suggested in Chapter 4, although specific questions are different.

- *Use photographs and books that accurately depict a wide range of People of Color and their daily lives in the United States to elicit children's thoughts and feelings about different groups.* With individual children and with small groups, you might ask questions such as, "What do you notice about this person?" "What might she or he do for fun or for work?" In addition to seeking children's ideas about different aspects of diversity, note their emotional reactions: Do any children laugh? Ask questions? Seem interested? Scornful? When children see pictures or hear stories about people with more/less money, how do they react? Do they blame poor people for their plight, or are they more sympathetic and respectful? Do they assume that rich people are better or happier than poor people are? Ask children, whom of the people depicted in the photographs would they like to join their classroom or live in their neighborhood. Then explore the reasons behind their selections. Encourage children to make up stories about the people in some of the pictures.
- *While listening to children's conversations and dialog during play, note any comments that imply that People of Color are deviant or inferior.* For example, early childhood teachers have reported hearing the following: "His skin looks like mud. Yuk!" "Chinese people can't see good because their eyes are kind of shut," "Look! I am sitting 'Indian style,'" "Arabs kill people," and "Vietnamese people talk funny." These comments can become the starting point for planning activities to challenge beliefs that may be precursors to prejudice.
- *Ask family members about children's previous contacts with people in racial/ethnic groups other than their own.* What groups are represented in their neighborhoods, social groups, places of worship, and workplaces? Have families traveled or lived in other cities and regions in the United States or other countries?

Were they tourists or did they live as members of the local community? How did their children react to unfamiliar people and situations? Incorporate these questions into your initial intake interview, as well as your ongoing conversations with families (as described in Chapter 5). How families tell their stories provides a glimpse into their views of people who are different from themselves. For example, do they describe unfamiliar customs/lifestyles with respect or disdain?

- *Observe how children and family members view possessions.* How often do children come into school reciting a catalog of their new purchases? How much attention do they pay to one another's new clothes? New toys? Do they tease children who wear worn clothing or shoes? Do they use new, hot toys to entice or control other children? Do they appear to be highly influenced by television commercials? How do the families feel toward consumerism and social-class differences? Do they talk a lot about possessions? Expensive trips? How competitive or cooperative are they with other families in the program? Do wealthier families ignore families with lower incomes?
- *Observe how children respond to the natural environment.* How do children react to the animals and plants in your classroom? Do they take an interest? Think about what other living things need? What do children do when they are outside? Do they express curiosity and concern about plants and animals or do they try to conquer nature (pretend to chop down trees, pull up grass, avoid or destroy bugs)? Do they notice litter and other local environmental problems?
- *Watch how children react to unfair situations.* How do children react to situations in which classmates are unfair or mean to each other? Do children stand up for themselves and others? Do they seem to understand the concept of fairness (not just use it to justify what they want)?

STRATEGIES FOR WORKING WITH CHILDREN

The following activities focus on nurturing children's attitudes and skills to thrive in a diverse society and to work with others to create a more equitable society. The strategies in this chapter build on children's previous exploration of similarities and differences and their development of caring connections within their immediate world (Chapter 4).

Implementing Learning Theme Four

This set of activities focuses on differences and similarities beyond White children's immediate environment. They resemble those found in other anti-bias and multicultural curriculum resources (e.g., Derman-Sparks & Edwards, 2010; Ramsey, 2004; Wolpert, 2002; York, 2003). Remember to connect this learning theme to children's understanding of similarities and differences among themselves.

Model inclusive practices. How you set up and use your aesthetic and material environment sets the stage for expanding your children's learning about racial and cultural diversity. A visual and material environment filled with diverse images immediately tells children and families that you value diversity. Therefore, while displaying images of the children in your program is essential, it is equally essential to bring the diversity of people in the United States into children's daily lives. For infant and toddler groups, introduce unfamiliar images slowly, while balancing them with depictions of familiar people and situations, and limit the amount of images and materials (Janet Gonzalez-Mena, in Derman-Sparks & Edwards, 2010).

One common error made by many teachers is to use pictures of people from countries other than the United States as the way to depict diversity. However, we believe that this approach doesn't work well with young children—unless a child in the group actually comes from a family that has recently immigrated from another country or is only temporarily living in the United States. Children attempt to make sense of what is new by connecting it to what they already know. So, if pictures of Mexican people living in rural villages and wearing sombreros is all that children see at school, they are likely to presume that Mexican American children they meet also live and dress like that.

Make an inventory of your current educational materials and work on building a collection of materials that accurately depict the diversity within all groups (including Whites) in the United States. The goal is to include materials that reflect the many ways that people live (urban, rural, suburban; poor, working class, middle class, wealthy; small and large families); how they look (different skin tones, facial features, and body types); what they wear (traditional or contemporary clothing); and what they do (people with a number of abilities and disabilities; women and men in a range of occupations and roles). In particular, be sure that many of the images counteract common stereotypes, as well as the incorrect ideas you hear from your group. Displaying a photograph of President Obama and his family is one way to support children's identity and broaden their awareness of the value of people from all backgrounds.

Use these materials regularly in your on-going curriculum, not just at special times, to enhance children's sense of connection with others. Choose books with People of Color to explore basic early childhood themes such as friends, a new baby in the family, the first day of school, grandparents, birthdays, or holiday celebrations. Help children to learn that we meet similar needs in different ways by exploring variations in how people manage day-to-day life (carry babies or put them to sleep, live in different types of houses, prepare food).

Expand children's awareness of the range of roles that People of Color carry out. Paying attention to children's ideas about what different People of Color can or cannot do, choose books and posters, arrange field trips that counter incorrect and stereotypical ideas. Be sure to include a wide range of roles: working in factories and farms, in professional jobs, as artists. Read children books that provide a positive message about African American men to challenge racist messages about African American men and President Obama, in particular, that are circulating on the web and other media.

Watch to see if children avoid playing with certain materials and try to challenge their aversion. For example, if children are not playing with an African American or Asian doll, join their dramatic play and make a point of holding and taking care of that doll, emphasizing how much you are enjoying playing with it. Unobtrusively incorporate the doll into their play rather than coerce the children to play with it.

Regularly schedule people from different racial and ethnic groups to do a series of specific activities with your children. Ongoing face-to-face contact is probably the best way to break down barriers, recognize similarities, and see differences as enriching rather than frightening or distasteful. Look for people who are able to come to your class several times; one-time visits are usually not sufficient to counter children's incorrect ideas or discomforts. Be sure that visitors are introduced as complex real people (with families, specific interests and tastes, particular ways of doing things) not as representatives of a class of people. Hoffman (2004) explains, "When I ask someone to be an 'example' for my curriculum, I don't want the children to think of that person in only one way. . . . I ask the person beforehand for three things he or she would like the children to know about them and focus on those" (p. 166).

Tell persona doll stories that explore differences and similarities beyond children's immediate experiences in meaningful and empathic ways. These stories expand on those you told to help your group of children learn about the differences and similarities among themselves (see Chapter 4). As you create new persona dolls of people not in their children's immediate environment, make sure the stories authentically reflect "ordinary" lives in the larger community by getting help from colleagues or friends from that group. Always use more than one doll of a particular group and tell stories that are about everyday experiences to illustrate similarities as well as differences between your children and the dolls. Also maintain a balance between positive experiences, such as family visits and celebrations; and challenging ones, such as handling prejudice.

Talk about why people have different skin colors. Heighten children's awareness of skin color differences by providing skin tone crayons, markers, and paints, and images and books that depict people from many different racial groups. When children ask questions or make comments, listen to their confusions and assumptions, and provide simple and accurate explanations. When appropriate, challenge misinformation by asking questions and providing new information. Two excellent children's books for guiding these discussions are *Shades of People* (Rotner & Kelly, 2009) and *All the Colors We Are* (Kissinger, 1994).

Help children gain accurate information about and connections with new immigrant families in your community. Increasingly in all regions of the country, previously predominately White towns and cities are becoming more diverse, as immigrant families from many parts of the world join the community. Strong feelings and debate, as well as misinformation and stereotyping, about new immigrants of color abound in the media and in many homes. Listen for any negative comments from children, and follow the guidelines about contradicting bias described under learning theme five. Find ways, including working with interpreters, to build relationships with the children's families, so that you can incorporate aspects of their home culture into your group. Invite community leaders among the new immigrant populations to meet with teachers and children and share stories about their lives and communities. Make sure you intentionally promote the inclusion of children who are English language learners in all activities. (Some children may stay on the sidelines unless they receive encouragement to participate.) Encourage English-speaking children to find ways to communicate with classmates who have limited English skills.

Create a learning environment that supports dual-language learning. Early childhood programs are serving increasing numbers of children whose home language is not English. An AB/MC approach includes finding ways to support children's home language as an essential component of respecting and integrating home cultures into early childhood programs, while also fostering their learning of English. There is no "one size fits all" learning environment to support English learners and native English speakers on their important path to bilingualism. Whatever combination of strategies you choose to use in your program, the commitment to address this issue is one of the central principles of effective anti-bias education (Derman-Sparks & Edwards, 2010).

Here are some ideas for supporting children's home languages: Hang welcoming signs in all languages, label classroom materials, and display pictures labeled in children's home language(s) for each curriculum area and for food, water, and the bathroom. Provide home language books, stories, and songs on tape (which families and other community members can help make). Learn key words and phrases (greetings, requests for help, terms of comfort and encouragement, etc.) in the children's home language(s). Be brave about using the words, ask family members to keep correcting your pronunciation and be appreciative of their help. If several home languages are represented in your group, individual staff members can learn key words in particular languages. Plan part of each day when you support English language learners in their home language. If you have the staff (or volunteers), you can plan story times in home language groups or build a full dual language program. Organize a group of people who will help you translate the program handbook, forms, and newsletters and other ongoing written communications into children's home language(s). Use photographs of all the activities and daily procedures, labeled in the home language(s), to communicate what is happening in your program. Encourage families to continue to develop their child's home language, including reading to their child in their home language. Create a lending library of children's books and invite families and friends to help you create some books in languages that are not currently available commercially.

In classrooms where all the children speak English, introduce children to a second language. Experience indicates that it works best to choose one other language to explore. Teach children everyday words for shared human activities (words for family members, expressions of feeling, foods, numbers, and colors) that people in their larger community speak. Use persona dolls to introduce words spoken in *their* families. Label materials around the room in more than one language. Learn songs in the second language.

Consider creating a dual-language program for English-speaking children. Bilingualism is important for *all* children who are growing up in our increasingly multilingual world. There is a long history of private schools for children of wealthy families teaching a second language from the early years. Why not for all children?

Explore the racial and cultural diversity that exists in the children's larger community, always making it concrete and individualized. With preschoolers and kindergarten-age children, focus on the immediate community and city (for instance, taking neighborhood walks). With 6- to 8-year-olds, you can move further afield (state and country), using photographic essays, books, and so on.

If you take field trips to visit people in the community, make the outings purposeful. Go to a store to buy materials for the classroom or visit people to learn about their interesting work. Avoid one-time, superficial field trips or visits, because these experiences may only reinforce children's stereotypes about unfamiliar racial or cultural groups.

With children 5 to 8 years old, begin to connect different ways of meeting similar needs with the environments in which people live. For example, you might create puppet shows or skits to show how someone from another type of community or climate finds your ways to be strange (a rural child wondering how city children manage without land and a creek to play in or a child who comes from a warm climate being surprised by snow).

Implementing Learning Theme Five

The following strategies build on the work you have done creating caring, respectful connections among the children in your program (see Chapters 3 and 4). Expect that, for some children, it will take a long time and many discussions to learn to resist the influence of misinformation they see and absorb in our society.

Always address children's biased remarks or behavior as teachable moments. Although children may not understand the full meaning of such comments, these can become the basis for more developed prejudice if adults do not respond to them. Consider them as teachable moments for which you provide both immediate responses and longer-term experiences, as illustrated by the following example from Eric Hoffman (personal communication, April 2005):

"Did you hear what those children said?" The parent's question drew my attention to four 4-year-olds sitting at a table, talking and giggling. To me, they looked like they had found a good way to get away from the crowd and relax, but when I focused on their words I understood the parent's distress. They were repeating a jingle that made fun of Chinese people. The children were clearly unaware that their language was racist. Their interest was in the silly sounds and their feelings of friendship.

"I hear you saying a rhyme that makes you laugh." They started to repeat the words, but I stopped them. "Do you know what the word *Chinese* means?" They all shook their heads. I explained that it referred to people from a part of the world called China, and that Chinese people would be insulted by the jingle. They were taken aback—that was not their intention.

"I know one that's not about Chinese," a child said, and he started saying another rhyme that made fun of Asian eyes. I explained that even though the new rhyme didn't mention Chinese people, it was still making fun of people. I started to explain about Asia and China, but I could see that my geography lesson was beyond their comprehension.

"It looks like you're not trying to hurt anybody's feelings. You want to be friends and laugh about silly words. So let's think of some that won't upset anyone." We came up with a great list of ridiculous rhymes that left them rolling on the floor with laughter. I felt good about how I handled the situation, until I heard one of the children say to another, "You shouldn't say Chinese. That's a bad word."

In discussing with my staff how we should respond, I was struck by a dilemma that is common in anti-bias work: How do you help people unlearn racism without hurting those who are the targets of that racism? We wanted to create curriculum that would help the children develop positive feelings about ethnic and national differences. However, we knew that we ran the risk of uncovering more racist ideas. We didn't want the children to censor themselves out of fear they would be punished; it felt important to get those misconceptions out in the open so they could be challenged. On the other hand, allowing children to voice racism, even when it is unintended, can damage children who are members of the targeted group. People of Color should not be forced to listen in while White people work out their racism. I find this especially important to keep in mind in groups where there is little ethnic or racial diversity, because it's so easy to dismiss the feelings of the minority when there is no one around to express them.

One way to make sure those feelings are heard is through persona dolls. By introducing a variety of dolls at the beginning of the year, I can bring people to my class who can voice the unfairness of name-calling and discrimination. If I have used the dolls correctly and brought them to life, young children will respond to those voices with compassion and work hard to correct the injustice.

So when my staff and I planned our new curriculum we didn't start with lectures and geography lessons, we started with feelings. One of the dolls talked about her wonderful Vietnamese family and how much she hated being made fun of for her differences. She spoke with great pride and great pain. That opened the door for many discussions about ethnic labels, places in the world, ancestors, and how much it hurts to have someone make fun of the way you look, speak, or act.

Start exploring stereotypes by encouraging children to identify and re-think their gender-related assumptions. Preschool children actively work at figuring out gender identification and roles. In the course of this investigation, they often express gender stereotypes and demand that other children follow their ideas of what girls and boys "are supposed to do." For these reasons, addressing gender-related assumptions is often a good way to begin raising children's awareness of stereotypes. Children can test these beliefs against their own experiences. For instance, make a list with the children of the activities they think that only boys or girls like. Then take photographs of children playing in the classroom and playground and compare these photographs with the list. Ask if children think they should make changes to the list.

Help children learn to distinguish between stereotypes and accurate infor-mation. When you read stories or show pictures that have stereotypes, use accurate images to help the children identify the differences and talk about why stereotypes are not fair. With kindergartners and primary age children, Wolpert (1999) suggests playing a "stereotype or fact" game to identify how they are distinct. The teacher makes exaggerated statements that the children know from experience are obviously not true, such as, "All children hate ice cream." Then she asks if the statement is true or false and how the children know. Some of the teacher's exaggerated statements can also be tested by the children, as in "Only boys know how to run." After trying out several similar kinds of statements, the teacher explains that the untrue statements are called *stereotypes*, because they say *all* children or *all* boys, and so on, even when it isn't true for everyone. Then, when children make a stereotypical comment about a person/group, the teacher can refer to the stereotype or fact game to encourage children to rethink their statement.

Next, work in a similar way with children's ideas about People of Color to encourage critical thinking about racial stereotypes. Use the information you have gathered about attitudes in the community and in the classroom to select images and books that challenge common stereotypes and particular misinformation and concerns expressed by your children. Help children see and think about the contrast between what they may think and what is real. For example, contrast young children's common belief that all American Indians live in teepees or shoot people with bows and arrows with photographs and books by and about contemporary American Indians. Engage children in critiquing children's books that only include images of Whites or that depict inaccurate images of People of Color. Ask children to imagine each story with more diverse characters or accurate images ("Could this character be a person with dark skin instead of light skin?" "Do you think that this book tells the truth about Vietnamese people?"). Invite children to dictate or write letters to authors and illustrators about what they like and do not like in their stories and pictures and how they could make future books more inclusive.

Foster children's empathy about the hurt that stereotypes can cause and their capacity to respond effectively to incidents of prejudice and discrimination. Begin with events in your own classroom or in your children's lives, and then make the bridge to bias experienced by others. As we saw in the previous example of Eric Hoffman's use of a teachable moment with a group of preschoolers, persona doll stories are especially helpful for these explorations. You may want to start with stories about gender (e.g., a persona doll, told that she or he couldn't play with a particular toy because of being a girl or a boy). Invite the children to explore how the dolls might feel and what they might do about it. As children become more skilled at recognizing and responding to bias, have a doll of color talk about being teased or excluded by her White peers or feeling uncomfortable in a classroom where there are no images of people who look like her. Involve children in exploring how it feels to be the target of prejudice or discrimination. Then, ask children to help figure out what they could do to stop the discrimination described in the story. Continue these stories over several sessions and throughout the school year, introduce new ones that address many different stereotypes, prejudices, and discriminatory actions. Also teach children how to use conflict-resolution strategies when they are being teased or rejected because of one of their attributes (excluding children on the basis of dress, always assigning a small child the "baby" role in dramatic play, teasing a child who wears glasses). Use these incidents to help children understand the impact of discrimination directed at people not in their immediate environment.

If you work with a racially diverse group, address biased remarks or behavior directed at a specific child or group of children. It is essential to stay calm, while responding quickly and clearly, as suggested in the following guidelines (adapted from Derman-Sparks & Edwards, 2010):

- *State what you observed.* Do so without making anyone feel shamed or humiliated.
- *Set limits.* Firmly, yet calmly, remind the rejecting child that it is not okay to make fun of, tease, or reject others because of who they are.
- *Explore feelings.* Let the injured child know that she is wonderful in your eyes. Treat the rejecting child caringly too, making clear that the problem is the behavior, not the child. Encourage *both* children to say how they are feeling, but do not expect that all children will want or be able to do this.
- *Find out what the child who was the target of bias wants to do next.* She may want to play with another child, do something with you, or figure out how to work with the other child in the incident.
- *Go beyond no; try to figure out what underlies the rejecting child's behavior.* Behind every child's inappropriate behavior is a feeling, question, or desire that deserves attention. She may want to be the "doctor" in dramatic play; he may not want to share his best friend's attention; she may be frustrated because the other child took the truck she wanted to use. Alternatively, children may be expressing real feelings of discomfort or anxiety about a new person or repeating biases they have learned at home. Once you understand some of the underlying feelings, help children figure out how to get what they want in positive ways.
- *Respect each child's learning process.* No one-time comment or intervention teaches anyone a new way of thinking. Children construct a positive view of human similarities and differences through many concrete experiences. This takes time.

Implementing Learning Theme Six

We now move on to strategies for promoting children's interest in the care of the environment and in sharing resources.

Nurture children's respect, love, and sense of responsibility for the well-being of the natural environment. Involve children in the traditional early childhood education activities of caring for classroom plants and animals as a first step. If possible, take field trips to explore different types of natural environments in your community.

Engage children in taking care of the environment around them. Pick up litter. Start a recycling program. Analyze the trash in your classroom and think of ways to decrease the use of disposable materials.

Help children identify and work on local environmental problems. Invite local environmental activists to tell the children about what they do. Find meaningful ways for children to participate in some of local projects, such as cleaning up a favorite park or growing plants that can be used to reduce erosion.

When engaged in cooking projects, talk about where food comes from. Help children think about the farmers who plowed the fields and nurtured and harvested the plants and what plants and animals need to survive. With primary age children, you can also talk about the part of the country or world a food comes from and what it would be like to live there.

Engage children in activities that develop a sense of community responsibility by sharing resources. Organize and participate in toy and clothing exchanges for families in the center and immediate neighborhood or food and toy collections for community organizations or food distribution centers. Be sure these efforts are not one-time superficial acts of "charity." Work closely with one organization, and if possible, have children spend time with some of their clients. If that cannot be arranged, invite a staff member to visit your program and talk about and show photographs of the program and individuals who receive the food and clothing. In these discussions emphasize similarities between the children and the clients of the program. Be careful to focus on several racial or ethnic groups to avoid reinforcing stereotypes (for an excellent example of this kind of action project, see Pelo & Davidson, 2000).

With children 5 to 8 years old, create situations that draw children's attention to economic inequities in the wider community. You can use role-playing activities to raise these issues. For example, in one kindergarten serving predominately White middle- and upper-middle-class children, the teachers set up a store in the role-playing area but gave children different amounts of money to spend, simulating economic disparities. In the follow-up discussions the children expressed their strong reactions to the situation and offered a number of solutions to make it fairer:

> Kyle, Ashley, and Blake (among others) suggested sharing the food with the group after each shopping trip. . . . Eva, Josiah, and Corey suggested that the

group should redistribute the money more evenly. . . . Josiah was adamant on this point saying, "everyone should have two [play dollars]" and later "I want to play the fair and square way." (Lee, 2004, p. 74)

The teachers initiated activities to explore economic class further. Using photographs and stories depicting people in different economic circumstances, the teachers helped the children make connections between their immediate "store" experience and broader equity issues.

Teach children about environmental activists who work on issues that the children are exploring. Enhance children's interest in plants and animals by learning about how environmental activists are working to help them. Many local groups advocate and raise money to protect and enhance waterways and open space in order to provide habitats for plants and animals. They may turn polluted fields into community gardens, clean up local rivers and streams, and reclaim wetlands, just to name a few of the activities. If children were interested in fish, then members of the local Waterkeeper Alliance might visit the classroom and talk about how they have cleaned up a local river or bay and the many kinds of fish that are returning. Children can see pictures and maybe visit a site and think of ways that they can get involved. In the Dandelion School in Cambridge, Massachusetts, children's interests in sharks and other fish sparked a wider concern about oceans. The teachers did some research about environmental activism and learned of diver Sylvia Earle's work to protect the oceans. While the children enjoyed playing deep-sea diver, Dr. Earl's work also intrigued them, and they began asking questions about how they could help to make the water cleaner (Kathy Roberts, personal communication, June 2008).

Horrific images of environmental destruction and dire predictions about the effects of climate change are not appropriate for young children, as the information is too abstract and overwhelming. However, watching frogs in a newly reclaimed wetland or visiting a community garden offer concrete evidence that people working together can make things better for plants, animals, and humans.

Implementing Learning Theme Seven

This final set of strategies continues building children's confidence and skills to be activists. These strategies are in addition to those we previously suggested for fostering children's sense of fairness and skills for taking action.

Engage children in democratic social processes by involving them in creating group/classroom structures that are fair to everyone. Include children in deciding on classroom procedures and rules. Obviously, the latitude that we give children in these decisions varies by age. However, children at all ages have ideas about helpful and hurtful interpersonal behaviors and eagerly contribute ideas about how to make the classroom safe for everyone (for example, no hitting). Children can also figure out ways for everyone to participate equitably in discussions and classroom decisions (Levin, 2003). Through these experiences, children learn to articulate their own needs, listen to the opinions of others, see their own needs in the broader context of the group, and practice being flexible. They also experience the interdependence of all members of the class, and learn, on a small scale, skills needed for democratic, equitable communities to work. (For more details on making decisions about classroom rules and routines, see Ramsey, 2004.)

Engage children in actions for fairness on issues that are meaningful to them and appropriate to their age and development. These activities are about children making their own worlds a little fairer—not about changing the world from an adult's perspective. Here are guidelines for designing appropriate projects:

1. Be alert to specific unfair situations and practices in the classroom or immediate community that directly affect the children's lives. For example, you might notice that only the boys use the block area or realize that the classroom space needs reorganization to accommodate a child who uses a wheelchair. In the community, you might draw children's attention to the fact that there is no safe way to cross the street to get to the park, or point out the lack of diversity in the dolls and puzzles that are offered in the school or available in the local toy store.
2. Discuss potential actions for fairness with the children. Guide them in exploring their ideas and feelings about the situation and what would make it fairer. Assess the possibilities for action that are appropriate to their ages and skills.
3. Work with children to design actions that are safe and workable for you and the children. Examples of children taking action reflect a range of issues. In one center, racist slurs appeared on a wall in a nearby playground used by the children. The children and their teacher discussed what to do and painted over the hurtful words. In a parent-cooperative preschool, the children, with their teacher's help, made signs asking people not to litter

in their favorite park. A 1st-grade class wrote letters to the local newspaper about the closure of a local library. In an early childhood special education program, the children put "tickets" on cars parked illegally in their school's handicapped parking spots. (For a fuller discussion of the process for generating and implementing emergent activism projects, see Hoffman, 2004; Pelo & Davidson, 2000.)

Help children appreciate that ordinary people working together can make a positive difference in their lives. There are now some excellent children's books for 4- and 5-year-olds about children engaged in actions that remedy unfair situations in their immediate environments. (See book suggestions on the websites listed in Appendix A.)

With children 5 to 8 years old, widen the focus to include activism to improve the lives of children in the larger community. As issues come up in the community, talk to children about them and see what strikes their interest. For example, children might write to and visit municipal officials to press to have swings, slides, and play areas added to a park that is close to a poor neighborhood. At this age they may also be interested in raising money for people in more distant areas who are suffering particular hardships, such as those caused by civil war or natural disasters.

Invite local activists, including members of children's and staff's families, to talk about what they are doing. Adult activism takes many forms, including cultural work, such as community art and children's theater. White people and People of Color work on campaigns to eliminate racial prejudice and discrimination through many educational, community, and faith-based initiatives. These unsung heroes often have rich stories to tell, which help children see activists as real people. Be sure that the message is about the power and impact of people working together to make positive changes; not about rescuing others. Document the visits of local activists and make books or chart stories. Invite the children to share these stories with their families.

Familiarize school-age children with the history of resistance to injustice to racism and other "isms" in our country. Be sure to inform them about activists of *all* backgrounds. Knowing about White anti-racism activists is essential to White children's building a new White identity. However, there is very little material for children on this topic. In fact, because this information is excluded from mainstream textbooks, you may need to build your own knowledge about anti-racism activism. One way to begin is to learn more about the people described in Chapter 6 and listed in Appendix C. With Internet resources, this information is much more readily available than it was only a few years ago. Learning about these activists and the movements in which they were or are participating will lead you to other people and resources. You can then turn this information into stories to share with the children. These stories should emphasize the collective nature of activism and the importance of ordinary people's involvement, as well as the roles of leaders. Be sure to include examples of Whites participating in organizations and movements that are led by People of Color. Send book ideas from you and the children to publishers, urging them to encourage authors to write stories about particular past and current activists.

By weaving learning themes four, five, and six, and seven into all parts of your program, you lay a foundation for the long-term goal of raising children who grow up committed to creating an equitable and sustainable world. Early childhood educators begin the work. Hopefully, children will continue to get the support from their families and teachers to develop the identities, skills, and confidence to engage fully, fairly, and effectively in a diverse world and to help make it one in which all children can thrive.

9

Cultivating Caring and Activism with Staff and Families

> Being an anti-racist is not founded on what racist attitudes a person doesn't have but rather is based on what anti-racist ideas, goals, and actions one takes part in to combat racism. So, for me this concept of anti-racist has been a very liberating one.
> —Pacific Oaks student, in L. Derman-Sparks and C. B. Phillips, *Teaching/Learning Anti-Racism: A Developmental Approach*

In this chapter the learning themes focus on adults moving on to a larger view of the human family and developing the disposition and skills for activism. The adage "Children do as adults do, not as they say" is especially pertinent in this work. As with curriculum for children, we build on White adults' explorations of their own racial and cultural identities and of diversity among White people.

OUTCOMES FOR ADULTS

The goals of working with adults parallel those for children described in Chapter 8. One desired outcome is that White adults will examine their own misinformation and prejudices toward People of Color, gain accurate knowledge, and broaden their range of relationships. A second is that, with greater skills and more in-depth knowledge about the inequities of our society, staff and families will want to participate in efforts to make our schools, communities, country, and the world more equitable.

Some families may disagree with these outcomes. They may be perfectly comfortable with the status quo, see no reason to become involved, and dismiss activists as destructive troublemakers. Alternatively, they may feel vulnerable and afraid that they could lose their job, their housing, or the respect of their community or religious group if they dare to rock the boat. To engage families, we need to help them see the connection between their dreams for their children and making their school, community, and the broader world a more sustainable and equitable place. For instance, persuading the city to allocate more funds to early childhood programs will result in a better future for *all* residents; taking a stand against the polluting practices of a local company will create a healthier environment for *everyone's* children.

Doing AB/MC work with adults has similarities to eating an artichoke —it is necessary to peel off one layer at a time, and the amount of tasty substance on each layer gets greater as you get closer to the heart—the place where change can happen. Then, surrounding the heart of an artichoke, you encounter White fuzzy hairs, which taste terrible and can be difficult to remove. But the reward of reaching the heart is worth the effort.

As you consider the ideas for working with staff and families in this chapter, you may want to review the phases of adult anti-racist identity development described in Chapter 1. In addition to helping you think about your own anti-bias journey, this information can help you guide reflections and discussions with families and staff.

LEARNING ABOUT YOURSELF

The questions in this section will help you reflect on your own views related to people beyond your immediate family, circle of friends, and colleagues, and on your engagement (or lack thereof) in social activism. You can also adapt these questions to spark small-group discussions among staff and families. Getting to know one another's experiences and views will lead to topics for further learning together. First, ask yourself the following questions:

- Over the past 5 years, how much contact have I had with individuals and groups from backgrounds different from mine and in what situations and roles? How have I felt in these situations?
- Of the people who are part of my daily life (family members, closest friends, colleagues, family physician, mentors, clergy, supervisors, supervisees), how many are White? How many are People of Color? How many are from a cultural, language, or social-class background that is different from mine? How truly diverse is my immediate world? Do I want to change the balance?
- When I meet or work with a family with a very different cultural lifestyle from mine, how do I react? Do I want to "educate" them to

live more as I do? How open am I to learning about their lives and using that knowledge to reflect on my own choices and values?

- What stereotypes about people based on race, religion, language, or culture do I know? Which stereotypes do I hold? (Just write what comes to mind without self-censuring. Remember that all of us learn the stereotypes that pervade our society, even if we do not agree with them. You may surprise yourself with how many you hold.) How do these stereotypes affect my initial perception of people? When I watch a movie or television show or read the newspaper, how conscious am I of stereotyped roles and messages? Are there some stereotypes that I notice more than I do others?

- How do I react when new information contradicts my assumptions about different groups? Do I dismiss it as just an exception to the rule? Do I notice it and then file it away without further thought? Do I use the experience as an opportunity to rethink my original assumptions?

- How do I feel when others stereotype my own gender, racial, cultural, economic, or religious group? How do I respond? What do I do in these situations? What do I want to do in the future?

- How do I feel when I hear or see others (family, friends, or coworkers) make prejudiced remarks, or act in discriminatory ways? What do I do? What keeps me from acting? What helps me to act?

- How do I feel when I hear children making stereotypical or negative comments about people's identity? How comfortable am I talking with children about their ideas and attitudes? What are the sources of any discomfort I may feel?

- If I knew from this point on that, every person on the planet would have adequate shelter, food, and clothing forever, how would I feel? How would this change my views about material goods? My perceptions of other people? How would a more equitable distribution of wealth affect my life?

- What are my beliefs about the growing disparities in wealth in the country and world? Who or what is responsible? What (if anything) do I think should be done about these inequities?

- What role does consumption (shopping, looking through catalogs, watching infomercials) play in my life? How do I feel when I purchase something new? When I cannot afford something I would like to have? Do I consider the environmental impact or disparities in resource distribution when I think about buying a new item or planning a trip? How aware am I of different

companies' labor and environmental practices? How does this information (or lack of it) influence what I buy?
- When I think of doing anti-bias and anti-racist work, what images of being an activist come to mind? Where do these images come from? Direct experience? My education? The media?
- Do I think of myself as an activist? If not, why not? If yes, what experiences have I had as an activist that can help me to do AB/MC work? What values/behaviors in my family's history support my being an anti-bias/anti-racist activist? Which ones make it difficult?
- Which social activists—from any group and any historical period—are potential role models for me? Why? Which of their attributes and activities are most appealing? Least appealing?

LEARNING ABOUT YOUR CHILDREN'S FAMILIES

Approach the process of gathering information as a shared exploration, not as a one-sided interrogation ("I would like to learn more about your child's and family's experiences so I can do a better job of being her teacher"). Often family members feel reassured if you also talk about your own experiences, especially about times when you have felt uncomfortable talking about racial issues and blunders that you have made in these conversations. If people start to become uncomfortable or resistant, then back off a bit and shift to another focus (if a parent is reluctant to talk about the racial composition of the community, he or she might be willing to talk about its different religious groups, which may be very informative). This flexibility does not mean abandoning the conversation but rather finding a more effective approach.

The following questions are only suggestions and should be adapted for specific groups. We hope that they will act as catalysts for more extended conversations.

- What is your community like? Who lives there? What racial, ethnic, or religious groups are there? Where do people work? What kinds of jobs do they have?
- How much contact has your family had, and, in particular, have your children had, with people from other racial, cultural, religious, and social-class groups? How have they responded to differences?
- Have your children asked questions or made comments about race? About poverty? About someone with an unfamiliar accent or a disability? If so, what have they said? How have you responded?

- With what institutions are your children familiar (workplaces, churches, stores, the welfare system)? What is the racial composition in those institutions? What messages do you think your children are learning about which people hold different types of jobs? What have they learned about which groups are in authority and which ones hold more subordinate positions?
- What messages about race, culture, and social class do you think your children are learning from the television programs that they watch? Books that they read? Have you and your children ever had conversations about these messages? What are some of the questions or reactions they have expressed?
- What do you want your child to learn about racial and ethnic diversity?

STRATEGIES FOR WORKING WITH FAMILIES AND STAFF

The strategies described in this section work with a wide range of people —those who are just beginning to consider these issues and those who are at the later phases of their anti-racism journey. What will vary is people's depth of discussion and willingness to take action on specific issues. *Remember that the activities in this chapter rest on the activities in Chapter 5, so be sure to do those first.*

As you learn about family and staff members' experiences with racial and cultural diversity, as well as where they are in their anti-racist identity journey, you will be able to tailor activities to meet their specific needs. As we stressed in Chapter 5, you need to be open to many different ways in which people respond. See your role as generating interest, providing information, and encouraging—but not forcing—people to stretch and take risks. Respect participants' unique histories and perspectives and the different paths they will take. Adapt your approach according to the racial and cultural composition of the group.

Pay attention to two undermining dynamics that teachers report occurring rather frequently. One is the tendency of some White participants —often, although not always, male or affluent individuals—to dominate the discussion, thus silencing others. Second, as we pointed out in Chapter 5, in a racially/ethnically diverse group, White participants often want the participants of color to "teach us" about racism. While learning about each other is important, the danger is that White individuals do not take responsibility for exploring their own ideas about race and racism, instead they are passive listeners. At times, having separate discussions within racial groups may be effective. Groups can then reform to share key ideas with each other.

Implementing Learning Theme Four

The following activities complement and support those for children described in Chapter 8: expanding awareness, appreciation, and respect for people beyond one's immediate world. In some cases, work with families and work with children can become a single project.

Explore ways that families can expand their experience with People of Color. Most communities have more diversity than White adults realize. Encourage families to identify specific ways they can build connections with individual People of Color in the larger community (joining an integrated place of worship, building a relationship between two places of worship, getting to know people through participating in cultural or social-action groups, seeking out professional People of Color such as a pediatrician or dentist, being committed to building a more diverse staff in the center). Note that employing a person of color as a gardener or housekeeper does not meet the spirit of this guideline, because it is a hierarchical relationship in that the employer has the power to hire and fire the employee. Although young children may not understand the terms of employment, they do notice concrete indicators of power such as the widespread practice of calling the employer "Mr. _____" or "Mrs. (or Ms.) _____" and the employee by the first name only. Such power relationships reinforce messages of White superiority.

Help families to consider how they might bring racial and cultural diversity into their home environments, as you are doing in the classroom. Encourage families to provide their children with materials (such as skin tone supplies for art projects) and children's books and toys with characters and stories that reflect a range of ethnic and cultural groups within the United States. Collaborate with families to create a lending or exchange library in your center with books, toys, cassette tapes, videos, CDs, and DVDs that authentically represent a wide range of people.

Invite family members to develop their skills to hear and address children's questions and comments about diversity. To stimulate interest, document questions and comments you hear from the children and use these as a starting place. Ask family members to share with you any statements or queries their children raise at home. They can convey these via email, a short note, or in person. Assure them that the child's name will not be associated with the comment. When you have several of these comments, they can become the basis for discussing strategies for addressing children's ideas.

Organize conversations between parents and local leaders and activists of color who can directly describe issues that children and families in their communities face, and about current efforts to address these issues. This personal contact often catches people's attention and motivates further learning and possible involvement in changing unjust conditions.

Organize discussion groups focused on books and articles that tell authentic stories or experiences of individual people and families. There are many excellent novels written by People of Color (Julia Alvarez, Bebe Moore Campbell, Toni Morrison, and Amy Tang, to name just a few) that draw White readers into new perspectives and help them to see that their way of life is only one of many realities in the United States. As important, they illuminate the effects of racism and help Whites recognize their unconscious racist assumptions and actions.

Implementing Learning Theme Five

Provide opportunities for adults to learn how to identify stereotypes and discrimination and to understand the pain that these assumptions and actions cause. In addition, create opportunities for families to figure out ways to teach their children how to recognize and challenge stereotypical information and unfair actions.

Invite staff and family members to talk about their childhood experiences of being teased, humiliated, or rejected because of some aspect of their identity. Use their stories as a bridge to addressing the racism directed at People of Color. Facilitate discussions in which participants explore how these experiences have affected their feelings about themselves and others. Perhaps in conjunction with books or short films, use those experiences to help participants identify with the pain of discrimination suffered by People of Color. These discussions may lead to ideas about participants' hopes for how their children will treat others. If participants believe that children are "color blind," you can talk to them about research that shows how readily young children notice race and absorb common prejudices(see Chapters 3 and 7). To bring the discussion closer to home, you can also present examples from your program (with names completely disguised, of course) that illustrate children's discomfort and stereotypes about People of Color.

Explore staff and family members' stereotypes of different racial and ethnic groups and how these influence their attitudes and behaviors about those groups. Pass out index cards and ask people to describe stereotypes they have learned or heard (without identifying themselves) and place the cards in a bowl. Read the cards out loud or list their contents on easel paper. Ask people to talk in dyads about how they learned these stereotypes. Then, in the whole group, talk about how stereotypes harm everyone and how people can unlearn their prejudices.

Involve participants in critiquing popular children's films, television programs, and books for stereotypes and misinformation. Ask family members to keep records of the stereotypes in programs and ads on television that their children regularly watch. Bring in a selection of children's books that contain stereotypical messages and ask staff and family members to critique these. (See Appendix A for guidelines on evaluating books.) Collect and critique holiday decorations and greeting cards, among the most obvious being images of Native Americans that are portrayed in the Thanksgiving context (see Bisson, 1997, for further examination of holiday issues from an anti-bias perspective). Describe the strategies you are using to teach children how to recognize and resist stereotypes and explore how families might use them at home.

Follow these guidelines when a family exhibits prejudice toward a specific group and expects the teacher to act on the family's beliefs (adapted from Derman-Sparks & Edwards, 2010, pp. 41–42). They might tell you they want their child told that a lesbian or gay headed family is not a real or good family, or that they do not want a "crippled" child in the class, or insist that their child not play with the Arab American children in the group. A child may also reflect his family's biases in what he says and how he acts to classmates.

The quickest (and often most tempting) response is to assert immediately: "In this classroom, we encourage all the children to respect each other and all kinds of families. If this is not acceptable to you, then you can decide to take your child to another class or program." While this bottom line approach ultimately might be necessary, it is not the way to begin.

Instead, invest some time and energy with the family. Try to find out what factors underlie the family's stance. Listen carefully and with an open heart—none of us is free from prejudice. It may be based on a lack of—or incorrect—information, or over-generalizing one negative experience with one individual into an attitude against a whole group. It may be a lack of validation in the person's own life. Some people use racism, sexism, ableism, or another "ism" as an outlet for their own frustration, anger, and fear, or as an excuse for greed—and our society often allows them to do so. These facts do not make the prejudice okay, but they help us to see the whole person and not just the biased behavior.

Explain to the family why you think it is so vital to children's healthy development and future life success to develop comfortable and respectful interactions with all kinds of people. Remember that this is a dialogue, not a monologue; make sure that family members have ample opportunity to express their views and that you are open to learning from their views, just as you are hoping they will learn from yours.

Talking with a family about their prejudiced views and discriminatory behavior may not always succeed. Some people will not want to talk; some, even after a number of conversations, will hold fast to their original stance. When this is the case, the bottom line approach is appropriate: "We will not allow prejudice and discrimination in our classroom. If this is not acceptable to you, we can help you find another program for your child." Then it is up to the family to make a decision about what they want to do. If it becomes clear a family cannot stay in the program, it is important that the director help them identify other resources in the community and handle their departure as respectfully as possible.

Implementing Learning Theme Six

The following set of strategies dovetails with classroom activities about caring for the resources of the earth. As children and their families become more mindful of the environment and the unequal distribution of material resources, they can work together to make changes in the classroom, in their homes, and in the community.

Invite family and staff members to talk about ways that they feel pressured by consumerism and its effects on their children. Be alert to issues that are on families' minds. For example, as the November and December holidays approach, many families feel that they have to purchase the latest expensive toys, clothes, and sports equipment for their children. They often feel torn between financial constraints and the barrage of mesmerizing commercials directed at their children. Brainstorm ways to counter the pressures on their children and themselves. For example, you might plan a joint school-family project in which you work together to make needed learning materials for the school or where family members make books about family events over the past year for their children. (Provide needed materials for these activities and also invite families to contribute additional specific materials as they can.)

Facilitate a discussion or workshop to talk about families' goals for their children and their child-rearing values related to possessions. To raise awareness about the impact of consumerism, you might invite the families to join an evening conversation on the theme "How Much Is Enough?" This event might provide a timely opportunity for families to share their concerns and think about ways to put more emphasis on caring connections within the family rather than on material things. Ask families to brainstorm and share activities they already do that do not involve buying new and expensive objects for their children (picnics, visits to a local park or zoo, a dinner where everyone cooks together, family game night, a day during the vacation that their child plans).

Pay attention to families' economic realities and tailor discussion questions for the range of incomes within your group. For relatively affluent families, you might pose the idea that they collectively commit themselves to buying less for their children. They can mutually support each others' efforts to counteract their children's arguments about how much other kids are getting and to resist gift-giving pressures from members of their extended families. As an alternative to purchasing expensive gifts or throwing lavish birthday parties, families can learn about local social justice organizations and choose one or two to support, or contribute to aid for people suffering from natural disasters or civil strife. Engaging children in these conversations and decisions exposes them to the hardships of many people and enables them to participate in organizational and individual efforts to achieve more equity. For lower-income families, agreeing to support each other in not succumbing to the competitive pressures of consumerism is critical. Family members can brainstorm strategies to provide gifts that are within their income range, including making gifts. Familiarize all families with children's books in which family members show their love for one another through creativity and ingenuity rather than spending money.

Involve families in environmental activities that contribute to the school and to the community's improvement. Tending a school garden and setting up recycling programs are a few of the many environmental projects that can be done collaboratively with families, children, and staff. Pelo and Davidson (2000) describe how families and schools can also work on community projects such as planting and caring for trees in a neighborhood park or creating a community garden.

Raise people's awareness about environmental justice issues in the city and state. While many people may know about efforts to preserve wildlife and habitats, they may not be as aware of issues that particularly affect working-class and poor communities, such as lead pollution, proliferation of waste-disposal plants, nuclear-waste dumps, or poorly ventilated factories. Collect material from national environmental justice organizations and invite local activists from these groups to talk about their work. Out of these meetings, further ideas for discussion and activities may emerge.

Expand consciousness of national and global environmental and consumerism issues. You might organize staff and family evenings in which you show and discuss videos/DVDs that highlight the interactive relationships between the environment, consumerism, race, class, peace, and democracy. For example, "The Global Banquet: Politics of Food" (2001) examines how American food choices affect the environment and worldwide economy, and "The Child Behind the Label" (1995) looks at the child laborers who produce goods bought by Americans. Both can be purchased through Teaching for Change (see Appendix B). "Consuming Kids: The Commercialization of Childhood" (by the Media Education Foundation in 2008) is a compelling account about the sophisticated advertising techniques used to hook children on the media and a wide range of products from toys to sugary cereals.

Implementing Learning Theme Seven

Acquiring skills and confidence to work for social justice in our schools, in our communities, and in the larger society and world are integral to AB/MC work. In this section, we suggest several strategies for engaging families in social change.

Explore images of activism that family and staff members hold. Being an activist has a range of meanings for people; many hold stereotypical images based on distorted media representations. As a starting place, invite family members and staff to share the images or key words that define activism for them. Reflect together on the authenticity of these images and words.

Think about the meaning of citizenship in a democratic society and the value of ordinary people taking responsibility to act in the face of injustice. Ask people to relate stories about how they themselves and their family members, neighbors, and friends have participated in social justice work.

Learn about the stories of ordinary people who have worked or are working for racial justice. Go to the website of Voices of Civil Rights, which is a joint project of the American Association of Retired People (AARP), the Leadership Conference on Civil Rights, and the Library of Congress. This website has wonderful stories from people throughout the United States (see Appendix B). You can also invite local social justice activists to talk about their experiences. Families and staff can work together to create teaching materials for the children based on these stories.

Encourage staff and families to collaborate on addressing pressing AB/ MC concerns in the school and in the community. For starters, involve families in children's action projects (see Chapter 8). To generate interest and participation on a wider scale, display information about local and national social justice movements and organize car pools to specific local events. Recognize families who take action by posting this information and related photographs on the family bulletin board or including it in class and school newsletters. At the school level, invite families and staff to work together to assemble and make materials that will bring greater diversity to the program's environment. At the community level, they could work with local libraries, toy stores, and bookstores to help develop a wider range of diversity in their selections. They could also get involved in actions to pressure the town to provide more services for low-income residents. Participants who are interested in politics might investigate and challenge local inequities and state and federal policies that create or perpetuate them. Check out the website of the Civil Rights Coalition for the 21st Century for current information and links to several other national groups (see Appendix B).

NEXT STEPS: INVESTIGATING RACISM AS A SYSTEM

Continuing on the anti-racism and social justice journey requires learning how the system of racism operates in our country. Although it may not be realistic to go further with all your families and staff, some individuals may be interested in meeting more regularly to engage in this study. We also urge you to find ways to continue your own study (see the resources in Appendices B and C). Here are a few strategies you can use with staff and families who wish to deepen and expand their AB/ MC work.

Gain a broader perspective of United States history. One enjoyable and compelling way to begin is to read aloud the dramatic readings in Howard Zinn's book *The People Speak* (2004), a collection of diverse voices telling stories that celebrate the enduring spirit of dissent throughout the history of the United States. For people who enjoy reading, assign various chapters of Ronald Takaki's *A Different Mirror* (1993), a portrait of the history of several different ethnic groups. Then ask each person or small group to report to the whole group. James Loewen's *Lies Across America: What Our*

Historical Sites Get Wrong (1999) reveals the gaping holes in most people's education. You can also suggest the books we list in For Further Reading in Chapters 2 and 6.

Learn about the history of the construction of "Whiteness" and how it has affected different groups. Study how the pressures to "be White" affected various European ethnic groups (see Allen, 1994; Brodkin, 1998 [Jewish identity]; Ignatiev, 1995 [Irish identity]; Roediger, 1991, 2005). Ask participants to consider what it would mean to them if the current social-political construct of "Whiteness" no longer existed. How might this shift affect their view of themselves and others? How might it change how they live their lives?

Learn about the dynamics of systemic racism. One excellent resource for opening up this topic is a video titled "Ending Racism: Working for a Racism Free 21st Century." Made by Crossroads (1996), an interfaith, community-based, anti-racism education and training organization, it comes with a detailed discussion guide (see Appendix B for contact information). For a group that enjoys reading, Joseph Barndt's *Understanding and Dismantling Racism: The Twenty-First Century Challenge to White America* (2007) offers a detailed analysis of how racism works and suggestions for how to recognize and transform it. Paul Kivel's *Uprooting Racism: How White People Can Work for Racial Justice* (2002) is a reader-friendly book that also provides self-growth activities. Apply what you learn about the dynamics of racism to current hot topics, such as immigration or the so-called "achievement gap" of children of color in the schools.

Explore staff and families' visions of a society free of racism (and other isms). After working together to analyze systemic racism, group members may be motivated to explore and share their visions of a society free of racism. In small groups of 4 to 5 people, ask participants to envision, for example, high quality child-care centers, schools, or community health-care centers that are open to all regardless of individuals' economic resources or their racial or cultural backgrounds. A key ground rule is to put aside all preconceived ideas and limitations and assume a free hand and ample resources to create these new institutions. Then, ask each group to relate their ideas and to describe their feelings as they imagine living in such a society. End by suggesting that they hold on to these visions as you all work toward improving your own program and community.

Form or join a support/action group. Because AB/MC work is complex and takes time, teachers or families who try to go it alone may end up feeling discouraged and burned out. Experienced AB/MC educators and activists often credit their networks for enabling them to go from being bystanders to taking action and for staying involved for the long haul (Alvarado et al., 1999). Support groups provide opportunities for participants to deepen their knowledge about racism and other isms, to find and give support for personal changes, and to continue to develop new ways of thinking and acting in their work and communities.

Some support/action groups are program based, with families and teachers meeting regularly (weekly, biweekly, or monthly) to discuss their own experiences and ways to build AB/MC work in their school. One teacher called her school support group a "Circle of Girlfriends" (Annette Unten in Alvarado et al., 1999). Others organize or join support groups made up of teachers and community people outside of their center or school, perhaps through a local AEYC or other professional organization, or a faith-based or community organization. Some teachers have formed chat rooms or email discussion groups to have a place to express their concerns and to get feedback and support. For example, the Wisconsin Early Childhood Association created an online book club format for their discussions, using NAEYC as the website server.

Support groups require a long-term commitment and regular attendance, consistent with the complexities of learning to do effective AB/MC education. Group members' experiences, interests, and ideas about where they need to grow determine discussion topics. Personal storytelling and analysis of the themes that arise from the stories are the most common methods, often supplemented with discussions about books, videos/DVDs, and invited speakers. Successful support/action groups find it is most productive to balance discussions related to personal growth with those focused on ways to take action in their school and community.

Certain group dynamics can derail discussions about race and racism, even among dedicated people. Some members may feel superior to others because they see themselves as being further along in dealing with racial issues. To have useful discussions, people must put aside their feelings of competitiveness and superiority and listen to themselves and others with openness and humility. Establish that no one is ever free of the effects of racism and that everyone in the group is striving for a deeper understanding of how racism has influenced their lives and the larger society.

Members may act out societal hierarchies of gender, economic class, or race; or the power differentials between teachers and families. When these dynamics emerge, use them as teachable moments to examine how they undermine the creation of equitable relationships. When members avoid conflict and discomfort, conversations may become superficial. Confronting these dynamics opens up an opportunity for people to delve deeper into their anxieties and to gain the courage to be honest with themselves and others.

Above all, it is vital to understand that racism is, in its essence, hurtful and dehumanizing. Undoing it—whether in ourselves, our families, or in our early childhood programs—can also be painful, even while it is humanizing and liberating. Learning how to manage conflict enables group members to express disagreements and to hear and understand the complexities of multiple perspectives. (For ideas about creating and maintaining support/action groups, see Chang et al., 2000, and Cronin et al., 1998.)

Ultimately, AB/MC work "is a path where we walk in companionship. . . . And through these relationships . . . [we] realize that no one does this work alone, that they travel with friends and . . . a 'suitcase full of hope'" (Eric Hoffman in Alvarado et al., 1999, p. 210).

A Tale of Two Centers
EPISODE TWO

The second episode of the centers' narratives illustrates how the teachers implemented aspects of learning themes four through seven.

THE MOTHER JONES CENTER

In the first episode, the children had made books on the theme "Everyone Works in My Family." The teachers—Liz, Charlie, and Marina—wanted to build on the children's enthusiasm about the topic to expand their ideas about families and work beyond their immediate experience (learning theme four). At circle time, the teachers made charts with the children showing how many tasks all families share and the many ways families get their work done. They used multiracial/ethnic persona dolls to broaden the range of family approaches and jobs—which led to an unexpected and troubling conversation. One of the persona dolls, Samantha, has an African American identity, and a daddy who is a schoolteacher. Adding Samantha to the chart, Liz asked the children, "What do you think Samantha's daddy does to help his family?" One of the children said, "He's a garbage man." The other children nodded. Liz, taken aback, said, "No, he's a teacher. He teaches 3rd grade." The children shook their heads. "Unh unh," said Bradley firmly. "Black guys pick up the garbage."

Liz did not know what to say. In fact, in their neighborhood, the only African American men most of the children had contact with did indeed collect the garbage. Two African American men collected even the school garbage. It was clear that she needed to broaden the curriculum, but Liz was not sure how to do it.

After talking it over, Liz, Charlie, and Marina decided that, despite a lack of racial diversity, they could at least be sure that the children got to know those few People of Color who were in the community in order to help dispel children's assumptions based on their limited information (learning themes four and five). They decided to have the children interview the center's support staff, most of whom were People of Color, to get to know them as individuals. They arranged for the children to interview the school secretary, the cook, and the mail carrier. It took some major arrangements to get one of the garbage collectors to come to school, but when he did, he became an instant hero, as he also brought the huge truck and showed the children how it lifted up the dumpster and crushed the trash. The teachers invited him to talk about his children (aged 3, 5, and 9), and his hobby (fixing motorcycles). After each visit, the children gave the people they interviewed a bouquet of "flowers" made at the art table and followed up with a thank-you letter. The teachers put the information the children had gathered into a book with a snapshot of each person, which they added to their "Everybody Works" collection.

Wanting to broaden the "Everybody Works" curriculum, and to address the incipient racism inherent in the children's lack of contact with People of Color, the staff moved on to a curriculum they named "We Are All the Same—We Are All Different" (learning themes two and four). They decided to first strengthen the children's exploration and sense of comfort with the differences within the classroom and within their neighborhoods and increase their sense of comfort with talking about differences and similarities.

To encourage the children to *see* one another accurately, Marina made a matching game with digital photos of the backs of children's heads and of their faces. The ease with which children identified slight differences, such as the length of a boy's hair, or the degree of wave in a child's hair, surprised her. At circle, they made eye charts, counting how many people had blue, green, hazel, or brown eyes and how many wore glasses. The classroom persona dolls extended the conversations and were included in all the charting. One of the dolls, Pilar, wore glasses, and the children helped her solve the problem of children teasing her about the glasses.

The curriculum continued to build with ideas such as "Everybody sleeps, but we sleep in different places" (shared beds, bunk beds, cribs, hammocks, mats on the floor, with grandparents, alone in a bed). "Everybody eats but we eat different foods" (all the different kinds of breakfasts children have, who gets to drink coffee and who does not, the different ways that people make bread and other pastries).

Charlie, Liz, and Marina also began to discuss what they could do to build a caring community among the families (learning themes three and five). To prepare for this, the three teachers talked about specific families with whom they were struggling. Of particular concern was the Curtis family. JoAnn Curtis never seemed to be able to get it together. She was inevitably late, her twins still in their pajamas at 9:30 or 10:00. She rarely returned forms on time (or at all) and never participated in the parent meetings.

Liz, who had been silent through most of the meeting, finally spoke up. "I know how hard it is," she said. "I remember when I was working and going to school and the kids were little. It is hard when your car breaks down and you have no money to fix it. The buses are unreliable, crowded, noisy, and never run when you need them. I used to be so ashamed to show up at parent meetings because I could never get there on time, and I couldn't talk the way the other parents did." She fell silent again. Marina and Charlie looked at each other feeling embarrassed and ashamed. Charlie said slowly, "You know I have to say that I had not thought about it from that perspective. I had only been thinking about my own annoyance and the inconvenience it has caused for us. Let's try to figure out how *we* can help her get the twins here on time." Marina nodded and said, "What about keeping some clothes for the twins here, so that we can change them if they need to come in their pajamas?" Charlie agreed, "Good idea. Also, let's see if there are any parents who live near her who might be able to help with transportation."

There was a pause, and then Marina turned to Liz and said softly "Are you afraid to talk to us?" (She was indicating Charlie and herself.) "Sometimes," Liz admitted. "You're both so educated. You're really intelligent and I feel . . . sort of dumb sometimes." The teachers were silent for a few moments and then Charlie said, "I wonder how many of our kids are learning that they aren't 'intelligent' too? I think you're brilliant, Liz. I wish you shared more of your thinking. I mean, look at how you turned around that first parent meeting!"

During the first parent meeting, the teachers had asked the families to talk to one another about their goals for their children during the school year. The conversation had not gone well. Many of the participants were silent, and those who spoke focused on the issues they themselves had struggled with in the elementary schools. "I want her to learn to pay attention." "I want him to learn to read and write." "I want the kids to learn not to get into trouble." "He can't sit still." Charlie was disgusted that the families did not have "age-appropriate goals." Marina felt discouraged that there were some parents who seemed to have no goals at all for their children. Liz, however, suddenly spoke up and began to talk about what it had been like for her as a low-income single mother putting her children through school. She talked about pressuring her children to stay clean no matter what, remembering her own childhood experience of other children teasing her because of her old, dirty clothes. Now that her children were older, she divulged, she regretted not letting them play freely and putting so much pressure on them. She then asked the family members to go into groups of three and talk about experiences in their own childhoods that they wanted to protect their children from also experiencing. The conversation was lively and intense. The teachers then talked a little about how they saw the center curriculum providing strength for the children and skills for healthy survival. Liz brought the conversation back to the participants and asked them what qualities in their families they most wanted to pass on to their children. Those became the list of values, which the teachers wrote down and then posted in their classrooms.

Despite the successful outcome of the first meeting, it was clear to the three teachers that tensions and distrust continued to exist between the families. Those parents who were working seemed hostile to those on public subsidy. The student parents sought one another out and appeared to avoid the other families. Some of the employed parents made critical comments (often in front of the children) about the "welfare families" who "took" their tax dollars, and they were uneasy about their children playing with "*those* kids, from *those* families." The staff wondered how much of such messages were communicated to children.

While the staff was thinking through what they wanted to do, three of the mothers asked to meet with them. Nervously, but very firmly, the women informed the teachers that they did not want their children playing with food. The cornmeal table, the bean collages, the macaroni necklaces could feed their families for a week. "Food is for eating," one of the moms said sternly, "not for wasting." Chagrined, the teachers agreed at once to stop using food for curriculum projects, and as they discussed their obliviousness to the issue, they began to discuss the amount of wasted food at snack and lunchtime. After the staff meeting, the teachers thought the food-wasting issue might be something that could build bridges for all the families. They decided to launch a compost plan and plant a small garden. Parents agreed to help build planter boxes and seek donations of small tools and good dirt, and put up a compost box in the yard (learning theme six).

The children were fascinated with the project. Watching food scraps turn to dirt was as interesting as watching seeds sprout. The seedlings also entranced everyone; the teachers had to set limits on the children's enthusiasm to water the plants. The children could hardly wait until the lettuce and carrots came up.

As family members began to help in the school garden, they also began to eye the vacant lot down the block from the school. Planting in boxes was fine, but planting in the ground would be a lot better. In the ground, the children could grow strawberries. Perhaps families could have their own plots and grow their own vegetables—or even flowers! A small delegation of the parents got together, for the first time working across the lines of difference among them. They researched the ownership of the lot and found it could be for sale. No one had enough money, but Charlie thought that if they gathered enough neighbors together perhaps they could get the city to lease the lot as a community garden (learning themes six and seven).

Excitement ran high as family members organized a newsletter, set up a petition, arranged for their county supervisor to make a visit. The staff displayed the petition in front of the school with a bulletin board of pictures of the children working in the garden, and with copies of some of their artwork. Many neighbors began dropping in to the school to see what the children were doing and to offer small supplies (a pair of garden gloves, some sweet-pea seeds, and a tube of sunscreen).

Meanwhile, it occurred to Marina that the garden might be a tie to the nearby community of Central American farm workers. After careful discussion with Liz and Charlie, a new curriculum was born: "Food—Where Does It Come From?" The children went on field trips to see the people who planted and picked the strawberry fields, and then, of course, they tasted strawberries. How did the strawberries get from the fields to the store? Who took care of the food in the store?

Marina felt that things were going very well, until she heard Bradley say to Michael, "We're going to visit those aliens tomorrow!" Stunned, she asked Bradley what he thought an alien was. "You know," he replied, "those brown people from Mars who pick the strawberries." Checking with the morning teachers, she discovered that some of the parents had been uneasy about the field trips. There had been conversations about illegal aliens, and some anger from parents with family members who had lost their union jobs when the frozen-food plant moved to Mexico.

The three teachers decided to address these issues directly with the families and called a meeting (learning theme five); Liz facilitated, with the support of Marina and Charlie. Speaking as a member of the neighborhood, Liz led a discussion about how people often scorn and mistreat farm workers, who are often very poor. She named these attitudes and behaviors as stereotypes, misinformation, and social oppression. From there, she and Marina began to talk about the conditions of the families who worked in the fields. They made the connections between the struggles that many of the center families were having and the struggles of the farm workers' families.

Not all the parents were convinced. However, when Charlie began to talk about the children's misinformation regarding "aliens," "garbage men," and "dirty skin," and the emotional pain that these terms inflict on people, most of the parents were concerned and wanted to learn more. Together parents and teachers identified ways that children had absorbed these biased assumptions from what they saw (and did not see!) in their community and in the media. They then brainstormed ideas for challenging the negative images and conveying ones that are more accurate. Ideas began to flow, and a new curriculum focus began to emerge.

And so the work continues . . .

THE LOUISA MAY ALCOTT CENTER

In the first episode, the teachers had implemented several changes to try to curb the children's competitiveness, which seemed to reflect their families' White privilege and desire to raise superstar children. After several weeks of emphasizing cooperative activities and encouraging the children to learn about their similarities and differences, Brenda and Vera noticed that the competition among the children had abated somewhat. Family members seemed more relaxed and less worried about their children's accomplishments. A tone of entitlement, however, continued to pervade the conversations, which often revolved around exotic vacations, expensive purchases, and seemingly unlimited budgets for children's activities. The teachers felt uneasy with how many families seemed to live in a bubble of restless affluence—never questioning their right to use as many resources as they could afford, yet never feeling satisfied. Brenda, from her perspective of having grown up in a working-class family, felt that there was an "invisible norm of affluence" that was going unquestioned in the classroom.

To tackle this issue, the teachers built on previous discussions with the children about the distribution of resources. Wanting to make inequities more real to the children, they took a step beyond already existing cooperative activities, this time setting up situations of scarcity (a small numbers of markers, a single pair of scissors) that required the children to wait, negotiate, and share. As they talked through the frustrations and conflicts that arose in these situations, the teachers introduced carefully selected pictures and stories that depicted people from many different groups (including Whites) living in less advantaged circumstances (learning themes four and six). The teachers challenged the children to consider how they might feel if they were living with very few resources.

Although the children were interested and concerned, a couple of them also made comments about poor people being lazy. The teachers were concerned that children were absorbing negative stereotypes about poor people and had no idea of what it really meant to be poor. They wanted to make poverty more real and meaningful to the children. Al, an old friend of Brenda's who worked at a homeless shelter, came to the classroom for several visits. He showed pictures and told the children about his work and about some of the families who lived in the shelter. The children asked many questions about the families in the shelter, and several talked about how it was not fair that some kids did not have a place to live. A few parents expressed concern about their children being exposed to "such depressing" information, but others were impressed at their children's thoughtful comments and questions about poverty and homelessness.

The teachers decided to address the issues of entitlement and superiority head-on and planned a family–staff meeting to talk about them. They anticipated that this discussion would be difficult and invited a highly trained outside facilitator to run the meeting. The facilitator started the discussion by asking participants to list the stereotypes that people had about them and their jobs (sleazy lawyers, overpaid corrupt executives, pampered homemakers) and to talk about how those made them feel. Then they asked participants to list (anonymously) on cards the stereotypes they had learned about different racial and income groups. Then the facilitator read the cards aloud and had participants talk in small groups about how they had learned those stereotypes and how they had influenced their attitudes about different groups. When the small groups were reporting out to the larger group, the conversation was lively, with some people talking about their feelings of embarrassment and guilt, while others reacted defensively (learning theme five).

A pivotal moment came when Susan, a corporate lawyer, said quietly, "You know the problem isn't the poor people. The problem is that they do not have access to the resources and opportunities that we have. I hate to say this, but I think that maybe *we* are the problem." The conversation stopped and the room fell silent. The facilitator thanked Susan and used her comment to shift the conversation from personal guilt to thinking about changes that they could make in their own lives and ways that they could pressure institutions to address the larger systemic problems that underlie poverty (learning theme six). Obviously, it was only the start of a very long conversation, but at the end of the meeting, many participants stayed behind to keep talking, and several asked to have some follow-up meetings.

Over the next few weeks, Brenda and Vera were pleased to notice that both children and family members begin to moderate their consumption patterns. For example, several family members mentioned that they had decided to forego lavish birthday parties and to have smaller, simpler events.

Meanwhile, to moderate children's fascination with new toys and games and to help them connect more closely with the natural environment, the teachers extended the time spent outdoors and used natural objects to teach concepts that they usually taught inside the classroom (counting trees, identifying leaf patterns). They also replaced some of the store-bought materials in the classroom with natural materials (grasses instead of paintbrushes, twigs and small logs instead of blocks) to encourage children to appreciate the qualities of these materials and to invent new ways of working with them.

Vera's husband, an environmentalist, came to the school and talked to the children about local environmental problems. The children started to keep track of the amount of trash that accumulated in their classroom and came up with ways to cut down on waste (drawing and writing on both sides of the paper, using only one paper towel to dry their hands).

To make the connections between preserving the environment and the unequal consumption of resources more concrete, the teachers incorporated images and stories showing how people from different regions use and conserve the resources that they have (learning themes four and six).

With the approaching holidays, the teachers organized a teacher-parent discussion group about the financial and social pressures that many families feel during the holidays. They began by having family members think about their favorite childhood memories. As people recalled special times with family and friends, they realized that very few of their happiest childhood moments had anything to do with new toys. Based on these memories, everyone brainstormed ideas about how to create enjoyable and meaningful family times that did not involve spending a lot of money.

A number of families decided to join forces to do some outdoor activities over the holidays (taking hikes, cleaning up a local park, skating and sliding on a nearby pond). Several families also decided to contribute some of the money they would have spent on presents to Al's homeless shelter. Some also arranged to volunteer at the shelter over the break. When school closed for the vacation, Brenda and Vera felt a glow of accomplishment. The children and families were beginning to let go of their competitiveness and sense of entitlement, and were reaching out to one another and to the community in new ways.

When the children returned to school after the holidays, however, Brenda and Vera were dismayed to hear the old competitiveness take over the children's conversations. Despite the fact that a number of the families had tried to cut back on gifts, the children were bragging about what they had received for Christmas or Hanukkah, which, of course, sidelined the three children whose families did not observe either of these holidays. When the teachers mentioned these observations to the parents, they heard stories of relatives who piled on the gifts (despite the parents' efforts to shift the focus away from purchased presents) and of children watching many hours of television loaded with holiday commercials. Several of the parents seemed discouraged and ready to "just give in to the culture—we can't do anything about it."

Vera and Brenda decided that it was time to move into a more activist phase (learning theme seven). Since parents and children were both talking about television commercials, the teachers decided to start there. They asked the families to record the commercials that their children saw most frequently. Then they showed these clips to the children and helped them to talk about what the advertisers were saying and how they made the products look so enticing. The teachers also had the children think about the roles that boys, girls, and people from different racial groups played in the commercials (learning theme five). To provide contrasting images, the teachers brought back the photographs of families who had many fewer material goods.

Brenda and Vera also had an evening meeting at which they showed the tapes and contrasting images to the parents. Spurred on by this meeting, a number of parents investigated groups that were trying to get legislation passed that would limit or eliminate commercials directed at young children. As they visited websites and received literature from these groups, parents became aware of some of the racist practices of advertisers such as targeting specific racial groups for particular products (for example, pitching high-priced sneakers and alcoholic beverages to young African American men). Almost without realizing it, a number of parents turned the corner and became activists. They connected with different groups on the Internet and started to go to meetings and write letters to newspapers, broadcasting companies, and national and state legislators. The children participated by providing pictures and stories about how commercials were dishonest and stereotyped.

As they became more involved, parents began to see the connections between the poverty that they had discussed earlier and the deeper structural inequities that fueled hyperactive consumption (sweatshops in poor countries, tax cuts that favored people such as themselves). As they learned more, a few parents began to question their personal priorities and the school admission and financial policies that effectively excluded children from lower-income families. These conversations made many families and staff members feel anxious and defensive, but they also forced people to begin to examine their roles in the larger social inequities.

As families began to understand the issues and join groups that were addressing them, they no longer felt helpless. Instead, they felt energized and determined to use their political and economic clout to make a difference. Of course, not everyone participated, but those who did created an excited buzz at the school that kept people thinking and talking about their values and priorities. As with all AB/MC work, it was messy and often difficult, but it was also alive, daring, and full of hope and enthusiasm.

And so the work continues . . .

Appendix A:
Guidelines for
Selecting Children's Books

Books provide excellent opportunities for children to explore their life experiences as well as the rich diversity among the many people on our planet. In a quality learning environment, children's literature enhances every child's sense of self and connections to the world.

However, some books may expose children to misinformation about themselves and others. Therefore, adults must scrutinize written material with a critical perspective. If possible, they should ask members of the group(s) represented in a book to review it for accuracy and representativeness. While a particular book may impressively address one aspect of diversity, it may also include stereotypical material about another aspect. We can decide to discard such a book, or we can use its flaws to nurture children's critical thinking. Furthermore, one book, even if excellent, can never depict the diversity within a group, so a range of stories and images are always necessary.

To help you make choices about selecting children's books, use these critical assessment steps (based on the work of the Council on Interracial Books for Children [CIBC, 1980]). These criteria would also apply to any electronic media including films or computer games.

ILLUSTRATIONS

Look for stereotypes. A stereotype is an oversimplified generalization about a particular identity group (e.g., gender, race, ethnicity, class, sexual orientation, ability/disability), which usually carries derogatory messages. People are objectified or de-humanized. As we suggested in Chapter 9 quickly list all the stereotypes you know about various groups of people, even if you do not believe them. This list will help you to recognize stereotypes when they appear. All books should depict people as genuine individuals with distinctive, rather than stereotypical, features. Use stereotypical images in books to engage children in critical thinking or simply eliminate those volumes from your collection.

Be alert for tokenism. Having only one example of any group—either in your book collection (e.g., one story about lower-income White children among many books about White middle/upper class families), or within a book (one African American child among many White children)—implies that the dominant group is universal and the "norm."

STORY LINES AND CHARACTERS

Check for stereotyped roles. Even if a book shows more visual diversity, the story line may carry messages of bias that may be obvious or quite subtle. Do the stories typically depict People of Color, female characters, low-income families, or people with disabilities as passive or needing help? Do they have to exhibit extraordinary qualities to gain acceptance and/or approval? How are problems presented, conceived, and resolved? Who typically causes a problem, and who resolves it? Your book collection needs a balance of different people in active and recipient roles. Are problems solved individualistically by one person or more collectively by a group of children and adults working together?

Be alert for biased views of different lifestyles. Do the lives of People of Color or poor White people in the story contrast unfavorably with the norm of White, middle-class suburban life? Are negative value judgments implied about cultures that differ from the dominant culture? Does the setting reflect current life or outdated assumptions about specific groups? Do the books in your collection depict diversity among people within a specific racial/ethnic group (e.g., range of family structures, living environments, economic class, and types of work, male/female roles within the family)?

Who are the heroes? Does your book collection include stories in which heroes are from a range of racial, economic, cultural, and gender groups? Does it include stories about people who are struggling for justice?

AUTHORS' AND ILLUSTRATORS' BACKGROUNDS AND PERSPECTIVES

All authors write from a cultural as well as from a personal context. Carefully read the biographical material on the jacket flap or back of the book. What qualifies the author or illustrator to deal with the subject? If the book is not about people or events similar to the author or illustrator's background and experiences, what specifically recommends them as creators of this book? What is the author's attitude toward her or his story characters? Do the images reflect respect and accuracy on the part of the illustrator? Do you have a balance of books by authors and illustrators that reflect a range of identities and experiences?

EFFECTS ON A CHILD'S SELF AND SOCIAL IDENTITIES

Will all of the children you serve see themselves and their family's way of life reflected in your book collection? See one or more characters with whom they can readily and positively identify? Does your overall collection reflect all of their backgrounds? Do your books reinforce or counteract messages that teach children to feel inferior or superior because of their skin color, gender, family income, able-bodylines, or type of family structure?

COPYRIGHT DATE

Copyright dates indicate the publication year, not the time of its writing (which might be 2 to 3 years previously). Although a recent copyright date is no guarantee of a book's relevance or sensitivity, copyright dates provide useful information. More children's books began to reflect the reality of our pluralistic society in the 1970s. Since then, many authors and illustrators have produced excellent books that reflect multiple aspects of diversity with accuracy and respect. When considering new books for your collection, begin with the most recently published ones and then continue with descending copyright dates.

SUGGESTED WEBSITES

Here are a few excellent websites to find suggestions for useful books, which are selected and updated by anti-bias/multicultural educators:

Teaching for Change,
    http://teachingforchange.org/publications/lists/earlychildhood

   Provides a regularly updated bibliography of anti-bias books for young children on a range of diversity and social justice topics.

The Children's Peace Education and Anti-Bias Library,
    www.childpeacebooks.org

   An interactive database permits you to look up books for young children by identity group, topics, or type of book.

Cooperative Children's Book Center, University of Wisconsin-Madison,
    www.education.wisc.edu/ccbc/books

   Lists of children's books pre-K through elementary school on several diversity topics, including categories such as "Family," "Labor," and "Spanish/English Bilingual." Check for age appropriateness for preschool children.

Always keep in mind the power of books—their words and their images—to nurture or to undermine children's sense of self and attitudes toward others.

Appendix B:
Organizations and Websites

A range of organizations offer resources for furthering your own development, professional work, and activism. The following selected list also leads to additional sites. Choose resources that meet your particular needs.

GROWTH AND ACTIVISM

American Civil Liberties Union, **www.aclu.org/immigrants-rights**: Among a wide range of civil rights activities, the ACLU takes education and legal actions to protect immigrant rights.

American Friends Service Committee, **www.afsc.org**: Programs related to economic and social justice, peace-building and demilitarization, and to youth in the United States and other countries.

Applied Research Center, **www.arc.org**: Public-policy research institute working on issues of race, racism, and social change in schools and in health-related institutions.

Center for New Community, **www.newcomm.org**: Education and community organizing for immigrants rights, anti-racism, and other social justice issues in rural areas and small cities.

Center for the Study of White American Culture, **www.euroamerican.org**: Resources and opportunities for discussions about the multifaceted issues of Whiteness.

Civil Rights Coalition for the 21st Century, **www.civilrights.org**: website of the Leadership Conference on Civil Rights and links to several other national organizations working on a range of civil rights issues.

Crossroads Antiracism Organizing & Training, **www.crossraodsantiracism.org**: Anti-racism work in faith-based, community and educational institutions. Resources for furthering learning.

Eliminating Racism and Claiming/Celebrating Equality, Kalamazoo, MI, **www.eracce.org**: Offers training and consulting to local educational and community groups.

Institute for Dismantling Racism (IDR), Winston-Salem, NC, **www.idrnc.org**: Educates, organizes, and supports people to develop anti-racist identity and build intentional anti-racist multicultural communities and long-term institutional change.

Leadership Conference on Civil and Human Rights, **www.civilrights.org/immigration**: Does educational, advocacy, public policy, and coalition group actions.

Let's Build a U.S. for All of Us: No Room for Racism, **www.usforallofus.org**: Network of White people working to counter racism and to stand with communities of color to build an inclusive democracy and equality for all.

Minnesota Collaborative Anti-Racism Initiative (MCARI), Saint Paul, MN, **www.mcari.org**: Provides consultation and training for non-profit institutions, business, community organizations, and colleges.

Newsreel, **www.newsreel.org**: Documentary, educational videos and DVDs addressing racism and other isms.

One Nation Working Together, **www.onenationworkingtogether.org**: Coalition of dozens of progressive organizations, organized to resist the efforts of right wing groups.

Poverty and Race Research Action Council, **www.prrac.org**: Generates and disseminates research on the relationship between race and poverty and policies and practices for local, state, and national advocacy groups.

Southern Poverty Law Center (SPLC), **www.splcenter.org**: Civil rights organization dedicated to fighting hate and bigotry, and to seeking justice for the most vulnerable members of society. Tracks and exposes the activities of hate groups and initiates law suits to protect their targets. Produces and distributes to schools, free of charge, documentary films, books, lesson plans, and other materials promoting tolerance and respect.

The White Anti-racist Community Action Network (WACAN), **www.wacan.org**: A protected online space to network, share in community, and act to transform our larger society to one that is racially just.

White Privilege Conference, **www.uccs.edu/~wpc/index.htm**: A yearly opportunity to examine systemic White privilege and develop strategies towards a more equitable world with a diverse group of people.

WORKING WITH CHILDREN

(Also see websites in Appendix A)

American Arab Anti-Discrimination Committee, **www.adc.org**: Material for supporting Arab American children and families and for teaching all children about Arab Americans.

California Tomorrow, **www.californiatomorrow.org**: Action research and resources for working with adults and children on issues of culture, language, immigration, and equity in schools.

Civil Rights Teaching, **www.civilrightsteaching.org**: Information to use with adults and to adapt for children.

Educational Equity Center at AED, Inc., **www.edequity.org**: Preschool to 3rd-grade resources for addressing equity issues related to disability, gender, and bullying.

Educators for Social Responsibility, **www.esrnational.org**: Resources on conflict resolution, violence prevention, and character education.

Gay, Lesbian, and Straight Education Network, **www.glsen.org**: Resources and information to assure equity in relation to sexual orientation and gender identity/expression.

Independent Living USA, **www.ilusa.com**: Information, news, resources, and numerous links for all issues related to children, adults, and families with disabilities.

National Association of Bilingual Education (NABE), **www.nabe.org**: Works to cultivate a multilingual multicultural society by supporting and promoting policy, programs, pedagogy, research, and professional development that yield academic success, value native language, lead to English proficiency, and respect cultural and linguistic diversity. Advocates for bilingual and English language learners and families.

National Association of Multicultural Education, **www.nameorg.org**: Annual conference, journal, and a listserv for keeping current on a range of diversity and equity educational work.

Oyate, **www.oyate.org**: A nonprofit Native organization working to see that the lives and histories of Native Americans are portrayed honestly, and that "all people will know our stories belong to us." Oyate does critical evaluation of books and curricula with Indian themes; conducts "Teaching Respect for Native Peoples" workshops and institutes; has a small resource center and reference library; and distributes children's, young adult, and teacher books and materials, with an emphasis on writing and illustration by Native people.

Rethinking Schools, **www.rethinkingschools.org**: Excellent journal on a range of educational equity issues. Curriculum ideas for working with elementary and high school students.

Syracuse Cultural Workers, **www.syrculturalworkers.com**: Social justice posters, bumper stickers, and pins.

Voices of Civil Rights, **www.voicesofcivilrights.org**: Personal accounts of Americans working to fulfill the promise of equality for all. Project of the AARP, Leadership Conference on Civil Rights, and Library of Congress.

Appendix C:
Selected Modern-Day
White Anti-Racism Activists

Name	Description	Period of Work	Source
Adams, Emmie Shrader	Grew up in Minnesota; worked in northern Mississippi organizing Black and White farmers to fight for their rights. On staff of Student Non-Violent Coordinating Committee (SNCC).	1961–1965	Curry et al., 2002
Addington, James	Co-founder, former co-director, and trainer with the Minnesota Collaborative Anti-Racism Initiative (MCARI), providing anti-racism consultation and training for non-profit institutions, business, community organizations, and colleges.	1990– present	www.mcari.org
Barndt, Joseph	Founder of Crossroads Ministry, now Crossroads. The organization engages in anti-racism education and organizing among faith-based congregations, community groups, and schools	1960– present	Barndt, 2007

Name	Description	Period of Work	Source
Bernstein, Hilda & Lionel (Rusty)	Life-long South African anti-apartheid activists and trusted colleagues of Nelson Mandela.	H: 1943–2002 L: 1938–2002	www.rusty-bernstein. com www. Guardian. co.uk/news/2006/ sep/18/ guardian obituaries.southafrica
Braden, Anne and Carl	Pioneering leaders, educators, and organizers against racist southern practices. Helped to found the Southern Organizing Committee and the Kentucky Alliance Against Racist & Political Repression.	C: 1954–1975 A: 1975–2006	Fosl, 2002
Brown, Babette	South African anti-apartheid activist and anti-racism educator and author in the United Kingdom. Created and led the Early Years Trainers Anti-Racism Network for 20 years. Currently, disseminates the persona doll technique in the UK and South Africa.	1950–present	www.persona-doll-training.org
Burlage, Dorothy Dawson	Dorothy influenced the White National Student Association to support the Civil Rights Movement. She organized in Texas for school desegregation, church activism, and voter registration.	1955–1970	Curry et al., 2002

Name	Description	Period of Work	Source
Campbell, Will D.	Challenged southern churches and Christians to support the ending of segregation and to establish civil rights for all. Organized interracial dialogue groups. Considered a "spiritual mentor" to the Whites in the Freedom Movement (Civil Rights Movement).	1950–1965	Curry et al., 2002
Chambers, Brad	Pioneered the movement for bias-free children's books and for children's book authors of color through the Council on Interracial Books for Children (CIBC) and its Bulletin.	1964–1984	
Christos-Rodgers, Jyaphia	New Orleans organizer, educator, sociologist, and community builder. Co-founder of the post-Katrina Rebirth Volunteer Center. Board Chair of the Center for Ethical Living and Social Justice Renewal.	1990–2010	www.crossroads antiracism.org
Curry, Constance	Active in the South before the first sit-ins, she helped organize the first Student Non-violent Coordinating Committee (SNCC) office. Pioneered work with White churches, student organizations, and White women's groups to promote school desegregation in the south.	1958–1966	Curry et al., 2002

Name	Description	Period of Work	Source
Dees, Morris	Co-founder of the Southern Poverty Law Center (1971), Dees has been its chief trial lawyer and conceptual leader. The Southern Poverty Law Center keeps track of and fights White-supremacist hate organizations in the courts. Publishes resources for educators through its magazine *Teaching for Tolerance*.	1970–present	www.SPLCenter.org
Del Pozzo, Theresa	Helped found the Northern Student Movement, an anti-racist group active against northern racism and raising funds for the Southern Non-Violent Coordinating Committee (SNCC).	1955–1970	Curry et al., 2002
First, Ruth	Life-long South African anti-apartheid activist and trusted colleague of Nelson Mandela. Assassinated by a mail bomb sent by the South African nationalist (apartheid) special forces.	1949–1982	www.anc.org
Gunderson, Margaret; Smeltzer, Mary; Ferguson, Lois and Charles—and 190 others	White teachers who taught school in the Japanese-American Internment Camps set up in the United States during World War II. They faced army and community hostility.	1940–1945	*L.A. Times*, 2/5/05, p. B1

Name	Description	Period of Work	Source
Goodman, Andrew	Along with James Chaney (African American) and Michael Schwerner, worked with the Mississippi Summer voting rights drive in 1964. Murdered by Ku Klux Klan.	1960–1964	Takaki, 1993
Greenberg, Jack	Head of the NAACP Legal Defense and Education Fund.	1947–1963	Takaki, 1993
Hayden, Casey	Worked with the Mississippi Freedom Democratic Party (MFDP) delegation at the 1964 Democratic Convention, by helping to organize committees in every Mississippi county. Later worked in Atlanta city programs when Andrew Young was mayor.	1961–1990	Curry et al., 2002
Hill, Herbert	Director of NAACP's labor drives in the South.	1949–1954	Takaki, 1993
Horton, Myles	Founder of the pioneering Highlander Center (Tennessee), which does anti-racist, labor, and environmental justice education and organizing in the South. Among many others, Rosa Parks studied at Highlander.	1940–1990	Horton et al., 1998
Lane, Jane	Long-time policy advocate, author, and educator, Jane was an education officer at the United Kingdom's Commission for Racial Equality, London.	1964–present	Lane, 2008

Name	Description	Period of Work	Source
Liuzzo, Viola Gregg	Previously not an activist, she decided to help with the Selma-to-Montgomery (Alabama) March and provide transportation to the marchers in her old station wagon. Murdered by the Ku Klux Klan.	1962	Brown, 2002
Mac Naughton, Glenda	Australian education activist, teacher, innovative researcher, author, and founder/director, Centre for Equity and Innovation in Early childhood (CEIEC), at the University of Melbourne.	1985–present	Mac Naughton & Davis, 2009
Olsen, Laurie	Co-founder and former executive director of California Tomorrow, which produces outstanding resources for combating racism in schools and for implementing culturally relevant and bilingual education for children.	1985–2009	www.california tomorrow.org
Schwerner, Michael	*See* Goodman, Andrew.		
Slovo, Joe	Life-long anti-apartheid leader, served in President Nelson Mandela's cabinet until his death from cancer. Mandela wrote, "Joe Slovo did not only interpret the world, he helped change it."	1942–1995	Slovo, 1995

Name	Description	Period of Work	Source
Thrasher, Sue	Active in the Student United Nations and the Methodist Student Union, she helped start the Southern Strategy Organizing Committee, a group of White activists and was the first archivist at Highlander Center.	1962–1989	Curry et al., 2002
Wilkinson, Frank	Pioneer in creating public housing in Los Angeles; fought for integrated housing. Worked in several multiracial coalitions to end segregation in all aspects of public life.	1950–1980	Brown, 2002
Zinn, Howard	Historian of social justice movements, current and historical. His best known, extensively selling book is *The People's History of the United States: 1492–Present*.	1950–2010	www.howardzinn.org

References

Aboud, F. E., & Amato, M. (2001). Developmental and socialization influences on intergroup bias. In R. Brown & S. L. Gaerther (Eds.), *Blackwell handbook of social psychology: Intergroup processes* (pp. 65–85). Oxford, UK: Blackwell Publishers.

Aboud, F. E., & Doyle, A. B. (1995). The development of in-group pride in Black Canadians. *Journal of Cross Cultural Psychology, 26*(3), 243–254.

Aboud, F. E., & Doyle, A. B. (1996a). Does talk of race foster prejudice or tolerance in children? *Canadian Journal of Behavioural Science, 28*(3), 161–170.

Aboud, F. E., & Doyle, A. B. (1996b). Parental and peer influences on children's racial attitudes. *International Journal of Intercultural Relations, 20*(3/4), 371–383.

Aboud, F. E., & Levy, S. R. (2000). Interventions to reduce prejudice and discrimination in children and adolescents. In S. Oskamp (Ed.), *Reducing prejudice and discrimination* (pp. 269–294). Mahwah, NJ: Erlbaum.

Acuña, R. (2011). *Occupied America: A history of Chicanos* (7th ed.). New York: Longman.

Allen, T. W. (1994). *The invention of the White race: Racial oppression and social control* (Vol. 1). London: Verso.

Allport, G. (1979). *The nature of prejudice* (25th anniversary ed.). New York: Perseus.

Alvarado, C., Derman-Sparks, L., & Ramsey, P. G. (1999). *In our own way: How anti-bias work shapes our lives.* St. Paul, MN: Redleaf Press.

Aptheker, H. (1993). *Anti-racism in U.S. history: The first 200 years.* Westport, CT: Praeger.

Archibold, R. (2010, April 23). Arizona Enacts Stringent Law on Immigration. *New York Times.* Available at http://www.nytimes.com/2010/04/24/us/politics/24immig.htm

Baker, C. (2007). *A parent's and teacher's guide to bilingualism* (2nd ed.). Buffalo, NY: Multilingual Matters.

Baker, V. C. (2010). *A window into four children's white identity: Exploring racial identity development among White children in a diverse preschool classroom located within a predominantly White community* [a project submitted in partial fulfillment of the requirements for the degree of Master of Arts in human development]. Pacific Oaks College, Pasadena, CA.

Banaji, M. R., Baron, A. S., Dunham, Y., & Olson, K. (2008). The development of intergroup social cognition: Early emergence, implicit nature, and sensitivity to group status. In S. R. Levy & M. Killen (Eds.), *Intergroup attitudes and relations in childhood through adulthood* (pp. 66–86). New York: Oxford.

Barbarin, O., & Crawford, G. (2006, November). Acknowledging and reducing stigmatization of African American boys. *Young Children, 61*(6), 79–87.

Barndt, J. (2007). *Understanding and dismantling racism: The twenty-first century challenge to White America*. Minneapolis, MN: FortressAugsberg.

Barrera, R. (2005). Visit the world with young children. *Scholastic Early Childhood Today, 20*, 36–40.

Barrett, J. R., & Roediger, D. (2002). How White people became White. In P. S. Rothenberg (Ed.), *White privilege: Essential readings on the other side of racism* (pp. 29–34). New York: Worth.

Beirich, H. (2010). *Essay: the anti-immigrant movement*. Available at http://www.splcenter.org/get-informed/intellinece-files/ideoglgoy/anti-immigrant/

Bernstein, H. (1967/2004). *The world that was ours*. London: Persephone Books.

Bigler, R. S., Arthur, A. E., Hughes, J. M., & Patterson, J. M. (2008). The politics of race and gender: Children's perception of discrimination and the U.S. presidency. *Analysis of Social Issues and Public Policy, 81*(1), 83–112.

Bigler, R. S., & Hughes, J. M. (2009). The nature and origins of children's racial attitudes. In J. A. Banks (Ed.), *Routledge companion to multicultural education* (pp. 186–199). London/New York: Routledge.

Bigler, R. S., Jones, L. C., & Lobliner, D. B. (1997). Social categorization and the formation of intergroup attitudes in children. *Child Development, 68*(3), 530–543.

Bigler, R. S., & Liben, L. S. (1993). A cognitive-developmental approach to racial stereotyping and reconstructive memory in Euro-American children. *Child Development, 64*, 1507–1518.

Bigler, R. S., & Liben, L. S. (2007). Developmental intergroup theory: Explaining and reducing children's social stereotyping and prejudice. *Current Directions in Psychological Science, 16*, 162–171.

Bisson, J. (1997). *Celebrate! An anti-bias guide to enjoying holidays in early childhood programs*. St. Paul, MN: Redleaf Press.

Boutte, G. (2002, Spring). The critical literacy process: Guidelines for examining books. *Childhood Education, 78*(3), 147–152.

Brodkin, K. (1998). *How Jews became White folks and what that says about race in America*. New Brunswick, NJ: Rutgers University Press.

Brodkin, K. (2002). How Jews became White folks. In P. S. Rothenberg (Ed.), *White privilege: Essential readings on the other side of racism* (pp. 35–48). New York: Worth.

Bronson, P., & Merryman, A. (2009, September 14). See baby discriminate. *Newsweek*, pp. 53–59. Available at www.newsweek.com/2009/09/04/see-baby-discriminsate.html

Brown, B. (1998). *Unlearning discrimination in the early years*. London: Trentham Books.

Brown, B. (2001). *Combating discrimination: Persona dolls in action*. London: Trentham Books.

Brown, C. S. (2002). *Refusing racism: White allies and the struggle for civil rights*. New York: Teachers College Press.

Brown, C. S. (2008). Children's perceptions of racial and ethnic discrimination: Differences across children and contexts. In S. M. Quintana & C. McKown (Eds.), *Handbook of race, racism, and the developing child* (pp. 133–153). Hoboken, NJ: Wiley.

Brown, N. (1998, August). *The impact of culture on the education of young children with special needs*. Paper presented at the biennial meeting of the Organization Mondiale de l'Education Preescolaire, Copenhagen, Denmark.

Browser, B., & Hunt, R. (1981). *Impacts of racism on White Americans*. Beverly Hills, CA: Sage.

Buhin, L., & Vera, E. M. (2009). Preventing racism and promoting social justice: Person-centered and environment-centered interventions. *Journal of Primary Prevention, 30,* 43–59.

Bush, M. E. L. (2004). *Breaking the code of good intentions: Everyday forms of Whiteness*. New York: Rowan & Littlefield.

Cadwell, L. B. (2003). *Bringing learning to life: The Reggio approach to early childhood education*. New York: Teachers College Press.

Carr, J., & Kutty, N. (Eds.). (2008). *Segregation: The rising costs for America*. New York: Routledge.

Carter, M., & Curtis, D. (1997). *Training teachers: A harvest of theory and practice*. St. Paul, MN: Redleaf Press.

Castelli, L., De Amicis, L., & Sherman, S. J. (2007). The loyal member effect: On the preference for ingroup members who engage in exclusive relations with the ingroup. *Developmental Psychology, 43*(6), 1347–1359.

Castelli, L., De Dea, C., & Nesdale, D. (2008). Learning social attitudes: Children's sensitivity to the nonverbal behaviors of adult models during interracial interactions. *Personality Social Psychology Bulletin, 34,* 1504–1513.

Chafel, J. A. (1997). Children's views of poverty: a review of research and implications for teaching. *The Educational Forum, 61,* 360–371.

Chafel, J. A., Flint, A. S., Hammel, J., & Pomeroy, K. H. (2007). Young children, social issues and critical literacy: Stories of teachers and researchers. *Young Children, 62*(1), 73–71.

Chafel, J. A., & Neitzel, C. (2005). Young children's ideas about the nature, causes, justifications, and alleviation of poverty. *Early Childhood Research Quarterly, 20*(4), 433–450.

Chang, H. N.-L., Femeneall, T., Louise, N., Murdock B., & Pell, E. (2000). *Walking the walk: Principles for building community capacity for equity and diversity*. Oakland, CA: California Tomorrow.

Chang, H. N.-L., Muckelroy, A., & Pulido-Tobiassen, D. (1996). *Looking in, looking out: Redefining childcare and early education in a diverse society*. Oakland, CA: California Tomorrow.

Chennault, R. E. (1998). Giving Whiteness a black eye: An interview with Michael Erik Dyson. In J. L. Kincheloe, S. R. Steinberg, N. M. Rodriguez, & R. E. Chennault (Eds.), *White reign: Deploying Whiteness in America* (pp. 299–328). New York: St. Martin's Griffin.

Clark, K. B. (1963). *Prejudice and your child*. Boston: Beacon Press.

Clark, K. B., & Clark, M. P. (1947). Racial identification and preference in Negro children. In T. M. Newcomb & E. L. Hartley (Eds.), *Readings in social psychology* (pp. 169–178). New York: Free Press.

Cobb, D. (Au), Cobb, D., & Fowler, L. (Eds.). (2007). *Beyond Red power: American Indian politics and activism since 1900*. Santa Fe, NM: School for Advanced Research.

Cohen, R. (2010, September 10). *A call to religious tolerance.* Available at www. splcenter.org

Colby, A., & Damon, W. (1992). *Some do care: Contemporary lives of moral commitment.* New York: Free Press.

Coles, R. (1977). *Privileged ones: The well-off and the rich in America.* Boston: Little, Brown.

Connolly, P. (1995). Racism, masculine peer-group relation and the schooling of African/Caribbean Infant Boys. *British Journal of Sociology of Education, 16*(1), 75–92.

Connolly, P., Fitzpatrick, S., Gallagher, T., & Harris, P. (2006). Addressing diversity and inclusion in the early years in conflict-affected societies: A case study of the media initiative for children—Northern Ireland. *International Journal of Early Years Education, 14*(3), 263–278.

Connolly, P., & Hosken, K. (2006). The general and specific effects of educational programmes aimed at promoting awareness of and respect for diversity among young children. *International Journal of Early Years Education, 14*(2), 107–126.

Cose, E. (2010, June 18). The race gap in the economic recovery. *Newsweek.* Available at www.newsweek.com/2010/06/18/the-race-gap-in-the-economic-recovery. html

Cristol, D., & Gimbert, B. (2008). Racial perceptions of young children: A review of literature post-1999. *Early Childhood Education Journal, 36,* 201–207.

Cronin, S., Derman-Sparks, L., Henry, S., Olatunji, C., & York, S. (1998). *Future vision, present work: Learning from the Culturally Relevant Anti-Bias Leadership Project.* St. Paul, MN: Redleaf.

Cross, W. E., Jr. (1985). Black identity: Rediscovering the distinction between personal identity and reference group orientation. In M. B. Spencer, G. K. Brookins, & W. R. Allen (Eds.), *Beginnings: The social and affective development of black children* (pp. 155–171). Hillsdale, NJ: Lawrence Erlbaum Associates.

Cross, W. E., Jr. (1991). *Shades of Black: Diversity in African-American identity.* Philadelphia: Temple University Press.

Cross, W. E., & Cross, T. B. (2008). Theory, research and methods. In S. Quotana & C. McKown (Eds.), *Handbook of race, racism and the developing child* (pp. 154–181). Hoboken, NJ: Wiley.

Crossroads. (1996). Ending racism: Working for a racism free 21st century [DVD]. Matteson, IL: Crossroads Organizing & Training.

Council on Interracial Books for Children (CIBC). (1980). Ten quick ways to analyze children's books. In *Guidelines for selecting bias-free textbooks and storybooks* (pp. 24–26). New York: Author.

Cowhey, M. (2006). *Black ants and Buddhists: Thinking critically and teaching differently in the primary grades.* Portland, ME: Stenhouse.

Csikszentmihalyi, M. (1999). If we are so rich, why aren't we happy? *American Psychologist, 54,* 821–827.

Csikszentmihalyi, M., & Schneider, B. (2000). *Becoming adults: How teenagers prepare for the world of work.* New York: Basic Books.

Curry, C., Browning, J., Burlage, D. D., & Patch, P. (2002). *Deep in our hearts: Nine White women in the freedom movement.* Athens: University of Georgia Press.

Damon, W. (1980). Patterns of change in children's social reasoning: A 2-year longitudinal study. *Child Development, 51*, 1010–1017.

Day, J. A. E. (1995, June). Multicultural resources in preschool provision—An observational study. *Early Child Development and Care, 110*, 47–68.

de Marquez, T. M. (2002). Creating world peace, one classroom at a time. *Young Children, 57*(6), 90–93.

Dees, M. (2001). *A lawyer's journey: The Morris Dees story.* Washington, DC: American Bar Association.

Dees, M. (2010, March 2). Radical right catches fire. *SPLC Newsletter*, p. 1.

Delpit, L., & Dowdy, J. (Eds.). (2002). *The skin that we speak.* New York: New Press.

Derman-Sparks, L., & A.B.C. Task Force. (1989). *Anti-bias curriculum: Tools for empowering young children.* Washington, DC: National Association for the Education of Young Children.

Derman-Sparks, L., & Edwards, J. O. (2010). *Anti-bias education for young children & ourselves.* Washington, DC: National Association for the Education of Young Children.

Derman-Sparks, L., & Phillips, C. B. (1997). *Teaching/learning anti-racism: A developmental approach.* New York: Teachers College Press.

Feagin, J. (2000). *Racist America: Roots, current realities, and future reparations.* New York: Routledge.

Foley, N. (2002). Becoming Hispanic: Mexican Americans and Whiteness. In P. S. Rothenberg (Ed.), *White privilege: Essential readings on the other side of racism* (pp. 49–59). New York: Worth Publishers.

Fosl, C. (2002). *Subversive Southerner: Anne Braden & the struggle for racial justice.* Lexington: University Press of Kentucky.

Fox, D. J., & Jordan, V. B. (1973). Racial preference and identification of Black, American Chinese, and White children. *Genetic Psychology Monographs, 88*, 229–286.

Furnham, A., & Stacey, B. (1991). *Young people's understanding of society.* New York: Routledge.

Glover, A. (1996). Children and bias. In B. Creaser & E. Dau (Eds.), *The anti-bias approach in early childhood* (pp. 1–16). Sydney, Australia: Harper Educational.

Goodman, M. (1952). *Race awareness in young children.* Cambridge, MA: Addison-Wesley.

Gordon, M. (2006). The power of empathy. In R. Cavoukian & S. Olfman (Eds.), *Child honoring: How to turn this world around* (pp. 153–162). Westport, CT: Praeger.

Gossett, T. F. (1963). *Race: The history of an idea in America.* New York: Schocken Books.

Guglielmo, J., & Salerno, S. (2003). *Are Italians White? How race is made in America.* New York: Routledge.

Hayashi, A., Karasawa, M., & Tobin, J. (2009). The Japanese preschool's pedagogy of feeling: Cultural strategies for supporting young children's emotional development. *Ethos, 37*(1), 32–49.

Hayes, C., & Juárez, B. G. (2009). You showed your Whiteness: You don't get a "good" White medal. *International Journal of Qualitative Studies in Education, 22*(6), 729–744.

Helms, J. E. (Ed.). (1990). *Black and White racial identity: Theory, research, and practice.* Westport, CT: Greenwood Press.

Hill, L. D. (2001). *Connecting kids: Exploring diversity together.* Gabriola Island, British Columbia, Canada: New Society.

Hirschfeld, L. A. (2008). Children developing conceptions of race. In S. M. Quintana & C. McKown (Eds.), *Handbook of race, racism and the developing child* (pp. 37–54). Hoboken, NJ: Wiley.

Hoffman, E. (2004). *Magic capes, amazing powers: Transforming superhero play in the classroom.* St. Paul, MN: Redleaf Press.

Hoffman, M. (2000). *Empathy and moral development: Implications for caring and justice.* Cambridge, UK: Cambridge University Press.

Horton, M., with Kohl, J., & Kohl, H. (1998). *The long haul: An autobiography.* New York: Teachers College Press.

Howard, G. R. (1999). *We can't teach what we don't know.* New York: Teachers College Press.

Husband, T. (2008). He's too young to learn about that stuff: An examination of critical anti-racist pedagogy in an early childhood classroom [Doctoral dissertation for Ohio State University]. *DAI Section A: Humanities and Social Sciences, 69* (5-A), pp. 1642.

Ibish, H. (2008). *Report on hate crimes and discrimination against Arab Americans: 2003–2007.* Washington, DC: American Arab Anti-Discrimination Committee.

Ignatiev, N. (1995). *How the Irish became White.* New York: Routledge.

Jacobson, T. (2003). *Confronting our discomforts: Clearing the way for anti-bias in early childhood.* Portsmouth, NH: Heinemann.

Johnson, D. W., & Johnson, R. T. (2000). The three Cs of reducing prejudice and discrimination. In S. Okamp (Ed.), *Reducing prejudice and discrimination* (pp. 239–268). Mahwah, NJ: Lawrence Erlbaum Associates.

Jordan, P. E., & Hernandez-Reif, M. (2009). Re-examination of young children's racial attitudes and skin tone preferences. *Journal of Black Psychology, 35*(3), 388–403.

Kareem, N. (2010). Why parents need to talk to their kids about race. *Race in America.* Available at http://race.change.org

Katz, L. G., & McClellan, D. E. (1998). *Fostering children's social competence: The teacher's role.* Washington, DC: National Association for the Education of Young Children.

Katz, P. A. (1976). The acquisition of racial attitudes in children. In P. A. Katz (Ed.), *Towards the elimination of racism* (pp. 125–154). New York: Pergamon.

Katz, P. A. (2003). Racists or tolerant multiculturalists? How do they begin? *American Psychologist, 58*(11), 897–909.

Katz, P. A., & Kofkin, J. A. (1997). Race, gender, and young children. In S. Luthar, J. Burack, D. Cicchetti, & J. Weisz (Eds.), *Developmental perspectives on risk and pathology* (pp. 51–74). New York: Cambridge University Press.

Kaye, J. (2010). *Moving millions: How coyote capitalism fuels global immigration.* Hoboken, NJ: Wiley.

Kelly, D. J., Liu, S., Ge, L., Quinn, P. C., Slater, A. M., Lee, K., et al. (2007). Cross-race preferences for same-race faces extend beyond the African versus Caucasian contrast in 3-month-old infants. *Infancy, 11,* 87–95.

Kendall, F. (1996). *Diversity in the classroom: New approaches to the education of young children* (2nd ed.). New York: Teachers College Press.

Kendall, F. (2006). *Understanding white privilege: Creating pathways to authentic relationships across race.* New York: Routledge; Francis & Taylor Group

Kincheloe, J. L., Steinberg, S. R., Rodriguez, N. M., & Chennault, R. E. (1998). *White reign: Deploying Whiteness in America.* New York: St. Martin's Griffin.

Kirchner, G. (2000). *Children's games from around the world* (2nd ed.). Boston: Allyn & Bacon.

Kissinger, K. (1994). *All the colors we are: The story of how we get our skin color.* St. Paul, MN: Redleaf Press.

Kivel, P. (2002). *Uprooting racism: How White people can work for racial justice* (Rev. ed.). Gabriola Island, B.C., Canada: New Society.

Kline, S. (1993). *Out of the garden: Toys and children's culture in the age of TV marketing.* London: Verso.

Knowles, L., & Prewitt, K. (Eds.). (1969). *Institutional racism in America.* Englewood Cliffs, NJ: Prentice Hall.

Kozol, J. (1991). *Savage inequalities.* New York: Crown.

Krejci, J. M. (2008). Allies, activists, and advocates: A dissertation on the analysis of the experiences and processes that led thirteen White men to *anti*-racist work. *Dissertation Abstracts International: Section B: The Sciences and Engineering, 68*(10-b), 7024.

Lalley, J. (2008). Activism brings us power: An interview with Hilda Magana. In A. Pelo (Ed.), *Rethinking Early Childhood Education* (pp. 183–186). Milwaukee, WI: Rethinking Schools.

Lane, J. (2008). *Young children and racial justice.* London: National Children's Bureau.

Leahy, R. (1983). The development of the conception of social class. In R. Leahy (Ed.), *The child's construction of inequality* (pp. 79–107). New York: Academic Press.

Leahy, R. (1990). The development of concepts of economic and social inequality. *New Directions for Child Development, 46,* 107–120.

Lee, C. E., & Lee, D. (2001). Kindergarten geography: Teaching diversity to young people. *Journal of Geography, 100*(5), 152–157.

Lee, R. (2004). *Developing measures to learn how multicultural activities affect children's attitudes about race and social class.* Senior Honors Thesis, Mount Holyoke College.

Lee, R., Ramsey, P. G., & Sweeney, B. (2008). Engaging young children in activities and conversations about race and social class. *Young Children, 63*(6), 68–76.

Leonardo, Z. (2007). The war on schools: NCLB, nation creation and the educational construction of Whiteness. *Race, Ethnicity and Education, 10*(3), 261–278.

Levin, D. (2003). *Teaching young children in violent times: Building a peaceable classroom.* New York: Educators for Social Responsibility.

Levitas, D. (2010, April). Essay: The White nationalist movement. Southern Poverty Law Center. Available at www.splcenter.org

Levy, S. R., Karafantis, D. M., & Ramirez, L. (2008). A social-developmental perspective on lay theories and intergroup relations. In S. R. Levy & M. Killen (Eds.), *Intergroup attitudes and relations in childhood through adulthood* (pp. 146–156). New York: Oxford.

Lewis, A. E. (2001). There is no race in the school yard: Color-blind ideology in an all-White school. *American Educational Research Journal, 38*(4), 781–811.

Linn, S. (2004). *Consuming kids: Protecting our children from the onslaught of marketing and advertising.* New York: Anchor Books (Random House).

Linn, S. (2009). *The case for make believe: Saving play in a commercialized world.* New York: New Press.

Lipsitz, G. (2002). The possessive investment in Whiteness. In P. S. Rothenberg (Ed.), *White privilege: Essential readings on the other side of racism* (pp. 61–85). New York: Worth.

Loewen, J. (1995). *Lies my teacher told me.* New York: Simon & Schuster.

Loewen, J. (1999). *Lies across America: What our historical sites get wrong.* New York: Simon & Schuster.

Luthar, S. S., & Becker, B. E. (2002). Privileged but pressured? A study of affluent youth. *Child Development, 73*(5), 1593–1610.

Lyman, K. (2008). Lessons from a garden spider: How Charlotte transformed my classroom. In A. Pelo (Ed.), *Rethinking early childhood education* (pp. 139–143). Milwaukee, WI: Rethinking Schools.

Mac Naughton, G. (2004). Learning from young children about social diversity: Challenges for our equity practices in the classroom. In A. Van Keulen (Ed.), *Young children aren't biased, are they?!* (pp. 65–75). Amsterdam: SWP.

Mac Naughton, G., & Davis, K. (2001). Beyond "othering": Rethinking approaches to teachering young Anglo-Australian children about indigenous Australian. *Contemporary Issues in Early Childhood, 2*(1), 83–93.

Mac Naughton, G., & Davis, K. (Eds.). (2009). *Race and early childhood education: An international approach to identity, politics, and pedagogy.* New York: Palgrave Macmillan.

Mac Naughton, G., Davis, K., & Smith, K. (2009). Discourses of "race" in early childhood: From cognition to power. In G. Mac Naughton & K. Davis (Eds.), *Race and early childhood education: An international approach to identity, politics, and pedagogy* (pp. 17–30). New York: Palgrave Macmillan.

Marsh, M. M. (1992). Implementing anti-bias curriculum in the kindergarten classroom. In S. A. Kessler & B. B. Swadener (Eds.), *Reconceptualizing the early childhood curriculum: Beginning the dialogue* (pp. 267–288). New York: Teachers College Press.

Mazzei, L. (2008). Silence speaks: Whiteness revealed in the absence of voice. *Teaching and Teacher Education, 24*, 1125–1136.

McDonald, J. P., Mohr, N., Dichter, A., & McDonald, E. C. (2007). *The power of protocols: An educator's guide to better practice* (2nd ed.). New York: Teachers College Press.

McIntosh, P. (1995). White privilege and male privilege: A personal account of coming to see correspondences through work in women's studies. In M. L. Anderson & P. H. Collins (Eds.), *Race, class, and gender: An anthology* (pp. 76–87). Belmont, CA: Wadsworth.

McIntyre, A. (1997). *Making meaning of Whiteness: Exploring racial identity with White teachers.* Albany: State University of New York Press.

McKinney, K. D. (2005). *Being white: Stories of race and racism.* New York: Routledge.

McKissack, F. (2009). We still aren't in a post-racial society. *Rethinking Schools, 23*(2), 32.

McLoyd, V. C., & Ceballo, R. (1998). Conceptualizing and assessing the economic context: Issues in the study of race and child development. In V. C. McLoyd

& L. Steinberg (Eds.), *Studying minority adolescents: Conceptual, methodological, and theoretical issues* (pp. 251–278). Mahwah, NJ: Lawrence Erlbaum.

Media Education Foundation. (2009). *Consuming kids: The commercialization of childhood* (DVD). Northampton, MA: Author.

Mednick, L. G., & Ramsey, P. G. (2008). Peers, power and privilege: The social world of a second grade. *Rethinking Schools, 23,* 27–31.

Memmi, A. (1965). *The colonizer and the colonized.* Boston: Beacon Press.

Mendoza, J., & Reese, D. (2001). Examining multicultural picture books for the early childhood classroom: Possibilities and pitfalls. *Early Childhood Research & Practice, 3*(1), 1–38.

Monteiro, M. B., de França, D. X., & Rodrigues, R. (2009). The development of intergroup bias in childhood: How social norms can shape children's racial behaviours. *International Journal of Psychology, 44*(1), 29–39.

Morland, J. K. (1962). Racial acceptance and preference of nursery school children in a southern city. *Merrill-Palmer Quarterly, 8,* 271–280.

Nesdale, D. (2008). Peer group rejection and children's intergroup prejudice. In S. R. Levy & M. Killen (Eds.), *Intergroup attitudes and relations in childhood through adulthood* (pp. 32–46). New York: Oxford.

Nesdale, D., Durkin, K., Maass, A., & Griffiths, J. (2005). Threat, group identification, and children's ethnic prejudice. *Social Development, 14,* 189–205.

Nesdale, D., Maass, A., Durkin, K., & Griffiths, J. (2005). Group norms, threat, and children's racial prejudice. *Child Development, 76*(3), 652–663.

Nesdale, D., Miller, E., Duffy, A., & Griffiths, J. A. (2009). Group membership, group norms, empathy, and young children's intentions to aggress. *Aggressive Behavior, 35,* 244–258.

Newman, M. A., Liss, M. B., & Sherman, F. (1983). Ethnic awareness in children: Not a unitary concept. *Journal of Genetic Psychology, 143,* 103–112.

Nimmo, J., & Hallett, B. (2008). Childhood in the garden: A place to encounter natural and social diversity. *Young Children, 63*(1), 32–38.

O'Brien, E. (2001). *Whites confront racism: Antiracists and their paths to action.* Lanham, MD: Rowman & Littlefield.

Omi, M., & Winant, H. (1986). *Racial formation in the United States.* New York: Routledge & Kegan Paul.

Oppenheimer, A. (2010). *Six questions for supporters of Arizona law.* Available at http://www.miamiherald.com/2010/05/15/1631828

Orlick, T. (1978). *The cooperative sports and games book: Challenge without competition.* New York: Pantheon.

Orlick, T. (1982). *The second cooperative sports and games book: Over 200 brand-new cooperative games for kids and adults and both.* Ann Arbor, MI: North American Students of Cooperation.

Parker, R., & Smith Chambers, P. (2005). *The anti-racist cookbook: A recipe guide for conversations about race that goes beyond covered dishes and "Kum-Bah-Ya."* Roselle, NJ: Crandall, Dostie & Douglas Books.

Patterson, M., & Bigler, R. (2007). Effects of physical atypicality on children's social identities and intergroup attitudes. *International Journal of Behavioral Development, 31*(5), 433–444.

Pelo, A. (Ed.). (2008). *Rethinking early childhood education.* Milwaukee, WI: Rethinking Schools.

Pelo, A., & Davidson, F. (2000). *That's not fair: A teacher's guide to activism with young children*. St. Paul, MN: Redleaf Press.

Perkins, D. M., & Mebert, C. J. (2005). Efficacy of multicultural education for preschool children: A domain specific approach. *Journal of Cross-Cultural Psychology, 3*, 497–512.

Picower, B. (2009). The unexamined Whiteness of teaching: How White teachers maintain and enact dominant racial ideologies. *Race, Ethnicity, and Education, 12*(2), 197–215.

Porter, J. D. (1971). *Black child, White child: The development of racial attitudes*. Cambridge, MA: Harvard University Press.

Potok, M. (2010, Spring). Rage on the right. *SPLC Intelligence Report, 137*, 1–3.

Quintana, S. M., & McKown, C. (2008). Introduction: Race, racism, and the developing child. In S. M. Quintana & C. McKown (Eds.), *Handbook of race, racism, and the developing child* (pp. 1–15). Hoboken, NJ: Wiley.

Quintero, E. P. (2004). *Problem-posing with multicultural children's literature: Developing critical early childhood curricula*. New York: Peter Lang.

Radke, M., & Trager, H. G. (1950). Children's perceptions of the social roles of Negroes and Whites. *Journal of Psychology, 29*, 3–33.

Ramsey, P. G. (1991a). The salience of race in young children growing up in an all-White community. *Journal of Educational Psychology, 83*, 28–34.

Ramsey, P. G. (1991b). Young children's awareness and understanding of social class differences. *Journal of Genetic Psychology, 152*, 71–82.

Ramsey, P. G. (2004). *Teaching and learning in a diverse world* (3rd ed.). New York: Teachers College Press.

Ramsey, P. G., & Myers, L. C. (1990). Salience of race in young children's cognitive, affective and behavioral responses to social environments. *Journal of Applied Developmental Psychology, 11*, 49–67.

Roediger, D. (1991). *The wages of Whiteness: Race and the making of the American working class*. London: Verso.

Roediger, D. (2005). *Working toward Whiteness: How America's immigrants became White*. New York: Basic Books.

Rogers, R., & Mosley, M. (2006). Racial literacy in a second-grade classroom: Critical race theory, Whiteness studies, and literacy research. *Reading Research Quarterly, 41*(4), 462–495.

Rogovin, P. (1998). *Classroom interviews: A world of learning*. Portsmouth, NH: Heinemann.

Rosenfield, D., & Stephan, W. G. (1981). Intergroup relations among children. In S. S. Brehm, S. M. Kassin, & F. X. Gibbons (Eds.), *Developmental social psychology* (pp. 271–297). New York: Oxford University Press.

Rothenberg, P. S. (2002). *White privilege: Essential readings on the other side of racism*. New York: Worth.

Rotner, S., & Kelly, S. (2009). *Shades of people*. New York: Holiday House.

SantaCruz, N. (2010, May 12). Arizona ethnic studies ban OKd as law. *New York Times*, p. A2.

Satterlee, D. J., & Cormons, G. D. (2008). Sparking interest in nature—family style. *Young Children, 63*(1), 16–20.

Sauer, A. (2009). *Barack Obama, racism and the internet: An annotated gallery*.

Available at http://www.theawl.com/2009/09/barack-obama-and-racism-an-annotated-gallery

Schor, J. B. (2004). *Born to buy*. New York: Scribner.

Sharp, A. (2006). How to educate the emotions in the context of the classroom community inquiry. In M. Schleifer & C. Martiny (Eds.), *Talking to children about responsibility and emotions* (pp. 151–159). Calgary, Alberta, Canada: Detselig Enterprises.

Skattebol, J. (2003). Dark, dark and darker: Children's negotiations of identity. *Contemporary Issues in Early Childhood, 4*(2), 149–166.

Slavin, R. E. (1995). Cooperative learning and intergroup relations. In J. A. Banks & C. A. M. Banks (Eds.), *Handbook of research on multicultural education* (pp. 628–634). New York: Macmillan.

Slovo, J. (1995). *The unfinished autobiography*. Johannesburg, South Africa: Ocean.

Southern Poverty Law Center. (2010a, Spring). Angry radical; right catches fire. *SPLC Report, 40*(1), 1, 3.

Southern Poverty Law Center. (2010b, Summer). SPLC exposes racist origins of new Arizona law. *SPLC Report, 40*(2), 1, 5.

Stabler, J. R., Zeig, J. A., & Johnson, E. E. (1982). Perceptions of racially related stimuli by young children. *Perceptual and Motor Skills, 54*(1), 71–77.

Swiniarski, L. B. (2006). Helping young children become citizens of the world. *Scholastic Early Childhood Today, 21*, 36–42.

Tabors, P. (2008). *One child, two languages: A guide for early childhood educators of children learning English as a second language* (2nd ed.). Baltimore, MD: Paul H. Brookes.

Takaki, R. (1993). *A different mirror: A history of multicultural America*. Boston: Little, Brown.

Tatum, B. D. (1992). Talking about race, learning about racism: The application of racial identity development theory in the classroom. *Harvard Educational Review, 62*(1), 1–24.

Tatum, B. D. (1994). Teaching White students about racism: The search for White allies and the restoration of hope. *Teachers College Record, 95*, 462–476.

Tatum, B. D. (1997). *"Why are all the Black kids sitting together in the cafeteria?" and other conversations about race*. New York: Basic Books.

Teichman, Y., & Bar-Tal, D. (2008). Acquisition and development of a shared psychological intergroup repertoire in a context of intractable conflict. In S. M. Quintana & C. McKown (Eds.), *Handbook of race, racism, and the developing child* (pp. 452–482). Hoboken, NJ: Wiley.

Terry, R. (1970). *For Whites only*. Grand Rapids, MI: Eerdmans.

Thomas, M. (2005). *On growing up White: Teachers relate their experiences*. Unpublished manuscript.

Thomas, R. W. (1996). *Understanding interracial unity*. Thousand Oaks, CA: Sage.

Trager, H., & Radke Yarrow, M. (1952). *They learn what they live: Prejudice in young children*. New York: Harper & Brothers.

Tropp, L. R., & Prenovost, M. A. (2008). The role of intergroup contact in predicting children's interethnic attitudes: Evidence from meta-analytic and field studies. In S. R. Levy & M. Killen (Eds.), *Intergroup attitudes and relations in childhood through adulthood* (pp. 236–248). New York: Oxford.

U.N. News Service. (2010, May 11). *Independent UN rights experts speak out against Arizona immigration law.* Available at http://www.un.org/apps/news/printnews

Van Ausdale, D., & Feagin, J. R. (2001). *The first R: How children learn race and racism.* Lanham, MD: Rowan & Littlefield.

Vasquez, V. (2007). Using the everyday to engage in critical literacy with young children. *New England Reading Association Journal, 43*(2), 6–11, 97–98.

Vaught, S. E., & Castagno, A. E. (2008). "I don't think I'm a racist": Critical race theory, teacher attitudes, and structural racism. *Race Ethnicity and Education, 11*(2), 95–113.

Vorrasi, J. A., & Gabarino, J. (2000). Poverty and youth violence: Not all risk factors are created equal. In V. Polakow (Ed.), *The public assault on America's children: Poverty, violence, and juvenile injustice* (pp. 59–77). New York: Teachers College Press.

Walters, S. (2008). Fairness first: Learning from Martin Luther King and Ruby Bridges. In A. Pelo (Ed.), *Rethinking early childhood education* (pp. 151–154). Milwaukee, WI: Rethinking Schools.

Warren, M. (2010). *Fire in the heart: How white activists embrace racial justice.* New York: Oxford University Press.

Wellman, D. (1977). *Portraits of White racism.* Cambridge, UK: Cambridge University Press.

Whitney, T. (1999). *Kids like us: Using persona dolls in the classroom.* St. Paul, MN: Redleaf Press.

Wight, V., & Chau, M. (2009, November). *Basic facts about low-income children: Children under age 6.* New York: National Center for Children in Poverty. Available at www.nccp.org/publications/pub_896

Wise, T. (2009). *Between Barack and a hard place: Racism and White denial in the age of Obama.* San Francisco: City Lights Books.

Wolpert, E. (1999). *Start seeing diversity: The basic guide to an anti-bias classroom* [Video and Guide]. St. Paul, MN: Redleaf Press.

Wolpert, E. (2002). Redefining the norm: Early childhood anti-bias strategies. In E. Lee, D. Menkart, & M. Okazawa-Rey (Eds.), *Beyond heroes and holidays: A practical guide to K–12 anti-racist, multicultural education and staff development.* Washington, DC: Teaching for Change.

Wu, F. (2002). *Yellow: Race in America beyond Black and White.* New York: Basic Books.

York, S. (2003). *Roots and wings: Affirming culture in early childhood programs* (Rev. ed.). St. Paul, MN: Redleaf Press.

Zernike, K., & Thee-Brenan, M. (2010). *Poll finds Tea party backers wealthier and more educated.* Available at http://www.nytimes.cpm/2010/04/15/us/politics/15poll.html

Zinn, H. (1995). *A people's history of the United States: 1492–present* (rev. ed.). New York: HarperPerennial.

Zinn, H. (Ed.). (2004). *The people speak: American voices, some famous, some little known.* New York: Perennial Books.

Index

Thomas, M., 18
Thomas, R. W., 102, 104, 106, 108
Thompson, Becky, 108
Tochluk, S., 111
Trager, H. G., 45, 46, 49–50
Tropp, L. R., 53
Tutu, Desmond, 41

United Nations News Service, 43
Unten, Annette, 157

Values
  Alcott Center activities and, 95, 167
  children learning about racism and, 115
  children learning to be activists and,
    123
  cultivating caring and activism with staff
    and families and, 152–153
  exploring White identities with staff and
    families and, 78, 81, 86, 87
  fostering children's identities and, 66
  and laying the foundation for working
    with families and staff, 81
  Mother Jones Center activities and, 162
  self-knowledge and, 20
Van Ausdale, D., 45, 46, 47–48, 50, 54, 55,
    59, 60
Vasquez, V., 118, 120
Vaught, S. E., 31
Vera, E. M., 49
Violence, 5–6, 7, 34, 40, 41, 42, 58, 64, 105,
    114
Voices of Civil Rights, 154
Volunteers in Service to America (VISTA),
    14
Vorrasi, J. A., 58

Wallace, Beth, 18
Walters, S., 112, 118, 120
Warren, M., 109
Wealth. *See* Economic issues
Wellman, D., 107

West, Cornell, 108
White nationalists, 6, 40, 41, 44, 110
White people
  costs of racial-power codes for, 49–50
  definition of, 11–12
  diversity among, 35–36, 61, 62, 65–66, 71
  domination by, 2, 148
  as indentured servants, 33
  as responsible for existence and
    elimination of racism, 107
White Privilege Conference, 108, 110
White supremacy, 34–35, 38, 39, 40, 86, 102
White/Whiteness
  benefits and advantages of being, 43, 46,
    88–89
  categories of, 34
  definitions and contradictions of, 33–34
  historic formation and evolution of, 11,
    31–44, 156
  norm of, 14, 21, 43, 48, 62, 114
  reflection questions about, 43
Whiteness studies, 108–109
Whitney, T., 117, 121
Wight, V., 36
Williams, Leslie, 51
Wilson, Joe, 5–6
Winant, H., 32
Wisconsin Early Childhood Association,
    157
Wise, Tim, 3–4, 37, 39, 44, 108
Wolpert, Ellen, 130, 136
Woolman, John, 102
World War II, 107
Wright, Theodore S., 103
Wu, F., 107

Yasui, Barbara, 17
York, S., 78, 86, 130

Zeig, J. A., 55
Zernike, K., 40
Zinn, Howard, 77, 108, 111, 155

370.117
D435
2011

LINCOLN CHRISTIAN UNIVERSITY

127042

About the Authors

Louise Derman-Sparks was a faculty member at Pacific Oaks College in Pasadena, California from 1974–2006. She taught in the Perry Preschool and in Early Childhood Projects (Ypsilanti, Michigan) and was a child-care center director in Los Angeles. Louise presents conference keynotes, conducts workshops and consults throughout the United States and internationally. She served on the Governing Board of the National Association for the Education of Young Children (1998–2001), and holds a Masters in Education from the University of Michigan.

Patricia G. Ramsey is Professor of Psychology and Education at Mount Holyoke College in South Hadley, Massachusetts. Formerly, she taught in the Early Childhood Education Departments at Wheelock College, Indiana University, and the University of Massachusetts. She holds a master's degree from California State University in San Francisco and a doctorate in early childhood education from the University of Massachusetts in Amherst. She is a former preschool and kindergarten teacher.

3 4711 00217 5869